The Selected Works of Maulana Abul Kalam Azad

Volume VII
(1953-54)

Chief Editor
DR. RAVINDRA KUMAR

Atlantic Publishers & Distributors

Published by
ATLANTIC PUBLISHERS AND DISTRIBUTORS
B-2, Vishal Enclave, New Delhi - 27
Phone: 5413460

Sales office
4215/1, Ansari Road, Darya Ganj
New Delhi - 110002
Phone : 3273880

Typeset at
APD Computer Graphics
B-2, Vishal Enclave, N. Delhi - 27

Printed in India at
Mehra Offset Press
New Delhi

To

Mother India

To

Mother India

Preface

Dr. Shri Ravindra Kumar is an admirer of Maulana Abul Kalam Azad. This is nothing unusual. Maulana Azad had numerous admirers in the course of India's struggle for freedom. The number increased appreciably after India attained freedom. Partition of India was the heavy price India paid for this freedom. Maulana Azad had throughout his whole political life opposed forces which encouraged separatist trends in our national life. It was in the partitioned India that people realised more vividly the soundness of the views Maulana had expressed on the communal problem.

Maulana Azad was among the major figures in our unique struggle for freedom waged under the leadership of Gandhiji. The Selected Works which Dr. Ravindra Kumar has edited bring out the greatness of Maulana Azad in several fields of life. He was most assuredly an outstanding scholar, a great journalist, a matchless orator but with equal ease he was also a great statesman who played a significant role in every crisis which India and, in particular, the Indian National Congress, faced from time to time in its struggle to make our country free and independent.

He had also his due share in shaping India's destiny in her first decade of Independence. He was an outstanding member of the union cabinet but what was more important was the mature advice he made available to his comrade and fellow warrior Pandit Jawaharlal Nehru as the latter sought to grapple with India's difficult and daunting problems in the first crucial phase of her independence.

Dr. Ravindra Kumar may not yet be a mature scholar but the enthusiasm he has shown in portraying the intellectual and political life of Maulana Azad deserves commendation. The country is still faced with problems which greatly exercised the Maulana's mind. What he thought and said on these problems would still be a source of inspiration and enlightenment to his countrymen in the difficult days through which we are all passing.

Sadiq Ali

Introduction

Maulana Abul Kalam Azad was a great Parliamentarian who proved himself to be a pillar of strength to the veterans of the Congress Party and the Union Cabinet headed by Pandit Jawaharlal Nehru. Being an outstanding educationist and thinker, he became the stoutest champion of all progressive causes in the fields concerned.

He was a man who through his ideas on the role of religion and politics, strengthened national unity and integrity. It was his fundamental belief that being a Hindu or a Muslim or a Sikh or a Parsi or a Christian or a Buddhist, a person can be a true nationalist by observing his or her religion. But in order to realise that it is necessary that India's old culture and civilization should be properly linked with modernism. He, in this regard, pointed out clearly:

'If in our midst there are Hindus who believe that there can be restoration of Hindu life of thousand years back then they should be clear in their mind that this is merely utopian and obviously such a dream can never be fulfilled. Similarly it applied to Muslims who if they labour under the illusion that they can revive their old culture and civilization of a thousand years back which they brought from Iran, Arab or Central Asia then this is also a well nigh impossibility. My only appeal to such people is that they should not entertain such a misconception because such a concept is far removed from reality.'

Thus, in Maulana Azad's thinking nationalism was a matter of faith and conviction and not merely based on antiquated concepts. To quote himself again:

'I am that fundamental element who has himself made India, therefore, I never abandon my claim to be Indian.'

I am grateful to the staff of National Archives of India specially to its Director General Dr. R.K. Parti and Assistant Director Shri P.R. Malik, Mrs. Meena Kapoor, Mrs. Manju Sehgal, Shri Pramod Mehra and Shri N.P. Sharma, President Shri Sadiq Ali and other staff of Gandhi National Museum and Library, Rajghat, New Delhi, Dr. Ravindra Kumar, Director, Dr. Hari Dev Sharma, Deputy Director, Shri A.K. Awasthi and others of Nehru Memorial Museum and

Library, Teen Murti House, New Delhi, Librarian and other staff of Parliament Library, Sansad Bhavan, New Delhi, officials and staff of Sardar Vallabhbhai Patel National Memorial and Navjivan Trust, Ahmedabad and staff and officials of Kakasaheb Gadgil Pratishthan, Pune for providing me important literature in their possession.

I am greatly indebted to His Excellency, Hon'ble Dr. Shankar Dayal Sharma, Vice-President of India, Hon'ble Shri Shiv V. Patil, Speaker, Lok Sabha, His Holiness, Maulana Syed Abul Hasan Ali Nadvi, Rector, Nadwatul Ulama, Lucknow, Hon'ble Dr. (Mrs.) Najma Heptulla, Deputy Chairperson, Rajya Sabha, His Excellency, Hon'ble Shri B. Satya Narayan Reddy, Governor of U.P., Dr. Karan Singh, Dr. Akbar Ali Khan and other officials of Abul Kalam Azad Oriental Research Institute, Public Gardens, Hyderabad, Shri Babubhai Jashbhai Patel, Shri V.N. Gadgil, Shri Hitendra Desai, Shri Jitendra Thakorebhai Desai, Com. E.M.S. Namboodiripad, Shri Nathubhai Naranji Naik, Shri A.J. Jalbi, Shri S.G. Mohiuddin, Mrs. Kamlesh Ravindra Kumar, Dr. Malti Malik, Prof. K.L. Malik and others for their kind encouragement, guidance and co-operation in many ways in preparation of this Volume (No. 7).

My special thanks are due to Dr. K.R. Gupta and Shri Manish Kumar Gupta of Atlantic Publishers and Distributors for undertaking the publication of Maulana Abul Kalam Azad's works courageously.

– RAVINDRA KUMAR

Abbreviations

A.B.E.	: Advisory Board of Education
A.B.T.C.	: Adult Board Training Centre
A.I.C.T.E.	: All India Council of Technical Education
A.M.	: Ancient Monuments
B.E.	: Basic Education
C.A.B.E.	: Central Advisory Board of Education
C.L.R.I.	: Central Leather Research Institute
D.E.I.E.W.	: Department of Education in Indian Embassy, Washington
E.M.	: Education Ministry
E.S.R.S.	: Establishment of Salt Research Station
G.S.D.E.I.	: Grants to Study for Development of Educational Institute
H.M.E.B.	: Hyderabad Money in England Banks
H.N.P.	: Housing and National Prosperity
I.A.D.D.M.	: Indian Academy of Dance, Drama And Music
I.C.T.E.	: Indian Council of Technical Education
I.M.	: Indian Musicians
I.N.C.C.U.	: Indian National Commission for Cooperation with UNESCO
L.L.	: Literature and Life
L.Z.	: Lead Zinc in Zawar
N.A.I.	: National Archives of India
N.A.L.	: National Academy of Letters
N.G.S.S.T.	: Non-Government Secondary School in Tripura
N.L.	: National Library
N.L.H.	: National Language Hindi
N.L.I.	: National Library of India
N.M.	: Nature and Man
O.S.D.	: Other Scientific Department

P.T.E.	: Progress of Technical Education
R.A.I.U.	: Research Aid to the Institutions and Universities
R.E.	: Reform in Education
S.A.R.L.	: Sindhi as Regional Language
S.C.G.O.T.	: Seminar on the Contribution of Gandhian Outlook and Techniques
S.I.S.S.A.	: Scholarships to Indian Students Studying Abroad
T.R.D.D.M.	: The Role of Dance, Drama and Music
T.S.E.C.R.	: The Secondary Education Commissions Report
T.S.T.B.W.N.	: The Solution of Tensions Between and Within Nations
U.C.S.	: Unesco Coupons Scheme
U.E.	: Unesco and the East
U.S.E.F.	: United States Educational Foundation
V.A.	: Visual Art
W.S.W.C.	: Welfare Scheme for Women and Children

List of Documents

S. No.	Subject	Date
1.	Address at the inaugural session of the Seminar on the contribution of Gandhian outlook and techniques	5-1-1953
2.	Welcome address at the Inaugural Session of I.A.D.D.M.	28-1-1953
3.	Opening speech at the Library of Alipur	1-2-1953
4.	Address at the Eight meeting of the All India Council for Technical Education	8-2-1953
5.	Replies in the House of People to the questions asked regarding quarterly report to be sent to the Ministry of Education about the institution assisted by the Government of India	16-2-1953.
6.	Replies to the questions asked regarding the House of Raja Nand Kumar of Kunjaghat	16-2-1953
7.	About the History of freedom Movement	18-3-1953
8.	About Sindhi Language	18-3-1953
9.	Regarding the guiding principle in the matter of giving grants to the Post-graduate Departments of Universities	18-3-1953
10.	About the Basic Education	18-3-1953
11.	About the Grants to States for Development of Educational Institutions	18-3-1953
12.	In connection with the Department of Education in Indian Embassy, Washington	18-3-1953
13.	About the Scholarships to Indian Students Studying Abroad	18-3-1953
14.	About the Central Leather Research Institute	18-3-1953

CONTENTS

Document No. 1

Maulana Azad's Address at the inaugural session of the Seminar on the contribution of Gandhian outlook and techniques, held in New Delhi on 5-1-1953

I have great pleasure in welcoming you to this Seminar to discuss the contribution of Gandhian outlook and techniques to the solution of tensions between and within nations. I am particularly happy that so many distinguished men and women from so many countries have responded to our invitation. The subject for their deliberations is one which is of overriding importance in the modern world and immediately concerns all individuals of all nations.

When the Indian National Commission for Co-operation with Unesco met for the first time in 1949, it resolved that steps should be taken at an early date to consider the Gandhian doctrines and their relevance to the problem of achieving world peace. Unesco which is concerned with the creation of an international outlook and the promotion of friendly feelings between different nations was naturally greatly interested in the proposal. Since then we have been considering how best to give effect to our plans of examining Gandhian methods as a means of achieving peace. You will agree that it was hardly necesary to have a Seminar only in order to draw attention to Gandhiji's thought. His ideas have been before the world for many years and are already a part of the intellectual heritage of modern man. In view, however, of the crisis which threatens the world today and the danger of war which is always in the background of our minds, it seems specially appropriate to consider Gandhiji's methods so far as they provide an alternative to war and promise a solution to international problems. That is why after much hesitation and thought, we have decided to call this Seminar to give distinguished thinkers of the East and the West an opportunity to discuss Gandhiji's methods in all their implications.

I am keenly conscious of the stupendous nature of the problem and also of how a solution has until now baffled the efforts of man. It is therefore in a spirit of humility that we have organised this Seminar in the hope that the co-operative efforts of thinkers from so many countries may throw some light on our pressing problems and suggest some method of dealing more satisfactorily with the problems of war and peace. The issues at stake are so vast and our aim so important that, whether we fully succeed or not, the effort is its own justification.

The progress of science itself makes it the more urgent to find a solution to these problems. In the past, wars were often due to the fact that man's lack of knowledge did not permit him to utilise to the full the resources of nature. One nation or group could therefore satisy its needs only by depriving others. If food or fodder was scarce, the only means of overcoming this shortage lay in forcible occupation of the fields or pastures belonging to others. Today, the progress of science has created conditions where all legitimate demands of man can be satisfied. We can now live in an economy of plenty rather than one of want. Secrets of nature have been revealed one after the other and those have made available to man the immense wealth of her hidden resources. The tragedy of the situation, however, is that this increase of knowledge and mastery over nature is being used not so much for the constructive purposes of society as to enhance man's powers of destruction. The energy of the atom has been unlocked and this can bring within the reach of all comfort and plenty. We are, however, concentrating on the use of atomic energy mainly to create terrible engines of destruction. Wireless has brought all mankind nearer to one another, but instead of using it to strengthen the bonds of fellowship among men, we are using it as an aid to a propaganda of hatred and discord. Aeroplanes are being used primarily to develop our offensive in aerial warfare. Greater knowledge of germs and bacteria promises mastery over disease and suffering, but such knowledge is often being sought to develop their use as weapons in bacteriological war. Not that these discoveries have no beneficent use, but such use seems subsidiary to the main purpose of employing them as weapons for the destruction of humanity.

Since the beginning of this century, technological and scientific developments have tended to make war and peace co-extensive with the whole world. In the past, some problems may have been solved by war. In any case such wars were confined to a section of the world. Today, it is clear that no problem can be solved by war. If an attempt is made to solve any problems by means of war, the consequences extend beyond the frontiers of the nations concerned and involve all mankind. Wars have reached a stage where they only succeed in intensifying the hatred between nations and leading to new hatreds. Thus, the only consequence of war today is to enhance the impulse to revenge and retribution. Forces are released that makes each war a prelude to further and more devastating wars.

This becomes clear if we consider the sequence of events since World War I. Originally the conflict arose between Germany, Austria and Russia but very soon France and the United Kingdom were embroiled. More nations joined till it became a world war which ended in the defeat of Germany. The victorious nations met at Versailles and drew up a plan of peace. President Wilson enunciated his famous Fourteen Points which aimed at bringing into being a world which would be free from the threat of war. He proclaimed the doctrine of the right of self-determination of nations. Eventually, however, a Peace Treaty was signed which was based not on the Fourteen Points but on a desire to impose the severest penalty on Germany. Certain sections of the German people were separated from the Reich and such heavy reparations imposed on it that the very basis of its economic life was shaken. The responsibility of World War II is generally laid on Hitler and the Nazi Party, but if we ask who created Hitler, we have to recognise that it was the Treaty of Versailles. In fact, we may say that the signing of the Treaty was the moment of Hitler's birth.

The Peace Treaty made every German feel his humiliation and helplessness. The Weimar Republic tried by negotiations to lighten the burden on the Germans so that democracy might have a chance in Germany but the U.K. and France paid little heed to her appeals. In fact, the victorious Allies characterised all German attempts to reduce reparations as attempts at blackmail. I cannot refrain from referring to the Lausanne Conference which met shortly before the rise of Hitler. On that occasion, Germany proposed measures for the removal of causes of misunderstanding and conflict between herself and France and was prepared even to have Joint Chiefs of Staff for the two armies so that they could always work together. This would have removed permanently French fears of German aggression and German fears of French military might. It is obvious today that there could have been no better solution of the long standing Franco-German conflict. If this proposal had been put into effect, World War II might well have been avoided. The proposal was, however, rejected. It is a strange irony of history that Mr. Ramsay Macdonald, who had been one of the foremost pacifists during World War I, should have been mainly responsible for its rejection. Would it be uncharitable to suggest that the reason why he opposed the German proposals was that such close collaboration between France and Germany would reduce the importance and power of the U.K.? It seems that while the U.K. wanted peace between France and Germany, she did not want such close friendship as was envisaged at Lausanne.

Germany became more and more embittered and frustrated and sought a leader who could cater for this mood. Hitler's rise to power thus became inevitable even though his party was in a minority in the country as a whole. World War II was therefore nothing but a release of the hatreds that had been generated in Germany, consequent upon of the Treaty of Versailles. While Germany was powerless, the Allies dealt with her claims, not from the point of view of justice but of their own military might. In 1939, when Germany regained her power, she also based her claims, not on justice but on might. It is not easy to decide in favour of either protagonist. Both were tarred with the same brush of hatred and vendetta. Both adopted in the day of their power the law of the jungle rather than the law of reason.

Like World War I, World War II also ended in the defeat of Germany. Perhaps her defeat would have come earlier if the Allies had not insisted on unconditional surrender. As early as 1942, a group had been formed in Germany who wanted to end Hitler's power. Faced with the Allies' demand of unconditional surrender, they were compelled to stay their hand and aid Hitler in carrying on the struggle as long as possible. During World War I, there was a demand that the Kaiser should be tried as a war criminal and hanged. Though this was not done, the trials at Nuremburg were held after the conclusion of World War II. This was in accordance with a statute of the victorious nations to set up a tribunal to try the German leaders.

The question may very well be asked: what authority other than sheer military might allowed this tribunal to brand as war criminals the German leaders who had been responsible for the war? It was a manifestation of the same spirit which led the Allies to frame and enforce the Treaty of Versailles. Hitler and his associates were guilty first and foremost before the German nation. If anybody had the moral authority to punish them, it was the German nation and the German courts. After the war, German courts condemned hundreds of Germans as Nazis. Why then were the accused at Nuremburg not tried by the same German courts? There is no doubt that Goering, Ribbentrop and Himmler were guilty of heinous crimes against humanity but the question is, who had the right to punish them? When the Pharisees put a question to Christ about the punishment of the adulteress, Christ said that only he who was free from guilt had the right to cast the first stone.

It is difficult to say what the definition of a war crime is. When the German bombers raided the United Kingdom, the civilised world was horrified by the indiscriminate attack on the civilians. When, however, the Allied Powers started their bombing raids, they did not spare the civilian population of Germany either. If the inventors of V2 were war criminals, cannot those who were responsible for dropping atom bombs on Hiroshima and Nagasaki also lay claim to the title? Since the beginning of history, conquerors have generally killed only those who took up arms against them. Cyrus formulated this as an explicit principle five hundred years before Christ. Tyrants have no doubt destroyed and pillaged cities from time to time and they have been regarded as enemies of man. The use of a weapon to destroy a whole city, containing thousands of innocent and unarmed men, women and children, is therefore an act that must be condemned as a crime against humanity. During the present war in Korea, there have been accusations and denials about germ warfare. The world is not in a position to give a final verdict on these charges but papers are full of accounts of experiments about germ and bacteriological warfare. We also read of the extermination of whole groups of people for the crime of belonging to a particular class or community. In such a world, how can we brand any particular group as the only war criminals?

World War I laid the foundations of World War II. The Second World War is now creating conditions for a Third World War. Who can say where this process of destruction will lead mankind? Such senseless destruction seems even more futile when we remember how at the end of each war the conqueror and the conquered alike have to pay the price of victory. After World War I, circumstances compelled the Allies to recognise step by step the need to rebuild Germany in order to restore the health of European economy. After World War II, we are again witnessing fervent efforts of the victorious nations to rebuild Germany. All these are evidence that so long as we adopt the way of hatred and revenge, there is no solution except the creation of new and more bitter problems. If the world is to survive, we must therefore find solution other than by a war.

It was in order to find a method of settling international disputes in a peaceful manner that at first the League of Nations and now the United Nations have been established. There is no doubt that their establishment is a step in the right direction, but equally there is no doubt that they have not been able to fulfil the hopes they had aroused. The League petered out because it failed to stand up to the aggression of the great powers. Today, we are witnessing the United Nations fumbling whenever the interests of the great nations are at stake. Nevertheless, UNO represents the only hope of mankind, and it is therefore our duty to find out what its shortcomings are and how best to remedy them.

It seems clear to me that two conditions must be fulfilled if UNO is to achieve its objective. The first is the recognition of justice as a value with the same validity in the international sphere as within national life. Individuals in a State have, through a long process, learnt to curb their impulse to private vengeance and submit to the arbitration of neutral judges appointed by the State. If an individual seeks to wreak private vengeance, he is punished even though he may have acted under grave provocation. We must learn to apply the same principle in the international sphere and lay down that the individual nation, society or State must never be the judge in its own case.

The second condition is clearly linked with the first and in fact arises out of it. Social peace became possible only when individuals gave up the right of private action and agreed to abide by the dictates of the State. International peace can be achieved only if States are prepared to recognise limits to their national sovereignty and submit to the arbitration of an international body. The position today is that States advocate arbitration on all issues which concern others but refuse to recognise the validity of neutral arbitration as soon as their own interests are touched.

If these two conditions are fulfilled, we may hope to find a way out of the greatest danger which threatens the world today. This is the prevailing cold war between the Communist and the non-communist countries. Whatever may be our personal attitude to Communism, we must recognise the fact that it counts a large section of mankind as its adherent. We must also admit the right of these people to their own way of life, provided they choose it freely and do not seek to interfere with the way of life of others. Once the two blocks develop an attitude of toleration for each other, discussions on specific issues will no longer be barren and disappointing as they are today. This will also make each block realise that other nations must be free to choose their own way of life according to their national genius.

To recognise justice as an absolute value is to substitute right in the place of might. This also implies that ends can never justify means. It was a basic principle of Gandhiji's thought that not only must we aim at truth and justice but must also adopt means that are truthful and just.

There is therefore no option before the world today but to turn to Gandhiji's doctrine and methods if we are to escape disaster. He preached that violence and hatred solved no problems and could only lead to further misery. He therefore appealed to men to settle their differences in the light of reason and justice. He held that the only victories were those based on moral principles. The lessons of history confirm his teachings, for history is full of the record of conflicts which seemed to end in victory but were only the prelude to further conflicts and, as often as not, ended in bitter defeat.

In essence, Gandhiji's message is not a new one. It is a message which India gave to the world six hundred years before the birth of Christ through Gautama Buddha. This was also the message which Jesus gave to the world on the Mount of Olives. Jesus, it is often said, was the first and the last Christian. This, however, does not seem to be fully correct. If we look at the history of the Christian Church, we find that it survived the persecution of the Roman Empire and in fact triumphed over it, not by the use of force and violence but by its readiness to suffer persecution and even death for the sake of its ideals. Even when these early Christians had become powerful, they refrained from the use of power. Tertullian gave expression to this attitude in his speech for the defence of the Christians against the accusations of the Gentiles. In an address to the Magistrates he said, "Our origin is but recent, yet already we fill all that your power acknowledges – cities fortresses, islands, provinces, the assemblies of the people, the wards of Rome, the palace, the senate, the public places and especially the armies. We have left you nothing but your temples. Reflect what wars we are able to undertake. With what promptitude might we not arm ourselves, were we not restrained by our religion, which teaches us that it is better to be killed than to kill?"

Islam appeared on the scene six hundred years after the advent of Christ. When the Prophet of Islam started his mission in Mecca, the whole country rose in determined opposition and sought to suppress his preachings through violence. The persecution became so bitter that it was impossible for him and his followers to continue at Mecca and ultimately he had to repair to Medina. A section of the people of Medina extended their support to him, but the Quraish of Mecca would not allow him to remain in peace even there. They organised a campaign and launched a violent attack against him. The Prophet was thus compelled to raise the sword in self-defence. He no doubt took recourse to arms but the spirit in which he did so is without parallel in the history of warfare. The Prophet of Islam was compelled to take to the sword but there was no hatred or desire for vengeance in his military operations. Even in the midst of the conflict, when he and his people were violently assailed and he himself had suffered physical injury, he could still say, "My Lord ! lead my people along the path of righteousness, for they know not what they are doing."

Can the faintest suggestion of hatred, ill-will and revenge attach to a spirit which even in a situation like this could give vent to such noble sentiments?

Then the day came when he returned victorious to Mecca at the head of thousands of faithful followers. This was an occasion when he could have taken revenge for their past oppression and persecution. No such thought occurred to him for even a single moment. He forgave without any mental reservation all those who for ten years had helped every conceivable type of persecution on him and his comrades. He declared, "I shall deal with you today in the same manner as Joseph dealt with his persecuting brothers." When they were brought before Joseph in Egypt, he had said, "Today is not a day of judgment for you. May God forgive you and forgiveness is indeed without measure."

In more recent times, we have seen Tolstoy deliver the same message of opposing evil by good, though he had no opportunity of putting his theory to the test.

Gandhiji's greatness lies in this that he prepounded non-violence not as a mere theoretical idea but as a practical programme. In fact, his life was a shinning example of this principle and that is why he was able to convert large masses of men to his way of thinking. In doing so, Gandhiji at the same time offered to the world a moral substitute for war. Until his time, even thinkers who had recognised the futility of war could offer no substitute for it. In his programme of non-violent non-co-operation, Gandhiji showed a way in which wrong could be opposed without resorting to arms. This is not an easy way and we do not yet see clearly how the method can be applied in the settlement of all international disputes. Since, however, there is no other alternative, if mankind is to survive, we must find a way of extending its application to all fields of conflict.

Beginning from 1920 up to the last days of his life, I have had the privilege of seeing Gandhiji at very close quarters and have in fact been one of his associates. The thing which impressed me most during all this long and close association was his unflinching faith in non-violence.

Non-violence was for him an absolute value and he regarded it as the ultimate truth. Two instances come to my mind of how uncompromising his stand was on this issue. When World War II started, his heart was heavy with the suffering of afflicted nations. His anguish was the greater that he could not share in their misery or do anything to stop the holocaust. His sense of misery came to a head during the heavy air bombing of Great Britain and he brooded over it till he came to the decision that he must do whatever lay in his power to bring the war to an end. He therefore wanted to send a message to the British people advising them to refrain from the use of arms and instead oppose Hitler non-violently. Even if this resulted in the military occupation of Great Britain, he wanted to advise the British people to refuse to surrender to Hitler and oppose his violence by non-violent non-co-operation.

I pleaded with him that this was hardly an appropriate message to the British people in the honour of their trial and it was likely to be misunderstood. He withheld his message for two days but then told me that he had pondered deeply over the matter and it was his conviction that he must give out his mind whatever be the consequences. Accordingly, he drafted his message and sent to the then Viceroy and Governor-General of India.

A second occasion arose during the war over the issue of Indian independence. Gandhiji held that if the British made an offer of independence on the condition that India should join the war, he for one would reject the offer. He believed that non-violence was an absolute value and he would not be justified in compromising on this issue even for the sale of Indian freedom. As the President of the Indian National Congress at the time, I could not agree with him. It was my view that the Allies were fighting for a just cause ad the only thing that prevented us from participating in the struggle was British domination over India. If this was withdrawn, India would have no reason to withhold her help to the democratic powers that were opposing Nazi aggression. These two instances show how complete his acceptance of the principle of non-violence was. He was not prepared to deviate from non-violence even for the sake of national freedom.

In this Seminar we are not, however, considering non-violence as an absolute value nor pacifism as a creed which allows no exception. We recognise that in certain circumstances a limited use of force may be necessary in order to prevent violence. If we take an example from civil life, the power of police in a State is the guarantee of the suppression of lawlessness and disorder. Our aim therefore should be to find out how this principle can be applied in the relations between nations so that war may be eliminated as an instrument of policy. International conflicts are often the result of internal conflicts. We have therefore to consider the application of Gandhian methods and outlook for the solution of both types of tensions.

In conclusion, I would like to welcome once again the distinguished thinkers from the East and the West who have met to consider this problem and suggest practical measures to give effect to them.

It is a matter of regret that we have today among us no representative from either the U.S.S.R. or China. The resonsibility for this is not ours as we made repeated attempts to associate thinkers from these countries in the work of the Seminar. In view of the many international peace conferences that these two States have been sponsoring in recent years, I would have expected that they would welcome this opportunity of meeting thinkers from the other regions of the world for promoting international peace. It is therefore a matter of regret and surprise that our invitations have not met with the response that we had a right to expect.

Document No. 2

Maulana Azad's welcome speech dated 28-1-1953 at the inaugural session of I.A.D.D.M.

Of the many questions that pressed for immediate attention after the achievement of independence, one of the most important was that relating to the revival of cultural activities. During the last 150 years, the fine arts, whether dance or drama, music or literature, did not receive the attention or the support they needed from the State for their full development. It is true that there has been a renaissance in India since the middle of the 19th century, but this was due to the release of new forces in society and owed little to the State. That is why, it was not as extensive or deep as it would have been if it had received the necessary State support. After the fall of the Moghul Empire, the centuries old tradition of State encouragement to different forms of fine arts was almost completely withdrawn.

The Indian States, which constituted about a third of India, have, no doubt, in their own territories played a significant role in supporting and developing these arts and thus deserve our gratitude, but their effort was not commensurate with the requirements of the situation. In any case, with the disappearance of the princely order, the patronage which they extended to the fine arts is also no longer available. In a democratic regime, the arts can derive their sustenance only from the people, and the State, as the organised manifestation of the people's will, must therefore undertake its maintenance and development as one of its first responsibilities.

Enlightened public opinion in the country has been conscious of this fact for over a decade. On January 26, 1945, a specific proposal in this behalf was put forward by the Asiatic Society of Bengal. The Society moved for the establishment of a National Cultural Trust as an autonomous body entrusted with the task of stimulating and promoting the culture of the country in all its aspects. The trust was to consist of three academies, *viz.*, an Academy of Letters to deal with Indian languages, literature, philosophy and history; an Academy of Art (including graphic, plastic and applied art) and Architecture, and an Academy of Dance, Drama and Music. It was intended that these academies should aim at maintaining and improving the standards of achievement in all these fields of culture.

The proposal was referred to the Central Advisory Board of Education which after examination by one of its committees accepted it and recommended that the Central Government should contribute half the amount while the Provincial Governments and the Indian States should contribute the balance. Owing to financial and other difficulties it was not possible for the Government to bring into existence the Cultural Trust though it had in principle agreed to do so.

Meanwhile the country attained its independence. The changed circumstances required fresh consideration of the issue. Accordingly, a Conference on Art was held in Calcutta in August 1949, followed by two more in March 1951 at New Delhi, on Letters, and on Dance, Drama, Music and Art to consider the position and advise the Government on measures for the promotion of cultural development in the country. These conferences appointed committees which after examining the various aspects of the problem recommended the establishment of three academies, *viz.*, an Academy for Dance, Drama and Music, an Academy of Letters, and an Academy of Art. We have met today for the inauguration of the first of these academies.

A brief enumeration of the functions of the Academy will give you an idea of what we expect it to do. Some important functions are:

(*i*) to promote research in the field of Indian dance, drama and music and for this purpose to establish a library and a museum;

(*ii*) to encourage the exchange of ideas and enrichment of techniques between the different regions in regard to the arts of dance, drama and music;

(*iii*) to encourage, where necessary, the establishment of theatre centres, on the basis of regional languages, and co-operation among different theatre centres;

(*iv*) to encourage the setting up of institutions providing training in the art of theatre, including instruction in the actor's training, study of stagecraft and the production of palys;

(*v*) to publish literature on Indian dance, drama and music, including reference works such as an illustrated dictionary or handbook of technical terms;

(vi) to encourage the development of amateur dramatic activity, the children's theatre, the open air theatre and the rural theatre in its various forms;

(vii) to revive and preserve folk dance and folk music in different regions of the country and to encourage the development of community music, martial music, etc.

(viii) to sponsor dance, drama and music festivals on an all-India basis, and to encourage regional festivals;

(ix) to award prizes and distinctions and to give recognition to individual artists for outstanding achievements in the fields of dance, drama and music; and

(x) to promote cultural exchanges in the field of dance, drama and music with other countries.

Since the Central Government would bear the main burden of financing the Academy, it was considered appropriate, at least in the initial stages, to leave the choice of the Chairman and the Treasurer to the President and the Government of India. The Academy will, however, be autonomous in its internal working and will include in its membership representatives of the State Government and of important arts organisations as well as distinguished artists in their personal capacity. A provision has also been made for the amendment of its constitution as and when desired by the Academy. Specially noteworthy is the institution of the office of Fellows of the Academy; election must be almost unanimous and the total number will be strictly limited so that it will be a real honour – the greatest in the country – to be a Fellow of the Academy.

India can be proud of a long heritage and tradition in the field of dance, drama and music. In the field of fine arts, as in those of philosophy and science, India and Greece occupy an almost unique position in human history. It is my conviction that in the field of music, the achievement of India is greater than that of even Greece. The breadth and depth of Indian music is perhaps unrivalled as is its integration of vocal and instrumental music.

The essence of Indian civilisation and cultural has always been a spirit of assimilation and synthesis. Nowhere is this more clearly shown than in the field of music. The amalgamation of Persian and Classical Indian styles during the Middle Ages gave rise to a type of music which combines the excellences of both. When the Muslims came to India, Persian music was already a fully developed system but it did not take

Muslims long to discover the special merits of Indian music. They not only adopted it as their own but added to it richly by adapting elements from the Persian tradition. Since then there has been no separate development of the two systems, but within India a combined stream has grown which, in richess and splendour, surpasses both the original tributaries.

Amir Khusro is a well-known name to every student of Indian history. He was a great poet but his inventive genius has left its mark on other fields of the fine arts as well. In music, he has created new forms through the combination of Indian and Persian melodies. *Aiman, Tarana, Qol, Sazgri*, and *Suhla* and other tunes, which are sung to this day by millions of Indians, are a living testimony to his genius and his power of synthesis. In the field of instrumental music, it was he who invented the *Sitar*. He found the *Veena* too elaborate and complicated an instrument and simplified it by reducing the number of strings to only three. The name *Sitar*, which in Persian means three strings, still bears testimony to this fact.

The same process of simplification and development is found in the field of vocal music. Sultan Husain Sharqy, King of Jaunpur, was a great lover of music, and it was he who introduced the *Khayal* style in Indian music. The old classical style of *Dhrupad* was too difficult and rigid for the fluent expression of emotions. In *Khayal*, he perfected a style which has the dignity of the *Dhrupad* without its rigidity and has become one of the most cherished forms of Indian music.

We find the same spirit of assimilation and synthesis in the evolution of the various musical instruments of India. There were *Tanpuras* of various types which were popular in Iran, and India adopted and adapted them to suit her own requirements. Another Persian instrument, *Qanun*, is placed even to this day by the people of Kashmir. There is therefore no better example of the composite culture of India than in the field of music. The co-operation of Hindus and Muslims for almost a thousand years has here brought about a consummation that has perhaps no equal in the world.

We do not know the full history of the development of drama. New researches into Egyptology for the last 50 years indicate that drama was popular in Egypt thousands of years before the advent of Christ. If we are to accept Breasted's theory, it would appear that the Memphite drama was well developed as early as the fourth millennium before Christ. In 800 B.C., the tradition was revived under the orders of Shakaba, the Ethiopian Pharaoh, and a small fragment of a play survives to this day. In Babylon and Nineveh also religious festivals were accompanied by drama. All these indicate that, as in the fields of science and philosophy, Greece received inspiration as well as models from the earlier traditions of Egypt.

There is no doubt that whatever might be the source from which the Greeks derived their inspiration, they developed drama and brought it to a level that is still unsurpassed. Comparisons in such fields are invidious, but we can still say that Kalidasa may be compared with the greatest among the Greek dramatists. We have also the works of Bhasa, Bhavabhuti and Banbhatta who raised the Indian drama to a level which is perhaps not inferior to that attained by the Greeks. In the field of the theory of drama, Indian achievements are perhaps still more remarkable and serve as models even to this day.

In the field of dance, the great variety of Indian styles has attracted the notice of all students of arts and culture. The range of Indian dance extends from the strictly classical styles, developed in the temples with their infinite variety of expression and modulations, to the wonderful rhythm and flow of folk dances in different regions of the land. In their variety they present a richness of forms that have few parallels elsewhere in the world. What is most remarkable is the continuity of these traditions and the vigour they display to this day.

This precious heritage of dance, drama and music is one which we must cherish and develop. We must do so not only for our own sake but also as our contribution to the cultural heritage of mankind. Nowhere is it truer than in the field of art, that to sustain means to create. Traditions cannot be preserved but can only be created afresh. It will be the aim of these academies to preserve our traditions by offering them an institutional form.

The Academy of Dance, Drama and Music is the first of our three proposed academies and I am happy that the President has kindly agreed to inaugurate it. I have now great pleasure in inviting him to do so.

Document No. 3

Opening speech of Maulana Azad dated 1-2-1953, at the Library of Alipur

When the Council of the National Library invited me to open it formally in its new home, my mind naturally went back to my first contact with it some 48 years ago. This was in 1904 when I was a boy of about 16. I had completed my studies, and according to the prevailing practice in our traditional system of education, was lecturing to a group of students on various subjects. I came to hear that the Buhar collection of the Library contained a rare copy of Al Beruni's famous work – *Al Qanun*. Accompanied by a friend, Mirza Fazal-ud-Din Ahmad, who later published my book, *Taskara,* I went to the Library. It was, as you no doubt remember, then known as the Imperial Library and was housed in Metcalf Hall. It was necessary to secure a reader's permit and Mirza Fazal-ud-Din was given one without any comment. When, however, he asked for a pass for me, the Library Assistant looked at me intently and enquired about my age. I said, I was about 16. On hearing this, he refused to give me a permit as he said no one below 18 was allowed to be a reader of the Library. Mirza Fazal-ud-Din interceded on my behalf and said that whatever my age was I was already a Professor in Logic, Philosophy and Muslim Law. I should therefore be given the facility to use the Library, if need be by making an exception to the rule. I looked at the Library Assistant and felt that he was not inclined to believe the statement. Mirza Fazal-ud-Din tried to see the Librarian but unfortunately he was not available. My first effort to gain admission to the Library thus ended in failure and I returned home in disappointment.

Some years later, when one of my personal friends, a great scholar, Harinath Dey, became Librarian, the entire wealth of the Library became available to me and I burrowed among its treasures. I do not know to this day whether I violated any rules, but I must confess that often I took home with me not only rare books but also precious manuscripts which I kept till I had an opportunity of copying them.

I am glad that it should be my privilege today to throw open to all who wish to use it, the doors of a library which were closed to me 48 years ago.

Now that the National Library has found a permanent home in this palace after its sojourn in various more or less ill-suited houses, I cannot help recalling to your mind the memory of the man who laid the first foundation of its future greatness. Lord Curzon has the same place in the history of the British Viceroys as has Lord Dalhousie in the history of the Governor-Generals of the East India Company. One created the situation which led to the great outburst of 1857. The other pursued a policy which was responsible for a new and intense national struggle. Whatever be our judgment on Curzon's political activities, I cannot but remember today his words when on January 30, 1903, in declaring the Imperial Library open, he said.

> "It will be a proud and happy reflection if I am able to say that I found Calcutta without a library worthy of the name and left it with a first-class and well-organised institution."

I am sure you will all agree with me that the hope which he then expressed has found its fulfilment today.

It is curious that about the same time that Curzon opened the Imperial Library, he also unveiled a monument built for the alleged victims of the Blackhole of Calcutta. History is no respecter of persons, and it is significant that while the Imperial Library opened by him not only exists but has developed into a national library, the monument he built to a myth has been swept away by the passage of time.

I do not want to bore you with details about the arrangments in the library or the different types of books, magazines and newspapers that it contains for the service of the public. All these will be available to you in the Jubilee Volume that is being published by the Library on this occasion. I would only like to draw your attention to the fact that when Curzon opened the Imperial Library, the number of books was less than a hundred thousand, while today the collection numbers more than seven and half lakhs of books and manuscripts. I realise that even this is not enough and that national libraries in other countries have far richer collections. I have, however, every hope that the library will continue to expand and will, in course of time, rival the splendid libraries of Europe and America. The Government of India will spare no pains in this behalf and have already increased the annual grant for new purchases. I may also refer to the action already taken by the Government to secure for the library a valuable collection of Chinese classics as well as the literature of different Indian languages.

I may, at this stage, pay a tribute to the munificent donors who have presented collections to this library. The first name that occurs to me is that of Munshi Sadaruddin of Buhar. He was Mir Munshi of Mir Jaffar and also held a responsible position under Shah Alam. His memory will, however, be cherished, not for the political office that he held, but because of his love of learning. He laid the foundation of the Buhar Library in Burdwan and collected precious manuscripts of all types. His collection, which is now one of the valuable possessions of this library, contains the 12th century manuscript of Al Beruni's *Al Qanun* to which I referred earlier. This has on it the Seal of Fazil Khan, a famous Amir of Shah Jahan, who later became Prime Minister of Aurangzeb. Fazil Khan was not only a statesman but also a great engineer. After the Shalimar gardens in Lahore were built, it was discovered that the engineers had forgotten that the Ravi flowed on a lower level and hence water could not be obtained from it. Fazil Khan, through his ingenuity and skill, constructed a system by which the water was raised to the level of the garden. If therefore the Shalimar blooms to this day, the credit goes to Fazil Khan's skilful engineering.

Among recent donors, pride of place must go to the sons of the late Ashutosh Mookerji. They have made a gift of his entire collection of some 75 thousand books, covering all domains of human knowledge, to the National Library. I hope that other rich patrons of learning will seek to emulate these examples.

When I visited the British Museum, what impressed me most was its Reading Room. Here was a vast hall, full of earnest men and women devoted to the pursuit of knowledge. There was an atmosphere of silence and dignity which marked it out immediately as a true temple of learning. Any one who had to speak did so in a hushed voice so that others might not be disturbed. I have often felt that we must create the same conditions and atmosphere in our reading rooms and libraries. When I first came to the new home of the National Library, I felt that in what was formerly the Ball Room of the palace we have a reading room which can, if only we wish, create the atmosphere and conditions of the Reading Room in the British Museum.

Old residents of Calcutta will, I have no doubt, welcome the transformation of what was a citadel of power into an abode of learning. Formerly, this palace was the preserve of State dignitaries and bureaucrats:

today it is a temple of learning for whoever seeks to worship at its altar. Formerly, it was a place which imposed decisions on the people regardless of what they wished or needed: today, it is a storehouse from which the nation can derive its intellectual sustenance in accordance with its wishes and needs. The noble building and grounds which formerly catered for the proud rulers of the land will, henceforth, be the resort of even the humblest seeker of knowledge and truth.

When I first walked through the halls of this palace and saw its spacious lawns, I was reminded of a famous quatrain of Hafiz of Shiraz. Once before, in opening the Delhi Public Library, I referred to these lines. They, however, seem so appropriate to the National Library that I cannot help quoting them once again:

Du yari Ziraku Waz Badai Kuhan du mani
Faraghati u Kitabi U gushai Chamni
Man in Maqam ba dunya U aqbat na deham
Agarche dar Paim.Uftand Khalq anjamani.

Two wise friends: two jügs of mellow wine: Leisure sweetened with books: and a corner of a garden.

If I can have these things, I would gladly give up all other pleasures of the world here and hereafter.

Books you will find here in plenty. Two friends also should not be difficult to find. The lovely garden stretches before you, and you can choose for yourself a lonely corner. I must, of course, say with regret that the fourth condition of the poet cannot be satisfied; but I hope that your imagination will supply the deficiency !

Document No. 4

Maulana's Address at the 8th Meeting of the All India Council for Technical Education, held at New Delhi on 8-2-1953

I have great pleasure in welcoming you to the eighth annual meeting of the All India Council for Technical Education. You are aware that the constitution of the Council has recently been revised in order to make it a more compact body and the Council, as reorganised, is meeting today for the first time. I will therefore crave your indulgence for a few minutes to refer to the circumstances in which the Council was originally set up and the work it has accomplished in the last seven years.

It was in January 1944 that the Central Advisory Board of Education recommended at the instance of the Technical Education Committee of that body that the Government should set up a central organisation to stimulate, co-ordinate and control the provision of technical education on an all India basis. The Government considered that recommendation and set up the All India Council of Technical Education to survey the whole field of technical education and to advise them on measures that might be taken from time to time for development in this field. Sri Nalini Ranjan Sarkar was appointed Chairman of the first Council and he served for two terms with conspicuous ability. I must take this occasion to recall to your memory the services which he rendered as the first Chairman of the Council. I am sure you will all agree that his death is a great loss to the cause of technical education in the country.

In retrospect we now see more clearly one of the reasons for the establishment of the Council. After the outbreak of World War II, the Government of the day felt increasingly that they must secure the co-operation of Indian national leaders in order to create the necessary enthusiasm for the war effort. They tried to associate leaders of the Indian National Congress with the Government, but the Congress refused the invitation as the terms on which it was issued were unacceptable. The Government realised that they must have at least a semblance of Indian support and therefore invited some selected individuals to come into the Executive Council. They also wanted to prove to the world that even if the Congress leaders had not agreed to accept office, they were themselves anxious to develop nation-building services in India.

Those who accepted the British invitation were thus in a position of advantage and utilised the pressure exercised by the refusal of the Congress to give effect to a programme of expansion of various nation-building services. It was these circumstances which explain the plan of Post-War Educational Development in India (popularly known as the Sargent Report), the institution of the system of Overseas Scholarships, the establishment of the Council of Industrial and Scientific Research and the All India Council for Technical Education.

I have watched closely the valuable contribution of the Council towards the development of technical education in the country since its inception. As Miniter of Education, I have naturally been interested in its working and I am happy that my association with the Council will henceforth be much closer than it had been in the past. Some of the landmarks in the history of the Council naturally come to my mind on this occasion. You are aware that it was primarily at the initiative of the Council that the Government of India decided to strengthen a number of under-graduate institutions in various parts of the country by providing grants, amounting to about 1.5 crores of rupees. It was also on the recommendations of the Council that the Government accepted the proposals of the Sarkar Committee to set up four higher institutes of technology in the country. The Council is also responsible for undertaking steps to establish closer relations between industries and educational institutions by establishing different types of industrial training schemes.

There has been a good deal of expansion of facilities in technical education during the last five years. Most of it has been provided, in the normal course, in the colleges preparing students for university degrees or college diplomas. I understand that the intake of engineering degree courses has increased from about 2,500 to over 3,700 in the last five years. The intake in engineering diploma courses has also increased from about 3,000 to almost 5,000 during the same period. In fact, there are some experts who hold that the expansion in facilities has been too rapid and that there is not enough scope for the employment of the persons trained. Others hold equally strongly that even today we do not have an adequate number of properly trained personnel for the various approved projects and purposes. What is therefore needed is a review of our requirements not only in terms of numbers but also in terms of the type of training necessary.

In January 1951, the Council appointed a committee to assess the requirements of technical manpower with a view to undertaking this survey and also estimating what the requirements are likely to be for our various development schemes. I understand that, as the Planning Commission had not, until recently, taken final decisions on the various schemes, the Committee was unable to come to firm conclusions. Now that the Five Year Plan has been approved in principle, I hope that the Committee will carry out the task assigned to it as speedily as possible.

The members of the Council are aware that one of the bottlenecks in our programme of expansion of education has been finance. I am, however, glad to say that in the Five Year Plan we have been able to provide an additional two crore rupees over what was proposed in the Draft Plan, mainly as a result of the representations made by the Seven-Man Committee appointed by the Council at its last meeting. The total provision for the various types of technical education under the Five Year Plan will therefore be of the order of about Rs. 11 crore, out of which Rs. 3.55 crore will be available for entirely new projects. You will appreciate that the expenditure in the first year is likely to be less, for no project should be undertaken until it has been carefully examined. I have every hope that once development has been initiated according to the plan, we shall be able to carry through the expansion at an accelerated pace.

I am happy to report to you that the Indian Institute of Technology at Kharagpur has made further progress since the Council met last. This year, apart from admissions to the basic under-graduate courses in engineering, the Institute has accepted students for degrees in naval architecture, agricultural engineering and architecture. Post-graduate courses in production engineering and combustion engineering have also been started and a few students have undertaken research in various fields. The Institute has also organised a short course in Management studies, the first of its kind in Asia, which will enable persons drawn from industries, commerce, Government departments and other lines of activity to come together and study the common principles of effective administration. The total number of students has risen to 700 and the next academic year will see a thousand students on its roll.

You are aware that the Council has recommended the setting up of four regional committees in order to establish closer relations between industries and educational institutions to their mutual advantage. The first of these committees, the Eastern Committee, was set up some time ago. The Western Committee has also now been set up and it held its first meeting at Bombay in October 1952. I hope that the committees for the South and the North will also start functioning before long. You will agree that the establishment of these regional committees will lead to a more effective reaslisation of the requirements and possibilities in these regions and help us to formulate an integrated plan for India as a whole.

One of the most important questions requiring the attention of the Council today is that of formulating a detailed plan to implement the recommendations of the Seven-Man Committee as incorporated in the Five Year Plan. General lines of development have no doubt been indicated by the Committee but it is for you to determine the steps that should be taken to give them a concrete shape. Facilities in technological study at the post-graduate level are inadequate and even though the two institutes at Kharagpur and Bangalore will go some way towards meeting our requirements, we still have to send a large number of students for training abroad. It must be one of the first priorities in our programme of expansion to develop these facilities within the country itself. I am sure you will agree that the highest consideration should be given to strengthening institutions which are in a position to fulfil the objectives we have in view.

Another field where concerted development is necessary is to provide facilities for proper training to the large body of untrained personnel in industries. A small beginning has been made in in-service training but this has to be expanded considerably. It will be no exaggeration to say that the future of the country's industries will largely depend upon our success in improving the quality of the personnel now employed in industries.

The Council has already had under consideration a scheme for the development of facilities in applied arts and crafts. A conference of the principals of the art institutions in the country was recently held to consider the question further and it has made some important and far-reaching recommendations. One recommendation, which is somewhat novel and involves a departure from the present practice of the other bodies associated with the Council, deserves your special attention. The conference has recommended that after the Council has satisfied itself about the standards of the institutions concerned, it should recognise the various examinations held by them for purposes of the national diplomas and certificates. If this principle of decentralisation, which, I may add, is in line with current practice in the United Kingdom, is accepted in other fields of technical education, I feel it will lead to a wider adoption of the Council's schemes throughout the country and result in an all-round improvement of standards.

You are aware that the Government of India make no grants to technical institutions until their case has been examined by the Council and its co-ordinating committee. The first programme for aid to institutions is almost complete and you may consider what further steps should now be taken. The last important issue to which I would draw your notice is the need of setting up an Assessment Board for the recognition of technical and professional qualifications for employment. There is today considerable confusion in regard to the recognition of the numerous qualifications and awards for purposes of employment in government service. Industries and commerce also depend largely on the Government for guidance in the matter of recognition of various qualifications. It is therefore necessary to set up suitable central machinery which will remove the prevailing confusion and place the recognition of qualifications on a proper basis.

In conclusion, I would like to welcome the new members to the Council and express, on your behalf and on my own, our appreciation of the services of those whose membership has ceased.

Document No. 5

Maulana's reply dated 16-2-1953 in the House of the People to the question asked by Sardar A.S. Sehgal regarding a quarterly report to be sent to the Ministry of Education about the institutions assisted by the Government of India

Maulana Azad: There is no particular necessity for issuing such instructions. Government of India has its own rules regarding those institutions to which it gives aid. According to one of these rules, they are to state how they have spent the money.

Document No. 6

Joint replies by Maulana Azad and Shri K.D. Malviya in the House of People dated 16-2-1953 to the questions asked regarding the House of Raja Nand Kumar

Shri A.C. Guha: Will the Minister of **Education** be pleased to state:

(a) whether Government are aware that the residential house of the late Maharaja Nand Kumar of Kunjaghat, District Murshidabad, is in a very dilapidated condition;

(b) if so, whether Government propose to declare this house as a protected monument; and

(c) whether Government have made any estimate of the amount that may be necessary for its repairs?

The Deputy Minister of Natural Resources and Scientific Research (Shri K.D. Malaviya): (a) Yes.

(b) No.

(c) Does not arise.

Shri A.C. Guha: Is not the Government aware that the late Maharaja Nand Kumar occupies an important place in the history of India, and as such his house deserves protection?

The Minister of Education and Natural Resources and Scientific Research (Maulana Azad): The hon. Member will recall that this matter came up before the Government in 1948 and it was fully inquired into. The Archaeological Department was asked to report after inspecting the house in Murshidabad said to be belonging to Maharaja Nand Kumar. Its report indicates that the portion of the house now intact is not the same which was his house. His house, whatever it was, was destroyed in the earthquake of 1897. There is a portion in which some people are living, but there is no portion remaining which needs to be preserved or repaired. A new house, of course, can be built there, but it is not the intention of the Government to do so. It has been considered sufficient to put up a memorial tablet there bearing his name and brief life story. Consequently that tablet has been put up and the Government of Bengal has expressed its satisfaction at this action.

Shri A.C. Guha: May I know if the Government has any intention of putting up a suitable memorial tablet in the place at Calcutta where he was hanged?

Maulana Azad: No. There is no such proposal before the Government and Government do not consider it very necessary.

Document No. 7

Oral answers to the questions raised in the House of People dated 18-3-1953 about the History of Freedom Movement

Dr. Ram Subhag Singh: Will the Minister of **Education** be pleased to state:

(a) whether the Government of India have set up a Board of editors under the Chairmanship of Dr. Syed Mahmud, M.P., to prepare a history of the freedom movement in India;

(b) if so, the terms of reference to that Board; and

(c) whether any time-limit has been fixed during which the work of the Board is to be completed?

The Deputy Minister of Natural Resources and Scientific Research (Shri K.D. Malaviya): (a) Yes.

(b) To compile a comprehensive History of Freedom Movement in India.

(c) Yes, Sir. Three years.

Dr. Ram Subhag Singh: May I know whether that history will be only an account of the freedom movement of India or it will also contain a picture of the awakening of the national consciousness and other matters?

Shri K.D. Malaviya: This history will be concerned with the Freedom Movement of India.

Dr. Ram Subhag Singh: May I know whether any other Committee was appointed before the appointment of this Committee, and if so, what work that Committee did and with what result?

The Minister of Education and Natural Resources and Scientific Research (Maulana Azad): Earlier a Committee was set up to find out the sources from which such material could be collected. But its report was not of much help. It was then that this Committee was set up.

Reply to the spl. questions of Dr. R. S. Singh:

Maulana Azad: Yes. If the hon. Member so desires, it would be laid on the Table of the House.

Shri N. Sreekantan Nair: May I know whether this history will include the contributions made by organized labour and the *kisan* movements in India?

Shri K.D. Malaviya: This history will cover all phases of the Freedom movement that culminated in the coming of independence to this country.

Shri B.S. Murthy: May I know whether this history will contain the aspect of the agrarian revolution that has enhanced the working of the Freedom movement?

Shri K.D. Malaviya: All these are suggestions and are likely to be considered by the Committeee.

Mr. Deputy-Speaker: We cannot go into the chapter and verse.

Shri Punnoose: May I know the members of this Board?

Shri K.D. Malaviya: The composition of the Committee is as follows:

Dr. Syed Mahmud – *Chairman.*

Acharya Narendra Dev, Vice-Chancellor of Benares Hindu University.

Shri Balwantray G. Mehta, M.P.

Dr. S.N. Sen, Delhi.

Prof. Habib, Professor, Muslim University, Aligarh.

Prof. K.A. Nilakanta Sastri, Professor of Indology, Mysore University, Mysore.

Shri D.V. Potdar, Poona.

Dr. R.C. Majumdar, Calcutta.

Shri S.N. Ghose, M.P., Member and Honorary Secretary.

Shri P.T. Chacko: May I know whether this will include that part of the movement which took place in the native states?

Shri K.D. Malaviya: I have just now answered the question.

Mr. Deputy-Speaker: Hon. Members need not ask for details as to what is going to be included.

Reply to the spl. question asked by S. Govind Das

Maulana Azad: The Committee will decide it. But things as they are, it would be desirable to write this History first in English and then to translate it in other langauges of India.

Shrimati A. Kale: May I know why no Maharashtrians have been included in the Committee in spite of the fact that Maharashtra has taken a substantial part in the political movement?

Shri K.D. Malaviya: I presume Mr. Potdar is from Poona.....

(*Interruption*).

Mr. Deputy-Speaker: Order, order. I find much interest being evinced by hon. Members.

Kumari Annie Mascarene: May I know whether there is any lady member on this Board? We also contributed to the Freedom movement.

Shri K.D. Malaviya: There is no lady member on the Committee.

Dr. Suresh Chandra: What efforts have been made by Government to collect information about the Freedom movement which was carried on in other countries?

Shri K.D. Malaviya: This history of Freedom movement will relate to our country only.

Shri T.K. Chaudhuri: May I know if there is any arrangement for contacting leaders of old revolutionary movements such as the Anushilan, Jugantar, Ghadar and such other parties?

Shri K.D. Malaviya: All these questions will be considered by the Committee.

Shri Veeraswamy: May I know whether the history of the Freedom movement will contain the activities of leaders who later on either joined other parties or founded new parties like, Periyar E.V. Ramaswamy Naicker, Leader of the Dravidian Federation?

Mr. Deputy-Speaker: Everything new will be included.

Shri N.R.M. Swamy: May I know the estimated cost of this scheme?

Shri K.D. Malaviya: The estimated cost of this will be between Rs. four to five lakhs or may be less.

Document No. 8

Joint replies dated 18-3-1953, of Maulana Azad and Shri K.D. Malaviya to the questions asked in the House of People

Sindhi as Regional Language

Shri Gidwani: (a) Will the Minister of **Education** be pleased to state whether Government have received any representations from Sindhis living in different States of India, that Sindhi Language should be recognised as the 15th Language in the Eighth Schedule to the Constitution of India?

(b) Have Government received any representation from Sindhis living in Bombay State, that Sindhi Language should be recognised as the Regional Language of the Bombay State?

(c) Have Government received representations that Sindhi Language in Devnagri Script should be taught in the Primary Schools to Sindhi Children, in all States where Sindhis have migrated from Pakistan?

The Deputy Minister of Natural Resources and Scientific Research (Shri K.D. Malaviya): (a) and (b). Yes. Representations have been received to the effect that (i) Sindhi should be included in the list of languages contained in the Eighth Schedule to the Constitution of India and (ii) a directive be issued by the President under article 347 of the Constitution for recognition of Sindhi as a regional language in certain States including Bombay.

(c) In 1948 the Government of India had advised the State Governments to have Sindhi text-books for schools published in Devnagri script. This brought strong protests from Sindhi Associations in several places and the Government realised that since the Sindhis themselves were not of one mind on this question, it was difficult for the Government to impose its own decision on them. The Government was thus obliged to come to the decision that for the present provision should be made for text-books in both the scripts, leaving the choice to local guardians in each place to decide in what script they would like their children to be taught. The Government hope that the responsible and representative Sindhi opinion will come to a common decision in this matter which the Government could adopt.

Shri Gadgil[1]: Are Government aware that in most of the States where Sindhis have settled, Devnagri Script is used both for official and non-official purposes?

Shri K.D. Malaviya: This question refers to the representations from Sindhis. They wanted Devnagri script. Later on, there was some opposition.

Shri Gidwani: Will not two scripts retard the progress for futher education? If the text-books are in two scripts students going from one State to another will be handicapped regarding their further education.

Maulana Azad: As has been made clear in the reply, this question came up before the Government in 1948 for the first time. Shri Jai Ram Das Daulatram, then, was a Minister in the Central Cabinet. I consulted him and after consultations we were of the opinion that it was advisable to adopt Devnagari script for Sindhi language for purposes of imparting education to the Sindhi children. It would have made their job easier because they would have learnt Hindi also side by side. But as soon as we took this decision and conveyed it to the State Governments, a storm of protest was raised by the Sindhis. To begin with, we received telegram after telegram and letter after letter; which was followed by the representations from the various Sindhi institutions of Bombay, Kathiawar and Rajasthan. They insisted that the decision of the Government was a wrong one, and as a result of it all the ancient Sindhi literature would go waste; further adding that it would create a barrier between the old and the new literatures. In view of these developments the Government had to give in and they decided to continue using both the scripts till the Sindhis themselves arrived at a unanimous decision in this matter. If the hon. Member has any interest in this matter, I would advise him to call a representative conference of the Sindhis and then to take some unanimous decision.

Reply to the spl. question of Mr. R. Singh

Maulana Azad: It is difficult to say.

Further reply to the spl. question asked by Mr. Gidwani

Maulana Azad: One of my friends said just now that the population of Sindhis in Bombay was five lakhs.

---

1. Mr. Narhar Vishu Gadgil.

Pandit D.N. Tewary: Is it the policy of the Government to recognise more than one language as Regional language in all States?

Maulana Azad: The hon. Member is aware how the Constitution has dealt with issues such as this. If in a particular area a certain section of population speaks a particular language and is desirous of preserving it, the Government may consider it.

Further reply to question asked by Mr. Singh.[1]

Maulana Azad: It is Arabic or Urdu whatever you may call it.

Shri C. Bhatt: I have got a number of questions to ask.

Mr. Deputy-Speaker: But the hon. Member did not rise. I have now called upon the Minister to answer the next question.

Shri C. Bhatt: I was not lucky enough to catch your eye.

---

1. Mr. Raghunath Singh.

Document No. 9

Replies dated 18-3-1953 of Maulana Azad and his Parliamentary Secretary to the questions asked in the House of People regarding the guiding Principle in the matter of giving grants to the Post-graduate Departments of Universities

Shri V.P. Nayar: (a) Will the Minister of **Education** be pleased to intimate what are the guiding principles in the matter of giving grants to the post-graduate departments of universities?

(b) Have Government drawn up priorities in the matter of eligibility of grants to post-graduate departments of universities, and if so, what are the priorities?

The Deputy Minister of Natural Resources and Scientific Research (Shri K.D. Malaviya): (a) A statement is laid on the Table of the House. [*See* Appendix VI, annexure No. 1(b)].

(b) No priorities have been drawn up.

Shri V.P. Nayar: May I know how these principles have been laid down, by whom they were laid down and also, if they were laid down by a Committee of experts, who constitute that committee?

Shri K.D. Malaviya: The Government ultimately are responsible for all the things mentioned by the hon. Member.

Shri V.P. Nayar: That is not what I wanted to know. I wanted to know whether these rules have been framed by a Committee of experts.

Shri K.D. Malaviya: The rules have been framed by the Government of India. But, there is the All India Council for Technical Education, and Central Advisory Board of Education which advises the Government on all matters and makes recommendations.

Shri V.P. Nayar: May I know whether there has been any request from the Travancore University for grant of money for post-graduate research?

The Minister of Education and Natural Resouces and Scientific Research (Maulana Azad): So far as I remember no such request has been received by us.

Shri V.P. Nayar: May I know whether in the matter of giving priorities, grants for post-graduate studies in technical and technological subjects will be preferred to other subjects?

Maulana Azad: Scientific and technical subjects.

Document No. 10

Joint replies dated 18-3-1954 by Maulana Azad and Shri K.D. Malaviya in the House of People to the questions asked about the Basic Education

Shri S.N. Das: Will the Minister of **Education** be pleased to state:

(a) what were the important recommendations of the Committee on the productive aspect of Basic Education;

(b) which of these recommendations have been given effect to; and

(c) whether the implementation of these recommendations has led to any improvement in the direction of useful production?

The Deputy Minister of Natural Resources and Scientific Research (Shri K.D. Malaviya): (a) A statement is laid on the Table of the House. (*See* Appendix VI, annexure No. 2.

(b) The report of the Committee, together with the observations on it made by the Central Advisory Board of Education, at their 19th meeting in March 1952 has been communicated to all State Governments for necessary action.

(c) The implementation of the new approach suggested will require several years and it is not possible so soon to offer any opinion on its results.

Shri S.N. Das: May I know whether the report of this committee has been published and is available in the Library or was supplied to the various State Governments?

Shri K.D. Malaviya: It was not laid on the Table of the House.

Shri S.N. Das: May I know whether the Central Advisory Board of Education has considered the recommendations of this committee, and if so, what is their decision?

Shri K.D. Malaviya: Yes, Sir. The Board considered the recommendations and expressed the view that the element of craft work in basic education is of such educational importance and value that even if no economic considerations were involved, it is necessary to replace ordinary primary education by basic education, in a planned way.

Shri S.N. Das: With regard to part 2, item 1, it has been stated that the Committee has suggested a proper integration of post-basic education with secondary and university education. I would like to know whether the Secondary Education Commission has been asked to consider this point also.

Shri K.D. Malaviya: All these questions will be considered by the Secondary Education Commission.

Shri T.N. Singh: Is it a fact that the Government have made certain grants for basic primary schools to various States, and may I know whether the States have been able to avail of these grants?

Shri K.D. Malaviya: This question refers to the aid that is to be given for post-graduate studies and researches.

An Hon. Member: No, this is the next one. This refers to basic education.

Shri K.D. Malaviya: I am sorry, Sir, you have rightly corrected me. But it is beside the point.

The Minister of Education and Natural Resources and Scientific Research (Maulana Azad): Would the hon. Member repeat his question?

Further reply to question asked by Mr. T.N. Singh

Maulana Azad: An amount has been earmarked for this purpose in the Five-Year Plan. It would be allotted to the different States provided they are prepared to make their contributions.

Reply to the spl. question of Mr. T.N. Singh

Maulana Azad: The Government are of the opinion that there is no reason for drawing any such conclusion. What we have provided is that any State which is prepared to subscribe seventy per cent. of the total amount would receive the remaining thirty per cent. from the Central Government. And I think this is a fair allocation.

Shrimati Khongmen: May I know, Sir, how many basic schools have so far reached a self-supporting state?

Shri K.D. Malaviya: Basic School training is still in a very preliminary stage, Sir.

Reply to the question raised by Mr. Jhunjhunwala

Maulana Azad: A Conference has been convened on 18th April. The matter would be discussed with the State Ministers. After that we would be able to know which of the States are willing to accept it for the present.

Document No. 11

Written answers dated 18-3-1953, of Maulana Azad in the House of People to the questions asked about the Grants to States for Development of Educational Institutions

Ch. Raghubir Singh: (a) Will the Minister of **Education** be pleased to state whether it is a fact that grants are given to State Governments for the establishment and development of various educational institutions?

(b) What is the basis of selecting these institutions for grants?

The Minister of Education and Natural Resources and Scientific Research (Maulana Azad): (a) Under the Five-Year Educational Development Plan, Government of India have given grants to the States for certain schemes of Basic and Social Education schemes of Basic and Social Education, a part of which will be utilized by the States for development of educational institutions. The question of giving financial assistance to Universities and other institutions of higher education for advanced studies and research in non-Scientific and non-Technical subjects is under consideration.

(b) The general basis of selection is that the institutions must come within the pattern of the schemes formulated under the Five Year Plan of Educational Development. In the case of Universities etc. care is taken to see that they are competent to undertake the type of advanced work for which grant is solicited.

Document No. 12

Maulana Azad's answers dated 18-3-1953 in the House of People to the questions asked in connection with the Department of Education in Indian Embassy, Washington

Shri H.N. Mukerjee: (a) Will the Minister of **Education** be pleased to state whether there is a Department of Education attached to our Embassy in Washington?

(b) If so, what are its functions and the amount of money spent by it up-to-date?

The Minister of Education and Natural Resources and Scientific Research (Maulana Azad): (a) Yes.

(b) The Education Department looks after the educational facilities and the welfare arrangements of Indian students in the Western hemisphere, and helps to foster cultural relations between India and the U.S.A.

The Department was set up in 1945. The total amount of expenditure spent on the Department year-wise is given below:

1945-46	.... Rs. 1,18,980
1946-47	.... Rs. 2,27,280
1947-48	.... Rs. 3,86,821
1948-49	.... Rs. 4,66,351
1949-50	.... Rs. 5,64,064
1950-51	.... Rs. 4,60,908
1951-52	.... Rs. 3,85, 240
1952-53 (Upto 31st January, 1953)	.... Rs. 3,28,619
	Rs. 29,38,263

Document No. 13

Answers, dated 18-3-1953, of Maulana Azad to the questions asked in the House of the People

Scholarships to Indian Students studying Abroad

Shri Viswanath Reddy: (a) Will the Minister of **Education** be pleased to refer to the reply to starred question No. 418 asked on the 2nd March, 1953 and state what is the method of selection of these scholars for overseas scholarships?

(b) How many of these scholarships, if any, are reserved for the Backward Classes?

(c) Do Government have any plan to absorb these scholars in suitable positions so that full advantage of their training abroad is taken?

(d) If so, what are the principal features of that plan?

The Minister of Education and Natural Resources and Scientific Research (Maulana Azad): (a) Selection for each category of scholarship is made by a duly constituted Selection Board appointed by the Government of India.

(b) None, but if two candidates possessing equal qualifications are available, preference is given to a candidate belonging to the Backward Classes.

(c) and (d) Except for the Central State Scholarship Scheme, scholarships are generally awarded only to persons for whom employment on return is guaranteed by the authorities sponsoring them. Under the Central State Scholarship Scheme, one scholarship is awarded each year to the most meritorious candidate from Part 'C' and 'D' States, without any guarantee of employment or obligation to serve.

Document No. 14

Joint Replies by Maulana Azad and Shri K.D. Malaviya in the House of People dated 18-3-1953 to the questions asked in connection with the Central Leather Research Institute, Guindy

Shri Jasani: (a) Will the Minister of **Natural Resources and Scientific Research** be pleased to state what was the total cost of the construction of the Central Leather Research Institute at Guindy?

(b) What are the functions of this institute?

(c) What is the progress of work so far done by this institute?

The Deputy Minister of Natural Resources and Scientific Research (Shri K.D. Malaviya): (a) The anticipated cost of construction and equipment of the Institute is Rs. 35 lakhs.

(b) and (c) A statement giving the required information is laid on the Table of the House. [*See* Appendix VI, annexure No. 1 (a).]

Shri Jasani: Is there any Committee appointed to supervise the work of this Institute? How is it constituted? Who are the personnel?

Shri K.D. Malaviya: There was a committee which was appointed by C.S.I.R. Mr. Das was the Chairman – to initiate and it recommended the establishment of the Research institute. The other Members were Messrs. K. Seshachalam Chaudhuri, G.M. Mausari, P.T. Quy and B.C. Guha. Subsequently another local Planning Committee was formed.

The Minister of Education and Natural Resources and Scientific Research (Maulana Azad): Generally speaking a local Committee is set up for every research institute which is established by the Council. In this case also a Committee has been set up.

Reply to the spl. question asked by Mr. Jasani

Maulana Azad: Though appointed by us, these are local Committees.

Shri S.C. Samanta: May I know whether any bulletin is published to show the progress of work there and whether any research publications have already been made available?

Shri K.D. Malaviya: The programme is to publish technical bulletins and other magazines which will disseminate information regarding the Institute.

Shri M.S. Gurupadaswamy: May I know whether any foreign expert is employed for doing work in this Institute?

Shri K.D. Malaviya: No, Sir.

Document No. 15

An Oral reply of Maulana Azad in the House of People dated 19-3-1953 to a question asked by Shri K.C. Sodhia regarding the establishment of any Salt Research Station

Shri K.C. Sodhia: Has any Salt Research Station been established this year?

The Minister of Education and Natural Resources and Scientific Research (Maulana Azad): This question relates to Natural Resources and Scientific Research. A Salt Research Institute is being opened in Kathiawar, but it has not yet been completed.

Document No. 16

Maulana Azad's speech dated 20-3-1953, delivered in the House of People in connection with the Demands for Grants

The Minister of Education and Natural Resources and Scientific Research (Maulana Azad): Sir, whenever there was any debate on the Budget in these past five years, the Members of the House adopted a special attitude. They felt that the matter of education was an important one, and so a debate should definitely be held. The most glaring thing that would come up before them was that there was countrywide illiteracy, literacy being not more than twenty per cent., and the dissemination of education, as such, should be maximum and speedy. This was the reason why the necessity was felt for revising the item on education every year. But nobody understood the necessity to consider the provision for a speedy dissemination of education in the country. This had fallen to my lot to repeat the difficulties of the Government every year, and I would say that the Government had not slackened as the schemes were there. But unless we had the provision for this, we could not proceed forward in this direction. And now I am glad to see that my colleagues did not adopt that very attitude this year. May be, the appeal made by me to them last year bore the fruit. And this is what I conclude from yesterday's proceedings. I had, in fact, drawn their attention to the fact that they should not be so illogical in this matter.

Some of my colleagues, however, pointed to certain things yesterday during the debate, and I shall say in brief something regarding those.

It was brought to our attention that the Central Government was responsible for education although that was a State subject, and that the Central Government could not be free from this responsibility by saying that education was a State subject. Quite correct! I fully agree with what has been said. It is clear that the Government would not have taken any steps in the past five years for the dissemination of education if it did not agree with this view. You will certainly be in the know of the fact that when I took over the portfolio of education, I appointed the

Kher Committee for investigation into basic education. The function of that Committee was to make a full survey of basic education and to suggest the ways and means for making this basic education universal and compulsory within the shortest period. And you know that the Committee functioned with full speed and submitted a report after a year. It is evident that there would have been much progress in the dissemination of education during the four years had not the financial difficulties hurdled our way. As you know the Kher Committee recommended that there should be countrywide basic education in a span of 17 years, junior basic education in ten years and therein they also fixed a period of seven years for Senior basic education. They proposed that 30 per cent expenses should be borne by the Central Government and 70 per cnet. by the State Governments. The main obstacle in our way was that finances could not be arranged by us. Could the arrangemnts be made, the Central Government would have started with a contribution of 2 crores which would swell to 25 crores in 17 years' time. The State Governments in this case would have to contribute more than an *arab* of rupees in this direction. As the money could not be arranged, the schemes could not be furthered. I would, therefore, like to convince my colleagues that the Central Government are not ignorant of these developments and that they fully understand this responsibility of theirs. Evident as it is, schemes can then only be given a practical shape when there are finances. Such questions, however, as mentioned by some colleagues that teachers are getting very low pays, concern the State Governments, and it is quite correct that those should be taken up by them, but so far as the Central Government are concerend, not even a day's delay has been made in considering such questions. You are aware that in 1948 the Central Government sanctioned for Delhi and Ajmer that very scale of salary which was recommended by the Pay Commission and which is not paid in any province at present. But such a case does not concern State Governments; and we can do nothing in this respect. Some friends said that the Central Government be given the directions. Well, we cannot give directions: Constitution does not allow us to do so. Yes, we make a suggestion and here we are suggesting. Some Governments have, no doubt, paid their attention to it. I congratulate the Punjab Government for the consideration they gave to the genuine question. The question was as to what should be the minimum salary in the present circumstances, and not the salary that should be given to the teachers. Considering the present circumstances some minimum limit of the salary should be fixed for a teacher, patwari or a constable. I would like to congratulate the Punjab Government for the valuable step taken by them while presenting their this year's budget, and also for the arrangements they made for Punjab by fixing for future the minimum salary at no less than Rs. 77 per month which includes dearness allowance etc., besides the basic pay. This has, however, been a very good step, but it is apparent that it concerns the State Governments and we have been of no help to them.

Likewise, attention has been drawn to the commitments in the Constitution that basic education shall be made common and compulsory in ten years' time throughout the country.

What has been done about it? Do you know that no step has been taken so far in this direction which would make us hope that this work would be completed in 10 years' time? But it is apparent that difficulties stand in our way and unless those difficulties are over, nothing can be done. I would like to make it clear to you that unless the Central Government curtail the expenditure incurred on defence, no more provision can be made for education; and to tell you the truth the expenditure on defence carries away half the amount of budget. Nothing can be said when such time comes, but I may assure you that the Central Government is duty-bound and cannot do otherwise. Even in these circumstances we have to see where our steps will carry us. You might be remembering that last year I drew your attention to the fact that the Planning Commission was considering the amount to be spent on education. I also told you that at least 10 crores of rupees should be apportioned annually to the item of education, and I made efforts for it. You are aware that the scheme was started in 1950. About two and a half years have elapsed and about three years are practically left; we have to complete the scheme within these three years now. I am happy that we have apportioned 10 crores annually. These 10 crores per year mean 25 crores collectively for the three years to come. This is quite apparent that we are not in a position to spend 10 crores of rupees from the very first day as we have to lay new foundations, erect new superstructures, and gradually as the superstructure goes up the expenses will multiply. We are taking these steps from the next year and do hope to further the scheme then so that it comes up to the mark in the third year. Whatever has been planned in its respect is known to you. It has been attempted to go forward with all the three sections of education, *viz.*, basic, secondary and university education; and we shall give all the possible help we can.

You are aware that our Constitution has entrusted the responsibility of University education to the Central Government also, because it says that Central Government should be a party to the maintenance of standard and co-ordination of the University education. Today we hear people say that University education has deteriorated and the standard is coming down day by day. They say that some steps should be taken lest the whole structure of education should succumb. Quite fine; but how to do it? Do you know when I told you last year that the Government wanted to present a Bill before the House? The Government considered the matter, and arrived at the conclusion that nothing would come out of the attention paid by the Universities only or the State Governments unless an agency would come into being which would remove the drawbacks of University education, bring in new reforms, and implement new schemes. The report of the University Education Commission is out. Three years have elapsed. Most of the recommendations made in that report concern the Universities and the State Governments, but nothing has come out so far. The Central Government drew the attention of the Universities and the State Governments but nothing came out in practice. We, in fact, intended to make an agency for the purpose. If at all we wanted to get it implemented, the Government could have their hand in it because the Constitution provides them the opportunity of maintaining the standard and co-ordination, but we never liked the idea. We thought it proper that an independent agency be made so that there would be no direct hand of the Government of India in it; the recognised representatives of education in this country, the representatives of the Universities be asked to be the members of the agency and the Parliament would empower them to work under some conditions till the work would be over. The Bill was, however, formulated, and was sent to the Universities and the State Governments. You must have seen in the papers that there was a lot of opposition against the Bill. I do not want to go in detail at the moment. We are calling a conference of Vice-Chancellors of the Universities and Education Ministers of the States on 18th April, and are going to debate on this matter. We shall arrive at some decision after full discussions therein. We have, however, felt that the discrepancies and drawbacks of these Universities and education therein cannot go off unless an agency to look after education comes into being. This is about the steps taken by the Government regarding the university education.

You are aware that we took on loan a certain amount of wheat from America and it was decided that the sum that would accumulate by way of interest on that amount would be spent on the Indian Universities. This amount has, however, gone upto two and a half crores of rupees; and since that will be in shape of dollars, that cannot be spent on education because this problem can only be solved with Indian rupee. This amount can, in fact, help us in purchasing books and apparatus for research institutes etc. Apparent as it is, we need these badly for the Universities. Progress of the varsities has stopped for the last ten years since the days of war; and it is intended to give away the amount of four and a half crores to the Indian Universities. Talks are going on about it at present. But even apart from all that we have apportioned different sums in this respect in our Five Year Plan. These sums will be given for basic education and to Universities. Besides these we have Community Projects which include education also. We have made plans for creating a complete model which will include basic school, junior, senior and secondary schools and a Janata College. These days we are in correspondence with them and want that a rural university be established in accordance with the recommendations of the University Commission. What will the shape of that University be and what type that will be are the things under consideration. We, however, hope to have full discussions on it in the Conference scheduled on 18th April. So this amount of 34 crores has been left apart and shall be spent in the three years to come. We are happy that we have gained speed in our progress in this direction.

I want to say some words about the Scheduled Caste Scholarships as well. Yesterday some friends of mine here made a mention of these and drew the attention of the Government to the fact that some more steps need be taken in this direction. You are aware that at the time when the National Government took over the charge of the Central Government, there was a provision of not more than three lakhs of rupees for the education and scholarships of the Scheduled Castes. That period was over in two years, but no deputation came to me nor did anybody approach me for the increment in the amount. We ourselves felt it as our duty to increase that amount of three lakhs. There was not a single penny sanctioned till then for Scheduled Tribes. So this item, too, was added. A sum of fifty thousand rupees was reserved as token grant for carrying on an experiment in this direction. We made an observation and came to the conclusion that we were crowned with success, and we had, therefore, to increase the amount. This sanctioned amount of three lakhs gradually increased to 40 lakhs in these three years. Clarifying the question raised by Mr. Bhoj[1] Maulana Azad: No, excuse me. You see that the amount went on increasing from 3 lakhs to 40 lakhs of rupees. Howsoever fast the figures of census move upwards, there cannot be anything otherwise. Apparent as it is, Government are not ignorant about it and are fulfilling their duties. The fact remains that all of us feel in our hearts that for centuries the society has sinned by being so very unkind and unjust to these backward brethren of ours; and now it is the bounden duty of our society to atone for what it has done to them by uplifting these down-trodden brethren as soon as it can be.

Shri P.N. Rajabhoj: Excuse me for one minute. I would like to ask a question.

Maulana Azad: My friend drew our attention to the fact that Delhi University did not grant exemption of fees. Apparent as it is, the question of exemption of fees does not arise in the education of Universities, be it of Delhi or of any other place. But, however, the Government have it in view and are considering the exemption of fees in Universities.

Now, I want to say a few words about the cut motions moved here. No debate was held, in fact, regarding those but I want to make it clear to you what actually was behind those cut motions.

There was a cut motion that the expenses on the establishment of the Education Ministry were very much. I do not know what actually the mover of the motion thought about the expenses incurred by the Governments on the management, nor do I know what he thought about the proportion between the expenses made by different State Governments and the different branches of the Central Government. I would like to convince you that the Ministry of Education maintains the least possible staff and can assure you with full responsibility that the burden shouldered by the Ministry of Education is more than its might. In 1949 the expenditure of the Ministry on the maintenance of the staff was not more than three crores and now when work has spread very much and the expenditure is seven to eight crores there has not been a proportionate increment in the staff. I would make it clear that today we need more staff for efficiency of work and lowering the strength of the staff, therefore, is out of the question. If you look at the expenses of the Ministry of Education, you will find that we are not

1. Mr. P.N. Rajbhoj, the then Member of Parliament from Sholapur (Bombay State).

spending more than 2 or 2.7 per cent., and you should know that the governments outside India are spending more comparatively. Those governments are spending four to seven per cent. on their establishments. In comparison to theirs our expenditure of 2.7 per cent. is the least amount incurred on the establishment. If you observe it keenly you will find it as the least expenditure incurred on the establishment. I wonder that such a point should have been made an issue for a cut motion.

Another cut motion drew our attention to this thing that the candidates who passed the Commerce and Diploma Course in 1948 were not given the diplomas. I don't know if the movers of the siad cut motion took at all the trouble of seeing the ruling given by the All India Council of Technical Education. Had they only studied their proceedings, there would not have been any necessity to table this cut motion. This All India Council gave a new ruling that passing their own course would not suffice for the students and they would not be entitled to get the diploma unless they got practical education through an apprenticeship for a year at least in some recognised concern. I was informed that there were ten students in 1948, out of whom only four had the practical experience and were given the diploma. Nothing has been said about the remaining six; and only if they had one year's experience they would have got the diploma, not otherwise. So I understand that moving a cut motion that the students who completed their course in 1948 did not get any diploma is improper and out of place.

Attention has also been drawn to the fact that the Archaeological Department does not look after the ancient relics in Karnatak and some other places. I do not know the basis of it. You know that the Archaeological Department of the Central Government takes into consideration for maintenance those buildings and sites only which are thought of national importance by the Parliament. An Act has also been passed for these under which many monuments have been taken over by us. About 515 monuments of Karnataka, seven archaeological places of Malabar and 515 monumental places of Maharashtra have been taken over by the Archaeological Department of the Central Government. We have not closed our doors as yet, but are prepared to accommodate as many places as are thought of national importance. Besides, States Governments have their own archaeological departments and the monumental places there are looked after by them. All these places taken over are looked after properly and lakhs of rupees are incurred as expenses on their maintenance.

Some friends drew our attention to the fact that the Central Government should make more efforts for propagating Hindi language.

They know that the Central Government have started full efforts in this direction since the Constitution was passed wherein it was decided to have Hindi as the Official and National language of India. Also, a special section in the Ministry of Education has been deputed for this pupose, and its function is to see how Hindi can be propagated amongst the non-Hindi speaking areas, and how the difficulties be removed. This special section for the purpose of finding out ways and means has on role responsible officers who are busy with the work for all the twenty-four hours. Besides, the Ministry felt that two things were of the utmost importance regarding the propagation of Hindi. Firstly, coining scientific and technical terms – without which neither the problem could be solved nor would the avenues of progress open and in the sphere of education a board has been set up since for this work which is functioning speedily.

Secondly, as I have already told you, ways and means are to be found out for propagating Hindi in the provinces where the mother language is not Hindi. The Central Government are, however, making efforts for this in a very speedy way. You should also know that 14 lakhs of rupees have been kept apart for this purpose and the amount will be spent in the three years to come. Besides this, efforts have also been made to make arrangements for imparting education to the employees of the Government of India who are in junior service. A special school has been opened for them, where their number is increasing day by day. This also was felt that steps should be taken for the propagation of the languages of our South Indian brethren so that they do not feel that Hindi is pressed upon them while their languages are ignored. I understand they are justified to some extent if they think in that light. North Indian people with Hindi as their mother language should take interest in the languages of the South, and also in Bangla and Marathi. We have, however, approved the resolution that the students who read in the four Central varsities and have Hindi as their mother language shall also be imparted education in the South Indian languages, their State languages and in Marathi, Bangla and Gujrati, besides, and shall take proficiency examination in any of those languages, and shall also get scholarships. Such a procedure has so far started in the four Central Universities only, but we want this procedure to start in other Universities of the country. We have nevertheless, drawn their attention to this side and told them to introduce such scholarships so that the South Indian languages also have an opportunity to grow as much as they possibly can.

I shall not take much time of the House, but would like to bring home to you that we are passing through critical times. The most critical time for a nation is when it starts its life anew. We are actually passing through that very stage. On one hand we want to have arrangements made for education, health and other welfare subjects, and on the other hand we say that our income is static. Both the things cannot go side by side. Income is the problem; and unless some constructive things are done, there cannot be any source of income. And if expenditure is incurred on other things wherefrom will the money come for education and health. Actually speaking we are confronted with a dilemma, which we shall have to come over somehow or other. I would like to tell you convincingly that we are not lagging behind in the race of time. We are moving onwards.

Further part of the speech after asking a question by Mr. P.N. Rajbhoj

Maulana Azad: Sir, the Government are not concerned with the foreign scholarships. The board set up by the Government comprises the representatives of Scheduled Castes. The board decided that it would be in our interests to give ten or twelve scholarships in India instead of spending huge amounts on education in foreign countries. Three years have passed since and the thing has come up before the Government, and the Government have put it up before this board. They are considering this and it is hoped that a decision will be made by them very soon.

It is evident that this Government are not concerned with such problems in Kashmir, but we shall, however, draw the attention of Kashmir Government towards these so that they do their best in this direction.

Mr. Deputy-Speaker: I shall now put to the House all the cut motions that have been moved.

The cut motions were negatived.

Mr. Deputy-Speaker: The question is:

> "That the respective sums not exceeding the amounts shown to the third column of the Order Paper in respect of Demands Nos. 17, 18, 19, 20, 21 and 115 be granted to the President to complete the sums necessary to defray the charges which will come in course of payment during the year ending the 31st day of March, 1954, in respect of the

corresponding heads of Demands entered in the second column thereof."

The motion was adopted.

[*The motions for Demands for Grants which were adopted by the House are reproduced below.*- Ed. of P.P.]

DEMAND NO. 17—MINISTRY OF EDUCATION

"That a sum not exceeding Rs. 30,41,000 be granted tot he President to complete the sum necessary to defray the charges which will come in course of payment during the year ending the 31st day of March, 1954, in respect of 'Ministry of Education'."

DEMAND NO. 18—ARCHAEOLOGY

"That a sum not exceeding Rs. 40,59,000 be granted to the President to complete the sum necessary to defray the charges which will come in course of payment during the year ending the 31st day of March, 1954, in respect of 'Archaeology'."

DEMAND NO. 19—OTHER SCIENTIFIC DEPARTMENTS

"That a sum not exceeding Rs. 1,75,83,000 be granted to the President to complete the sum necessary to defray the charges which will come in course of payment during the year ending the 31st day of March, 1954, in respect of 'Other Scientific Departments'."

DEMAND NO. 20—EDUCATION

"That a sum not exceeding Rs. 4,47,39,000 be granted to the President to complete the sum necessary to defray the charges which will come in course of payment during the year ending the 31st day of March, 1954, in respect of 'Education'."

Demand No. 21—Miscellaneous Departments and Expenditure under the Ministry of Education

"That a sum not exceeding Rs. 27,71,000 be granted to the President to complete the sum necessary to defray the charges which will come in course of payment during the year ending the 31st day of March, 1954, in respect of 'Miscellaneous Departments and Expenditure under the Ministry of Education'."

Demand No. 115—Capital outlay of the Ministry of Education

"That a sum not exceeding Rs. 5,50,000 be granted to the President to complete the sum necessary to defray the charges which will come in course of payment during the year ending the 31st day of March, 1954, in respect of 'Capital Outlay of the Ministry of Education'."

Mr. Deputy-Speaker: We will now proceed with the Demands for Grants relating to the Ministry of Labour.

Document No. 17

Extract of reply dated 2-4-1953 by Maulana Azad to the question asked in the House of People in connection with the National Language Hindi

The Minister of Education and Natural Resources and Scientific Research (Maulana Azad): According to our information, this has been kept in view by the Board ever since it started work. The Government of India themselves have drawn the attention of all the State Governments and of the various Central Government Ministries to this. Accordingly, whatever work had been done already by the various Ministries has been made over by them to the Board. Some material has also been received from the States and the Board has considered the same. I am afraid the hon. Member does not fully appreciate the difficulties of this task. He thinks it is like the work involved in the preparation of general dictionaries. This is quite a different type of work. For the first time we are going to coin scientific and technical terms in Hindi. We have really to establish a new mind and to strike new coins. This is not the kind of work that could be hurried through. Hurry in this case would spoil the whole game. I can of course say with confidence that the Board is working at full speed. The first volume on Chemistry and Physics has already been prepared. Only ten or twelve days back I passed an order that it should be sent to press. It will be got printed and published so that everybody in the country might have an opportunity of seeing it and of making his comments.

Document No. 18

Views Expressed on the Death of Shri Asaf Ali[1]

The Minister of Education and Natural Resources and Scientific Research (Maulana Azad): Sir, it has fallen to my lot to announce a very sad news in this House. Shri Asaf Ali breathed his last in Berne at mid-night yesterday. The information that we have received till now is not a detailed one but so much is known that he died of heart failure.

This sad incident has deprived us of many good things, but the first thing that strikes me is that we have lost a brave comrade who fought with us shoulder to shoulder in the battle for independence. In 1920 when the non-co-operation movement was launched Shri Asaf Ali was practising at the Bar in Delhi. He left his practice, joined the movement and after that courted imprisonment a number of times. Wherever the movement was started he always came to the front. When in 1924 the Swaraj Party was formed and the Congress decided to enter the legislatures, he also was elected to the Central Legislative Assembly. There might be some of us here who may remember the meritorious work that he did in the old Legislative Assembly. He was the Secretary of the Congress Party, then he was elected its Deputy Leader. When in 1942 after the Bombay Session of the All India Congress Committee all of us were arrested he was also put behind bars because he was a member of the Congress Working Committee. Thus in Ahmadnagar Fort we lived together for three years. Afterwards when the First National Government was formed he was selected to be a member of the Cabinet by virtue of his holding the portfolio of the Minister of Railways. Then we decided to send him to Washington and there he discharged his duties most admirably. Afterwards he became the Governor of Orissa and now he was posted at Berne. This was just a sketch of his public life. But as a human being also he was possessed of many good qualities of heart and soul, which will long be cherished by his friends. I hope that this House will express its sense of deepest regret on this sad incident.

---

1. .April 2, 1953.

Document No. 19

Joint Answers dated 8-4-1953, of Maulana Azad and Mr. K.D. Malaviya to questions asked in the House of People

SURVEY OF MEN OF LETTERS

Shri M.L. Dwivedi: (a) will the Minister of **Education** be pleased to state whether any survey has been made in the country, of various men of letters, authors and the like, in the Rashtra Bhasha?

(b) Is it a fact that the work of compilation of a suitable dictionary, terminology and preparation of various documents and papers of Government in the Rashtra Bhasha, is being delayed for lack of hands?

(c) Is there any proposal or plan under consideration to utilise the services of such men?

The Deputy Ministry of Natural Resources and Scientific Research (Shri K.D. Malaviya): (a) No, Sir.

(b) No, Sir. The work of the preparation of dictionaries in Hindi of Scientific Terms relating to various sciences has already been started under the guidance and supervision of the Board of Scientific Terminology and its ten Expert Committees on Physics, Botany, Chemistry, Mathematics, Social Sciences etc. The Hindi Section under the Ministry of Education is also helping the various Central Government Departments in finding suitable Hindi equivalents for such technical or other terms as are referred to that Section.

(c) No, Sir. The compilation of dictionaries or preparation of technical terms requires the services of scientists, philologists and translators who are already being utilised for the purpose.

The Minister of Education and Natural Resources and Scientific Research (Maulana Azad): The only proper way to tackle this job was through the constitution of a Board of Experts which was to prepare a dictionary after full deliberations, which could then be published so as to provide all great scholars with an opportunity of perusing it and forming their opinions. The opinions of all these people were then to be received by the Board which was to make whatever changes it deemed necessary in the light thereof. The work is proceeding on just those lines. As I just stated a portion of the work has already been done and sent to press for printing.

Shri Meghnad Saha: Has the Ministry engaged whole-time workers for this purpose or only honorary workers?

Shri K.D. Malaviya: Whole-time workers are also engaged for this purpose.

Maulana Azad: Madhya Pradesh had also been written to and we hope that they would also adopt the same means as the other States have done.

Shri T.S.A. Chettiar: May I know whether Government have not agreed that the international terminology should be accepted so far as scientific terms are concerned?

Shri K.D. Malaviya: As far as possible, the underlying concept is that international terminology for science words should be accepted.

Maulana Azad: Let me make this a little more clear. The matter had been referred to the Central Advisory Board of Education, who decided that we should, as far as possible, adopt the international terminology. This does not mean, however, that the task before the Board has been lightened and all that it has to do now is to reduce the international terms into the Devanagari script. It has to and must coin hundreds of Hindi terms. As is known, every science employs a number of words which are spoken commonly, but which become 'terms' when adopted by a special science. For instance, 'action' and 'reaction' are words commonly used in English but they are specific terms in Chemistry. Now, it would be wrong to accept 'action' and 'reaction' in Hindi. We cannot adopt common English words in Hindi. For words of that kind we would have to coin terms in Hindi. 'Action' and 'reaction' are common words of the English language; they are not international terms. But when we are confronted with the word 'oxygen' we have to admit that here is an international term and that we should adopt it in Hindi without any modification. It is on these lines that the Board is working. They have coined hundreds of terms in Hindi and also selected a number of international terms.

Shri T.N. Singh: Are Government aware of the fact that by various Provinces as well as by various associations the same type of work is being done, and may I know whether they have ever thought of co-ordinating these efforts?

Shri K.D. Malaviya: Yes, Sir, It is so.

Document No. 20

Replies dated, 8-4-1953, of Dr. Katju[1] and Maulana Azad in the House of the People to questions asked regarding the Education Experts Committee

Shri Raghuramaiah: Will the Minister of States be pleased to state:

(a) the terms of reference of the Education Experts Committee which has been appointed to enquire into the affairs of the Osmania University; and

(b) whether it will be open to the committee to elicit public opinion on all points including the proposal to transfer the University to Central control?

The Minister of Home Affairs and States (Dr. Katju): (a) A copy of the Resolution setting up the Committee, which contains the terms of reference, is placed on the Table of the House. [*See* Appendix VIII, annexure No. 36.]

(b) No.

Shri Raghuramaiah: May I draw the attention of the hon. Minister to the first line in the Resolution that "The Government of India in consultation with the Government of Hyderabad decided to reconstitute the Osmania University as a Central Institution.....". I recollect, last time when this subject came up and answer was given by the hon. Deputy Minister for Education (*Some Hon. Members*: This is a speech) that as final and irrevocable decision has not yet been taken. I would like to know how these two statements can be reconciled....

Shri P.T. Chacko: On a point of order, Sir, I want to know whether the answer given was to question No. 1232.

Dr. Katju: Yes.

Mr. Deputy-Speaker: What is the point of order?

---

1. Dr. K.N. Katju.

Shri Raghuramaiah: I was labouring to point out a certain inconsistency in the answers. Last time, in reply to a question whether an irrevocable and final decision has been taken on the Centre's taking over the Osmania University, the answer was, that no such decision was taken, and that the decision would be taken after the committee's recommendations are received. I find here, "The Government of India in consultation with the Government of Hyderabad decided to reconstitute the Osmania University as a Central Institution....". I would be grateful if the two statements can be reconciled.

Dr. Katju: I think the Resolution represents the correct situation.

Dr. Suresh Chandra: How many times has this Expert Committe met so far and what are the results of the deliberations of this Committee?

Dr. Katju: I do not think the Committee has met so far.

Dr. Suresh Chandra: May I know why this Committee has not met so far?

Dr. Katju: I think that question should be put to the Committee.

Dr. Suresh Chandra: The Committee is not before the House, Sir, the hon. Minister should tell us the reasons.

Shri Ramachandra Reddi: May I know whether the Inter-University Board has been consulted in this behalf?

The Minister of Education and Natural Resources and Scientific Research (Maulana Azad): No, it has nothing to do with this.

Shri Sivamurthi Swami: May I know whether the Ministry has received any representation from the people against the appointment of this Committee?

Maulana Azad: No, we have not received anything of that kind.

Shri Meghnad Saha: When a Committee does not meet, is it not the duty of the Ministry to see that it meets?

Maulana Azad: The Ministry will see to it but it is, in any case, the duty of the State Government to see how the work is to be carried on.

Further clarification to the question raised by Dr. S. Chandra

Maulana Azad: I do not think it was through lack of time that the Committee failed to meet; there must be some other reason.

Shri T.S.A. Chettiar: May I know whether the decision of its being made into a Central University will be taken on the recommendations of this Committee?

Maulana Azad: This Committee has been appointed to ascertain what are the problems that would arise as a consequence of its conversion into a Central University and which should have to be considered. We shall have a full picture before us only on receipt of the Committee's report.

Dr. Suresh Chandra: Does it follow from the statement of the Minister that an irrevocable decision has not been taken yet with regard to the transfer of the Osmania University to the Centre?

Maulana Azad: The question may please be repeated.

Maulana Azad: No, I did not mean that. I meant that the Expert Committee would consider the grave and important problems arising as a consequence of the creation of a Central University so that we might have a full picture before us.

Shri Raghuramaiah: In further clarification of the Statement laid on the Table of the House, may I know whether, considering that this University is the only University in Hyderabad, the present popular Government or the University Senate has been consulted in the matter before the Government of India took this decision?

Maulana Azad: Evidently the decision taken in this behalf by the Government of India was in consultation with the State.

Mr. Deputy-Speaker: Yes, it is in consultation with them.

Document No. 21

Joint Answers dated, 8-4-1953 by Maulana Azad and Mr. A.P. Jain to the questions asked in House of People

GRANTS FOR UNIVERSITIES

Shri Jhulan Sinha: Will the Minister of **Education** be pleased to state:

(a) the amount of grants sanctioned for the Banaras and Patna Universities for the yare 1952-53; and

(b) the purposes for which those grants were sanctioned?

The Minister of Rehabilitation (Shri A.P. Jain): (a) and (b) A statement is laid on the Table of the House. [*See* Appendix IX, annexure No. 37.]

Shri Jhulan Sinha: May I know whether the Patna University has made any request for grant for its general and educational expenses? I find from the statement that there was no allotment to Patna University.

The Minister of Education and Natural Resources and Scientific Research (Maulana Azad): I cannot answer it just now.

Further reply to question raised by Mr. Jhulan Singh:

Maulana Azad: How can the Government say? It is to be decided by the University.

Reply to question raised by Dr. Suresh Chandra

Maulana Azad: Apart from the four Central Universities, the grants are generally given for scientific and technical education.

Reply to the question raised by Mr. S.N. Das

Maulana Azad: Government will consider it.

Mr. Speaker: Let us go to the next question.

Document No. 22

Maulana Azad's Address at the Conference of S.E.M. and V.C.U. held in New Delhi on 15-4-1953

I am glad to welcome you today to this conference. As you are aware, our object is to discuss problems of universities with special reference to the improvement of standards and co-ordination of facilities for higher education. It was my intention to call this conference in January but on account of pressure of work this could not be done.

The problem we have met to discuss is not new, though it has acquired a new urgency after the attainment of independence. You are all aware that for the last thirty years or more there have been persistent and at times well-founded criticism of our universities. The great increase in the number of students has been accompanied by a fall in the standard of attainment. Ill-equipped and ill-trained graduates have increased the number of the unemployed. Their indiscipline and lack of purpose have added to our difficulties at a time when the attainment of independence has posed great problems of reconstruction and development before the country.

It was in order to examine the existing defects and make recommendations for the remodelling of university education in conformity with the needs of free India that the Radhakrishanan Commission was appointed in 1948. The Commission made a careful survey of the entire field and made recommendations for necessary changes in the academic, financial and administrative set-up of our universities in the new context. It redefined the aims and objects of university education and placed special emphasis on the establishment of proper relations between the universities on the one hand and the Central and State Governments on the other. One of its basic recommendations was for the creation of a machinery for the most economic utilisation of our existing resources by avoiding wastage or unnecessary duplication in the fields of higher study and research.

The problem of university education was also considered at the time when the Indian Constitution was being framed. There were detailed discussions as to whether university education should be made a Central or a State responsibility. The Radhakrishnan Commission had recommended that the "all-India aspects of university education, the repercussions and interchanges necessary and desirable between universities, and the need or a national guarantee of minimum standards of efficiency" require that university education should be a concurrent responsibility of the Centre and the States. The Commission had, in particular, mentioned that co-ordination of facilities in special subjects, the liaison between the universities and national research laboratories and scientific surveys, the adoption of national policies and the maintenance of standards of efficiency should be the special concern of the Government of India. That this view carried due weight in the framing of the Constitution may be seen from the inclusion of a specific item in the Constitution making co-ordination and maintenance of standards the exclusive responsibility of the Central Government. I am referring to entry 66 in List 1 of the Seventh Schedule of the Constitution defining the exclusive jurisdiction of the Union Government, which reads as follows:

> "Co-ordination and determination of standards in institutions for higher education or research and scientific and technical institutions."

The co-ordination of facilities in higher education and the maintenance of standards of university education is thus an exclusive Central responsibility. This makes it necessary for the Government of India to take an immediate and direct interest in the affairs of all universities in order to ensure that the provisions of the Constitution are carried out. The Government has considered the matter carefully and reached the conclusion that this responsibility cannot be discharged without the creation of an agency which would enable the Government to carry out the necessary supervision and over-all guidance. Since this duty is an exclusive Central responsibility, the Government would have been entitled to set up, for these purposes, an official body composed of its own officers and nominees. The Government did not, however, do so. The Government recognises the value of university autonomy and desire that the necessary reforms in universities should, as far as possible, be initiated by the universities themselves. The Government is also of the view that in all such steps for the improvement of standards of higher education in the country, the co-operation of the States at every step is not only desirable but essential. It is or this account that the Government of India prepared a draft Bill entitled "Universities

(Regulation of Standards) Bill." Before introducing it into Parliament the Government of India referred it to the State Governments and the universities for their advice and guidance.

I must confess that I have been somewhat surprised by the response of the universities to this gestures of co-operation by the Central Government. The Inter-University Board, in its Madras session, has expressed itself against the Bill and raised doubts about its purpose and provisions. Nevertheless, the Board itself had to recognise the need of a machinery to effect co-ordination and improvement of standards. In view of this recognition, the suggestion that the draft Bill indicates a desire of the Government of India to interfere with the internal autonomy of the universities is quite unfounded, and it is difficult for me to understand the grounds for such suspicion. As I have already said, the Government could, if it so wished, introduce the Bill without referring to the universities. That it has not done so is itself evidence of the Government's regard for university autonomy. Further, the constitution of the body proposed in the Bill is such as to ensure that the autonomy of the universities will be respected. The Government could have proposed the appointment of a body under its own control to look into the affairs of the universities but, instead, the Government has proposed that it should be an autonomous body, set up by legislation, consisting of representatives of universities and other distinguished educationists.

The statutory character of the body and the composition of its membership are in themselves evidence of the Government's desire that there should not be too much departmental interference with the internal affairs of the universities, while, at the same time, ensuring that proper standards are maintained and some of the glaring defects of university education removed. I am sure you will agree with me that if the Indian universities have already fallen into comparative disrepute, much of the responsibility lies with the universities themselves. Their administration has, in many cases, become slack and standards impaired through mainly non-academic causes, into the details of which I need not go. However, since the Inter-University Board has raised objections, I felt it desirable to summon a conference of Vice-Chancellors and Education Minisers and find out what they base their objections on. I need hardly add that I am always willing to consider any constructive suggestions they might make for the improvement of standards in universities and better co-ordination of their facilities.

I assume that we have met with a common objective, *viz.*, the reform of university education, with a view to making the universities agencies of national regeneration in independent India. I have made a passing reference to the fact that universities do not today enjoy the public esteem accorded to them in the past. The reasons for this are many but two may be especially mentioned. One is the largely academic character of the instruction in the universities which, instead of developing the personality of the student and enabling him to make a place in society for himself, often converts him into a misfit who adds to the number of the unemployed, if not the unemployable. The other is that even the standards of academic education have fallen so much that persons who have reached the highest stage are not only ill-informed and ill-educated about the affairs of the world but are sometimes ignorant of the elementary things in their own fields of study. Inefficiency and corruption, which have also crept into some of the university administrations, have contributed to the public's loss of confidence in them.

While no one is more keenly conscious of the defects of the present position, I should, at the same time, like to say that I do not believe that a sweeping condemnation of the universities and university education is justified. Today, it has become almost a fashion for everyone to get up and condemn all universities outright but they forget that if our universities have many defects, they have also many virtues. Nor can we forget that they have made a solid contribution to the achievement of Indian independence by awakening a new political consciousness among large numbers of their alumni.

I must also point out that not all the present defects of the universities are due to faults of the staff or the administration. Many of them are a direct outcome of the system which has been set up. The fact that a university degree is an indispensable condition for employment in most types of service has induced a rush for degrees and led to overcrowding in the universities. As a degree is regarded as a passport to any employment, some universities felt that they should not deny this passport to their students. There was thus a tendency to pass as many students as possible, if necessary even by lowering the standards. Once this downward trend began, it was difficult to check it, for any university which sought to maintain a high standard faced the risk of losing its students to other universities with lowered standards. The fact that degrees are essential pre-requisites for employment had an undesirable effect on students as well. It made them pay more attention to the passing of examinations than to the acquisition of knowledge.

On the other hand, the lack of adequate financial support for the universities leaves them with no option but to encourage the inflow into universities of as large a number of students as possible. In a situation where many of the universities derive a major portion of their income from the tuition and examination fees of students, it is difficult, if not impossible, for the university to exercise adequate control on the discipline and standards of study of its students. I may tell you that the Government is aware of these problems and we are now considering various measures to ease the situation. In many countries the possession of a degree is not an essential condition for employment in government service. We are therefore also considering whether a change can be made in our present practice. A proposal is under examination that we should not insist on degrees for employment except only in specialised posts which require high academic qualifications. This can be done only if we are able to devise some alternative method of recruitment to different types and grades of public service, which will be objective, flexible and free from the defects of the present system.

I have mentioned that one defect of the existing system of university education is its abstract and academic character. This, in itself, would not have been so serious a defect in a country with a different social background. University education must, in any case, involve a high degree of specialisation and abstraction. Unfortunately in India, this emphasis on the intellectual and academic aspect has been accompanied by the loss of manual skills, and, what is worse, a repugnance for various types of manual labour. Instead of recognising the dignity of labour, university students are often inclined to look down upon manual work. The Government of India have for a long time been in correspondence with the universities to devise measures to inculcate a sense of the dignity of labour among students and develop in them the habit of doing manual work. One suggestion which was sent for your consideration was to find out whether students could not be utilised for some of the work which is now performed by paid labour. There is also no reason why students should not help in the maintenance and repair of roads, gardens, furniture and some of the buildings of educational institutions. Colleges could also adopt a village, preferably one that is easy of access, and try to effect improvements in housing, sanitation, communications and education through the voluntary labour of students.

With the acceptance of the Five Year Plan in which a co-ordinated effort is being made to improve rural areas through community development projects, a field of acvtivity has opened up where University students can render the greatest service to the country. I would suggest for your consideration that each university might undertake a project by which a selected rural area is adopted by the university and the university undertakes the responsibility of carrying out developmental programmes – educational as well as material – within that area. I should be happy if you would consider this question also during your deliberations today and tomorrow and make specific proposals to the Government to this end. I may add that if the universities undertake any such programme of activities, the Government may be in a position to place small funds at the disposal of the Vice-Chancellors to enable them to set up an agency, which will plan, execute and supervise such activities.

I would also like you to consider carefully what exactly we mean by university autonomy. As I have said before, I am against any undue interference by the Government or any other body with the internal affairs of the universities. At the same time, I would like to say categorically that university autonomy is not an end in itself but a means to an end. That end is the achievement of satisfactory academic standards and the maintenance of the high dignity of the universities as seats of learning and culture. If therefore these ends are not fulfilled, the community has a right to demand such change as will make their achievement possible. To resist measures for the purpose in the name of university autonomy is therefore totally unjustified. The universities do not exist in dignified isolation but are components of society and hence society has a right to determine what will be the character and aims of the university. The State, as the organised executive of the community, has therefore not only the right but the duty to ensure that the university fulfils those aims which society has a right to expect from them. The Government of India is aware of its responsibilities in this respect and is determined to discharge the duty it owes to the community.

What I have in mind will become clearer if we consider how the idea of academic freedom has developed. Our universities derive their traditions mainly from the British universities. You are aware that in a country which has party Government, there is a tendency for officials to change with the change of the party in power. Two Governors-General of India lost their office – one even before he could come out to India – on account of a change in the party Government in Britain. There was a risk that there might be similar interference with appointments in the universities. It is bad enough if officials change with a change in Government, but the position would be intolerable if learned and able teachers were dismissed to make room for incompetent and unqualified persons on political grounds. That is why, in course of time, a convention has grown up to give security to university teachers and see that the best men are placed incharge of the education of the future generations. University autonomy was therefore recognised in order to achieve academic freedom and higher educational standards. If there is a fall in academic standards, and the administration of the university becomes defective, you will surely agree that the plea of university autonomy cannot be used as a defence against effecting the necessary reforms.

We are today passing through an age when old traditions are crumbling and new values have to be built up in their place. The old order has passed but a new order is not yet born. The happiness and prosperity of millions demand that this revolutionary reconstruction of society should be carried out not by violent or disruptive methods but through a process of legislation and planned change. Obviously, the universities must play an important role in initiating such changes and serve as agencies for the creation of new ideals and the training up of workers in their cause. This, however, requires the reform and regeneration of the universities themselves in order to enable them to carry out this momentous task. The creation of a strong agency which will jealously guard their standards and co-ordinate their resources and facilities is essential if the universities are to regain their old prestige and become centres of a new national awakening. We have met today to find out the best method of doing so, and I have every hope that before we disperse we will have arrived at an agreed solution of one of the most pressing problems facing higher education in the country.

Document No. 23

Opening Address of Maulana Azad at the C.B.R.I., Roorkee on 12-4-1953

With the opening of the Central Building Research Institute at Roorkee, the last of the eleven National Laboratories included in the first plan of the Council of Scientific and Industrial Research, will start functioning formally. The establishment of these laboratories will form a landmark in the history of India's industrial development. They represent the first systematic and planned attempt to apply science and technology to the growth and development of India's national industries.

With the introduction of modern education in India in the beginning of the 19th century, colleges and universities were established and interest in the study of science grew. For a long time, however, they offered little, if any, encouragement to research or original work. It is perhaps significant that the first initiative in this direction came from private individuals and non-official agencies. The Indian Association for Cultivation of Sciences was established in Calcutta in 1876, mainly through the generosity of the late Mahendra Lal Sarkar. The generosity and foresight of Jamshed Tata led to the foundation of the Indian Institute of Science and Bangalore in 1911. The Bose Research Institute was the result of the developed work of Jagadish Chandra Bose and was founded in 1917. The establishment of these institutions marked a great step forward and led to the growth of a spirit of research in the universities. But these institutions as well as the different university departments had and have, as their main object, the quest of truth and the advancement of knowledge. While they have contributed to the enrichment of knowledge, they did not and were not in fact planned to serve as agencies for the economic and industrial development of the country.

There was, thus, in our educational and scientific institutions a gap whose existence hampered the growth and development of our national industries. The establishment of these eleven laboratories is therefore a step of the greatest importance for the future progress of the country, and I can say with confidence that, of the diverse nation-building activities undertaken after the attainment of independence, it will rank among the most important.

The history of the Indian Council of Scientific and Industiral Research is well known, but may well bear repetition. It was during 1942, when, on account of war, the import of all kinds of industrial goods from abroad ceased, and there was simultaneously an immense increase in the demand for them that the Council was established to find a solution of what appeared an almost insoluble problem. The work during this period was, from the nature of the case, of an emergency nature, and the real developmental programme of the Council began only after the attainment of independence. I have already referred to the achievements of the Council since 1947, and it appears to me that the one reason for its splendid success is that the Council is an autonomous body with its own budget and free from formalities and red-tape which slow down the administrative machine of the Government. Even the Minister-in-charge, who supervises the activities of the Council, does so not as a Minister but as an office-bearer of the Council. There is, thus, no outside interference with the activities of the Council, and to a large measure the success of the Council is due to this fact.

The Council functions through 27 research committes which deal with different branches of science and technology. These are advisory bodies consisting of experts from both science and industry. The Council thus includes, among its members, some of the best representatives from both these fields and I would like to pay a tribute to them for the efficiency and despatch with which its work is carried out.

I must also record that the work of the Council would not have progressed so rapidly unless it had had from the very beginning a Director marked by great imagination, drive and initiative. It is generally held that the place of the scientist is in a laboratory and not on the chair of an administrator. The Director of the Council has proved that an eminent scientist can fill the role of an administrator with equal distinction. I am of course referring to Dr. Shanti Swarup Bhatnagar whom I would like to congratulate on his achievement. I would also ask him to convey my appreciation to his colleagues without whose co-operation his work could not have been accomplished.

The establishment of a Central Building Research Institute is in accordance with the recommendations of the Building Research Committee set up by the Council of Scientific and Industrial Research. As a start, a Building Research Unit was set up at Roorkee to work in co-operation with the Thomson College of Engineering, now the Technical University of Roorkee. The Unit consisted of two sections – one entrusted with research on short-term problems and the other with the planning and establishment of the Institute. In 1950, the Unit was transformed into the Institute and the foundation-stone of its new buildings laid in February 1951. Work on them began in December 1951, and we are today celebrating the completion of the first stage of their construction.

The problems for investigation in an institute of this type are largely common to different countries, but there are some which are of special interest to India. The Institute will therefore pay special attention to problems like factors governing comfort and efficiency under tropical conditions, the study of soil stabilisation, the use of indigenous materials, the utilisation of industrial wastes, the construction of houses for persons of low income on an extensive scale, etc. The work of the Institute will deal with these problems under four main heads, *viz.* (a) building materials, (b) methods of construction, (c) performance of buildings, and (d) survey and information. I need not go into details which you will find in the brochure published for the occasion but may mention four typical problems whose satisfactory solution will have a great significance for the development of our building industry. They relate to the improvement in the quality of bricks, the possible use of bamboo as a reinforcing material, the investigation on novel methods of construction evolved by the Institute itself or by others, the prefabrication and assembling of building components, heat and sound insulation, resistance to moisture penetration, fire and weather, the consideration of new architectural and structural designs and problems relating to brick industry, lime industry, etc.

Surveys will also help to assess the capacity of the building industry of India and co-ordinate its development with the Five Year Plan. Practical results obtained by research investigation or useful information obtained from surveys will be made available to the building industry in a form suitable for ready application to practical works. Since building industry covers the development and manufacture of various building materials as well as the use of such materials in the actual construction of buildings, the Institute will have divisions dealing with the production and testing of materials as well as with the construction and testing of structures. In addition, the Institute will provide for scientific and technical work in its divisions of chemistry, architectural physics and engineering.

The Government of India have sanctioned a grant of Rs. 21 lakh for capital expenditure on the establishment of the Institute, and of this amount Rs. 18 lakh have already been spent. The present site of the Institute measures 10 acres but an additional area of 57 acres has been acquired to provide residential accommodation to the staff and for the further expansion of the Institute. The Institute has 41 persons on its technical staff while another 41 look after the administration and office work. The recurring expenditure, when the Institute is fully staffed, will be of the order of about Rs. 5 lakh a year.

I am sure you will all agree that the provision of better housing is one of the most important tasks which faces the nation. Without better living conditions in villages and towns the state of health of the people cannot be adequately improved. While India has been well known for its architectural achievements of the past, we have to admit that today the art of constructions does not exhibit the skill or standard which has been its pride in the past. Better houses in towns and the provision of cheap, durable and comfortable houses for villagers and industrial labourers is a prime need of the day, and I have every hope that this Institute will make a solid contribution to the solution of this national problem.

Document No. 24

Joint replies by Maulana Azad and Ajit Prasad Jain in the House of People, to the questions asked on 17-4-1953

EDUCATIONAL GRANTS

Shri S.C. Samanta: Will the Minister of Education be pleased to state whether Central Grants for education to different States vary according to the population of each State?

The Minister of Rehabilitation (Shri A.P. Jain): No.

The Minister of Education and Natural Resources and Scientific Research (Maulana Azad): Yes.

Reply to the supplementary question asked by Shri Samanta

Maulana Azad: No. So far as the Commission is concerned, it has made no such recommendation.

Document No. 25

Joint Replies of Maulana Azad and Mr. K.D. Malviya to the questions asked in the House of People on 21-4-1953

ANCIENT MONUMENTS

Prof. D.C. Sharma: Will the Minister of **Education** be pleased to state:

(a) the number of ancient monuments protected in the hill districts of the State of the Punjab; and

(b) whether any more monuments from these places are proposed to be taken over by the Archaeological Department and if so, the details thereof?

The Deputy Minister of Natural Resources and Scientific Research (Shri K.D. Malaviya): (a) Thirteen.

(b) No, Sir.

Prof. D.C. Sharma: May I know if the fort at Nurpur which has associations not only with Vedic times but also with Moghul and British times is being taken over as a protected monument?

Shri K.D. Malaviya: It has already been taken over.

Prof. D.C. Sharma: May I know if the fort at Kangra which is called in history books as Nagarkot is being taken over as a protected monument?

Shri K.D. Malaviya: Nagarkot has also been taken over.

Prof. D.C. Sharma: May I know which branch of the Archaeological Department looks after the Punjab and where is its headquarters?

Shri K.D. Malaviya: There is no State-wise division in the Central Department. The monuments have been divided according to importance and are either Centrally-controlled or State-controlled. All these which I have mentioned are Centrally-controlled monuments.

Prof. D.C. Sharma: Is there any proposal to have a branch of this Department in the Punjab, where you have so many monuments of religious importance?

The Minister of Education and Natural Resources and Scientific Research (Maulana Azad): That is the function of the Punjab Government and it would certainly look after the matter. It is not necessary of the Centre to open a separate branch. It is the duty of the State Government.

Document No. 26

Brief Statement of Maulana Azad dated 21-4-1953 in the House of the People regarding the research aid to certain institutions and Universities

The Minister of Education and Natural Resources and Scientific Research (Maulana Azad): I would like to clarify the position. As this question concerned the Universities, therefore in reply reference was made only to the Universities. Certain institutions like the Hoshiarpur Institute and the Bhandarkar Institute, Poona are carrying on research in Vedic literature or general Sanskrit literature. Government is giving aid to these institutions also, but these have not been referred to.

Document No. 27

Replies of Maulana Azad and Mr. A.P. Jain in the House of People to questions asked on 24-4-1953

DISTRIBUTION OF MONEY ALLOCATED TO SCHEDULED CASTES ETC.

Shri Muniswamy: Will the Minister of **Education** be pleased to state the proportion in which the amount of Rs. 40 lakhs allotted for Scholarships in the Budget for 1953-54 will be distributed among Scheduled Castes, Scheduled Tribes and Backward Communities?

The Minister of Rehabilitation (Shri A.P. Jain): The allocation of the amount of Rs. 40 lakhs amongst the Scheduled Castes, Scheduled Tribes and Other Backward Classes for the year 1953-54 will be decided after examining the recommendation of the Board. A meeting of the Scholarships Board is likely to be convened shortly for the purpose.

Shri Muniswamy: May I know whether the Government are aware that the scholarships sanctioned to the States are not properly distributed?

The Minister of Education and Natural Resources and Scientific Research (Maulana Azad): No. Government do not think so.

Shri P.N. Rajabhoj: What was the proportion allotted to the Backward Classes, Scheduled Castes and the Scheduled Tribes in the last scholarship distribution?

Shri A.P. Jain: Scheduled Castes: Rs. 14,50,000; Scheduled Tribes: Rs. 5,00,000; Other Backward Classes: Rs. 10,50,000.

Shri Muniswamy: May I know whether Government are contemplating to increase this amount during the current year?

Shri A.P. Jain: Yes.

Shri B.S. Murthy: May I know whether any complaints have been received that the grants now being given to the students are not sufficient to covery their expenses?

Shri A.P. Jain: No.

Shri Nanadas: On what basis is the allocation of moneys made?

Shri A.P. Jain: It is allocated, after taking into account the following factors:

1. The population of the three groups;
2. Educational backwardness of each group; and
3. Number of applications received from each group of candidates.

Document No. 28

Maulana Azad's reply in the House of People to the questions asked on 24-4-1953

LEAD-ZINC IN ZAWAR

Shri B. S. Mehta: (a) Will the Minister of **Natural Resources and Scientific Research** be pleased to state by what time the detailed Geological mapping of the lead-zinc deposits in Zawar is expected to be completed?

(b) How much reserves of lead-zinc ores have been proved by the survey made so far?

(c) What is the strength of the party working there for Geological mapping?

(d) How long will they continue to work?

The Minister of Education and Natural Resources and Scientific Research (Maulana Azad): (a) to (d). A statement giving the information required is laid on the Table of the House [*See* Appendix X, annexure No. 20.]

Document No. 29

Written Answers of Maulana Azad dated 24-4-1953 in the House of People to the questions asked about the Secondary Schools

Shri Dasaratha Deb: Will the Minister of **Education** be pleased to state:

(a) the number of non-Government secondary schools in Tripura and the number of students reading in those schools;

(b) the percentage of students reading in Government secondary schools and in non-Government secondary schools;

(c) whether any representation under the leadership of Shri Ramesh Chandra Neogi was made by the Tripura Sikshak Samity regarding scales of pay and other demands; and

(d) if so, what steps Government propose to take with regard to that representation?

The Minister of Education and Natural Resources and Scientific Research (Maulana Azad): (a) 40 and 7,151 respectively.

(b) 47 per cent. and 53 per cent. respectively.

(c) Yes, Sir, but the correct name of the person is Shri Ramendra Chandra Neogi.

(d) It is being considered by the Chief Commissioner.

Document No. 30

Written answers dated 24-4-1953 of Maulana Azad to the questions asked in the House of People about the U.N.E.S.C.O.

Shri K.C. Sodhia: (a) Will the Minister of **Education** be pleased to state the total worth of U.N.E.S.C.O. coupons sold by Government to universities and educational institutions under (i) scientific materials, (ii) films, and (iii) books during 1952-53?

(b) What is the amount realised under the heads mentioned in part (a) above?

(c) What is the object of issuing and purchasing these coupons?

The Minister of Education and Natural Resources and Scientific Research (Maulana Azad): (a) The total worth of UNESCO Coupons sold during 1952-53 is as follows:

(i) Scientific Materials Rs. 3,66,840-14-9.

(ii) Films Rs. 33195-0-0

(iii) Books Rs. 95,916-8-9.

(b) All this amount has been realized.

(c) The object of the Scheme is to overcome foreign exchange obstacles to the purchase abroad of publications, educational films and scientific equipment.

Further Clarification

Maulana Azad: I have jsut said that these amounts are for books, films and scientific materials. The question of cash does not arise.

Document No. 31

Statement, dated 24-4-1953 of Maulana Azad regarding the General Policy of the Government for old buildings of national importance

The general policy of the Government is that old buildings of national importance which are sought to be protected should not be used for any other purposes as far as possible.

Document No. 32

Written answers, dated 24-4-1953 of Maulana Abul Kalam Azad and Mr. A.P. Jain to the questions asked in the House of People in connection with the Plan of Government for the Work of building houses for the I.I.T. Kharagpur

Shri N.B. Chowdhury: Will the Minister of **Education** be pleased to state:

(a) how far the work of building houses for the Indian Institute of Technology, Kharagpur, has progressed.

(b) whether the work is proceeding according to the original plan; and

(c) when the construction work is likely to be completed?

The Minister of Rehabilitation (Shri A.P. Jain): (a) All staff quarters and 2 hostels have been completed. Three Wings of the Institute are nearing completion. Work on the 3rd hostel and the rest of the Institute building has been taken in hand.

(b) The work is proceeding according to the plan prepared by the Board of Governors of the Institute.

(c) By 1955.

Shri N.B. Chowdhury: May I know whether the Director of the Institute is connected with the work of supervision of this construction in any way?

The Minister of Education and Natural Resources and Scientific Research (Maulana Azad): No.

Shri N.B. Chowdhury: May I know whether the Government have received any complaints about the removal of any article from the premises of this Institute?

Shri A.P. Jain: No.

Maulana Azad: No.

Shri N.B. Chowdhury: May I know the total estimate of this construction work?

Shri A.P. Jain: I cannot give the total at the moment, but I shall give the separate figures, which are as follows:

1 Director's Bungalow – Rs. 64,350

12 'A' Class Bungalows – Rs. 3,70,056

2 'B' Class Bungalows – Rs. 6,43,918

65 'C' type Quarters – Rs. 6,48,802

40 'C-1' type Quarters – Rs. 6,25,070

93 'H' type Quarters – Rs. 6,40,908

4 Blocks-Bachelor quarters – Rs. 9,02,786

Shri K.K. Basu: May I put one short supplementary?

Mr. Speaker: There is only one more minute. If that is put, then it will bar the other question. Next question, No. 1410.

Document No. 33

Replies of Maulana Azad and Mr. A.P. Jain in the House of People to the questions Asked on 24-4-1953

INDIAN MUSICIANS

Shri Muniswamy: (a) Will the Minister of **Education** be pleased to state the total expenditure incurred by the Government of India on the recent celebration held at Rashtrapati Bhavan in honour of the Indian Musicians?

(b) Do Government proposes to hold such functions every year?

The Minister of Rehabilitation (Shri A.P. Jain): (a) An Expenditure of Rs. 7,330/7/- has been incurred by the Government of India for award to Musicians of the year for 1952-53.

(b) Yes, Sir.

Shri Muniswamy: May I know how the selection of these musicians was made?

The Minister of Education and Natural Resources and Scientific Research (Maulana Azad): The selection was made by the Academy.

Shri Muniswamy: May I know whether the same musicians who came this year will be allowed to come next year?

Maulana Azad: Sanads will be given to fresh persons every year.

Further reply:

Maulana Azad: They might be called. That is a different matter. But the awards will be given to fresh persons every year.

Document No. 34

Oral Answers dated 7-5-1953 of Maulana Azad and Malaviya to the questions asked in the House of People

Conference of Education Ministers and Vice-Chancellors

Shri A.M. Thomas: (a) Will the Minister of **Education** be pleased to state the recommendations, if any, of the conference of Education Ministers and Vice-Chancellors held on the 18th and 19th April, 1953?

(b) What are the proposals of the Government in the light of the views expressed at the conference?

(c) What will be the constitution and functions of the proposed University Grants Commission?

The Deputy Minister of Natural Resources and Scientific Research (Shri K.D. Malaviya): (a) The Government of India had originally proposed the constitution of two separate agencies: a Central Council of University Education and a Universtiy Grants Commission. The Conference has suggested that instead of two separate bodies, only one, namely, the University Grants Commission, should be constituted and vested with functions and powers which the draft Bill had intended to vest in the Central Council of University Education. The conference also considered the question of manual labour by students at the University and Secondary levels and made certain detailed suggestions. It has also recommended a survey of the work being done at present and the suggestions that the various educational authorities may like to put forward for the future.

(b) and (c) The matter is under consideration.

Shri A.M. Thomas: In answer to a question of mine in the last session of the Parliament whether, in view of the opposition of the University bodies, the proposal to bring a comprehensive Bill to control University education was dropped, the reply of the hon. Minister, Maulana Azad was an emphatic "NO". Reports again appear that the

Bill in the form prepared by Government has been dropped. Is that report correct and may I know the present position?

The Minister of Education and Natural Resources and Scientific Research (Maulana Azad): If the proposal of the Conference is accepted by the Government, the only change in that case will be that the Bill which it previously wanted to bring on behalf of the University Education Board will now be brought on behalf of the University Grants Committee.

Shri A.M. Thomas: Am I to understand that the proposal to appoint a Central Council of University Education has finally been dropped and it has been resolved that a University Grants Committee on the U.K. model will serve the purpose?

Maulana Azad: The proposal of the University Grants Commission was already before the Government. Now the Conference has decided that the function of the proposed Education Board should also be entrusted to it and it should also enjoy the power which was proposed for the Board.

Shri A.M. Thomas: May I enquire when can we expect a comprehensive legislation which will be introduced in Parliament?

Maulana Azad: Efforts are being made to introduce it at an early date.

Shri Meghnad Saha: The University Commission presided over by Dr. Radhakrishnan has laid down certain proposals for the constitution of a University Grants Commission. Does the proposed Bill intend to follow the same lines or different lines?

Maulana Azad: Yes. The Commission proposed to be set up by the Government will largely be on the same lines as have been recommended by the University Inquiry Commission.

Shri Meghanad Saha: The Radhakrishnan Commission has suggested that the University Grants Commission should be an autonomous body on the lines of the Union Public Service Commission. Is it going to be an autonomous body or a body subordinate to the present Ministry?

Maulana Azad: It is under consideration of the Government.

Shri Velayudhan: May I know whether there was any consensus of opinion in the conference of the Vice-Chancellors that Government control over these Universities should be slackened?

Mr. Deputy-Speaker: Was it the general feeling that Government's control over the Universities should be slackened?

Maulana Azad: It is under consideration and it is difficult to give any definite reply at the moment.

Shri Matthen: May I know whether the proposed university Grants Commissions is on the model of the U.K. Grants Commission?

Maulana Azad: The matter is under consideration of the Government and no final decision has yet been taken.

Document No. 35

Answers dated 7-5-1953, of Maulana Azad, to the questions asked in the House of People regarding the idea of two Commissions for Universities works

Maulana Azad: No. The proposal made by the Conference has just been read out.

Shri Punnoose: May I know why the original idea of two Commissions has been given up for one and may I also know how this new proposal would be useful to the Universities?

Maulana Azad: It is still under consideration. The Conference made the suggestion that instead of two separate bodies there should be only one body which should do the work of both. Apparently this does not seem to be an undesirable suggestion.

Document No. 36

Replies dated 12-5-1953 of Maulana Azad and Mr. K.D. Malaviya to the questions asked in the House of People

CONFERENCE OF VICE-CHANCELLORS AND STATE EDUCATION MINISTERS

Dr. Ram Subhag Singh: (a) Will the Minister of **Education** be pleased to state whether the Vice-Chancellors of all the Universities of India were invited to the Conference of Vice-Chancellors and State Education Ministers recently held in New Delhi?

(b) If not, who represented Delhi University in that Conference?

The Deputy Minister of Natural Resources and Scientific Research (Shri K.D. Malaviya): (a) and (b) All the Vice-Chancellors were invited; as, however, no one was holding the Vice-Chancellorship at the Delhi University, that University was not represented at the conference.

Dr. Ram Subhag Singh: Since how long was nobody holding the Vice-Chancellorship of the Delhi University, and what was the reason?

The Minister of Education and Natural Resources and Scientific Research (Maulana Azad): He hopes to take charge very shortly. I believe the post has remained vacant for seven or eight months, the reason being that after the resignation of the Vice-Chancellor the University took some time to consider the matter of the new Vice-Chancellor and the Committee set up for the purpose also delayed the matter for some time. Now a new Vice-Chancellor has been appointed and it is hoped he would soon assume charge.

Document No. 37

Maulana Azad's address dated 29-6-1953 welcoming the members of the British Everest Expedition

It gives me great pleasure to present to you this team of brave, resolute and courageous spirits who have achieved one of the most splendid triumphs of our time. My pleasure is all the greater because I know that the joy of this achievement is shared by the whole world. I present to you, Sir, the members of the British Everest Expedition who, having conquered the highest peak on earth, have now come in our midst.

We all know how difficult and arduous this enterprise was. The human spirit has faced in many field Nautre's most tremendous challenges. The history of science is one long story of such struggles. But the challenge which these friends faced 29,002 feet above us was in many respects unique. In other fields, man's endeavour has been greatly aided by human ingenuity and by instruments of science. It is these instruments which have often decided the fate of the combat. But in the battle waged by these friends, ingenuity and mechanical aid were of limited help only. No doubt they helped to overcome some obstacles on the way, but not the real and the most difficult of all obstacles. We all know what it is. It is the hostility of the environment which makes it almost impossible for the human organism to function on such heights. Here, where Nature assumes its most terrific aspect and the elements are most ruthlessly at war, the human body and mind, adapted to the exigencies of an environment, 29,000 feet below, feel powerless and almost cease to respond. In such a battle weapons are of little avail. Only invincible courage and undaunted will-power can help a man to succeed.

From 1921 to 1952, eleven attempts were made by brave and resolute men to conquer this field, but each time they had to retire before mightier forces. At last the time came when the issue of this great battle was decided in favour of the spirit of man. It was this heroic British Expedition, whom we have the pleasure of welcoming in our midst today, which finally succeeded in planting the banner of victory over this field. Like the Roman conqueror of old, they may well say—we came, we saw, we conquered.

There can be no doubt that the credit of this splendid triumph must go to the team spirit and the fine organising ability of the leadership of the expedition. The nature of the undertaking was such that no single individaul or even two or three individuals together, however brave and spirited, could have achieved this triumph. Only the collective heroism of a well-organised team could have achieved this feat which the British Expedition has achieved. It was essential that every member of the Expedition should be carefully selected and allotted his share in the division of labour and that all should be wholly and equally inspired by the spirit of team work, of selfless co-operation and, above all, by a high sense of discipline. All these conditions could not have been satisfied if the Expedition had not been fortunate in having so able and earnest a leadership. The experience of previous expeditions was fully utilised and all contingencies foreseen. Every necessity was anticipated and carefully provided for, from oxygen to powdered ink, and every aid that modern science and industry could give, was made use of. The utility of each one of these has now tested in this experiment.

The important problem that has to be faced in scaling Everest is to decide how many camps should be set up on the way and at what altitude the last camp should be. Up to the time of this Expedition, the highest camp built had been at a height of 25,000 feet, *i.e.*, the last stage of the climb was about 4,000 feet, without any camp on the way for emergency refuge. Needless to say, this was the most arduous of all the stages. If the weather took a sudden turn for the worse, or if darkness descended earlier than anticipated, the climbers had no nearby shelter and were wholly at the mercy of chance. Thus, many of them were suddenly caught in blizzards and had to spend the night in ice caves. Wiser for the misadventures of their predecessors, the present Expedition decided to build the maximum number of camps from the base of the ascent to the top. Eight such camps were set up, of which the last was at 27,900 feet. This meant that the final stage which formerly was of 4,000 feet, was now reduced to 1,100 feet. Whoever was to attempt the last ascent had now to cover, not 4,000 feet as before, but only 1,100 feet in one climb. This wise arrangement reduced the danger and difficulty of the final assault to the minimum. Although it is obvious how difficult an undertaking it must have been to build a camp at 27,900 feet, the wonderful sense of discipline and co-operative spirit of the team overcame all obstacles. On the evening of May 28 Sir Edmund Hillary and Sri Tenzing reached this last camp and spent the night there. On the following dawn they set out for the last lap of the journey and, thanks to their courage, skill and fortitude, stood on the top of the world at 11-30 in the morning.

Sir, you will agree with me that every member of the Expedition deserves to be congratulated for this heroic and splendid achievement. It was the joint and selfless contribution of all which made possible what had hitherto been possible. In particular we congratulate Sir John Hunt whose fine leadership planned the assault and Sri Tenzing and Sir Edmund Hillary to whom fell the heroic task of covering the last lap of the journey and who fulfilled it with splendid courage and extraordinary endurance.

Sir, the story of the conquest of the highest peak in the world is now at an end. If we turn back the pages of history, we will see that this story began more than 200 years ago. The earliest record we have of a survey of the Himalayas is in the 18th century. It was in 1711 that some French Jesuit Fathers trained a few Chinese Lamas to survey Tibet. This was done under the Chinese Government's instructions. In 1717, the Jesuit Fathers prepared a map of Tibet based on this survey, in which was shown a range of mountains which stretched for 40 miles along the southern boundary. This was the first map of the Himalayan peaks. In 1735, the famous French Geographer, D'Anville, published this map in Paris. The Himalayan peaks were thus put on the map of the world but their exact heights could not be ascertained. In 1849, a party of the Survey of India located the highest peak of the Himalayas and marked it in the map as XV. In 1852, it was first discovered that this was probably the world's highest peak. An Indian member of the Survey party, Radhanath Sikdar, first came to this conclusion but at that time the exact height of the peak could not be measured. This was achieved in 1865 when it was ascertained that peak XV was 29,002 feet high and was the highest on this earth.

Attempts were then made to find out the local name of this peak. The French Jesuits had called it "Tchoumou Lancma", basing it on the descriptions supplied by the Chinese Lamas. The names *Devadhunga* and *Gaurishankar* were also suggested by some documents. But after careful enquiry it was found that the Tibetan name did not refer to any particular peak but to the whole range of mountains. Nor was any sufficient evidence found to support the claim of *Devadhunga. Gaurishankar*, it was discovered, was not the name of the highest peak but of another peak which was lower by 5,500 feet. Since no authentic local name was available, the then Surveyor-General of India, Sir Andrew Waugh, with the permission of the Royal Geographical Society of London, named the peak XV "Mount Everest" after the ex-Surveyor-General, Sir George Everest. Between 1921 and 1924 the Royal Geographical Society and the Alpine Club organised three expeditions to climb Everest. As a result of these expeditions, a great deal of topographical information regarding the northern slopes of Mount Everest was collected. It is believed that on June 8, 1924, Mallory and Irvine had almost reached the summit, but as they did not return alive, no authentic information could be obtained. Mr. Odell had reached a height of 27,000 feet while Col. Norton and Dr. Somervell had achieved 28,000 feet. Thus, only the last 1,000 feet of Mount Everest remained to be conquered. This has now been achieved by the British Expedition. Thus the romance of the world's highest peak, which began in 1717, was completed on May 29, 1953.

Sir, I have now the honour to request you to decorate Sir John Hunt, Sri Tenzing Norkay Sherpa and Sir Edmund Hillary with the special medals made for this occasion and to present to every member of this distinguished expedition a silver shield as a memento of their great achievement.

Document No. 38

Replies dated 8-9-1953 by Maulana Abul Kalam Azad in the House of People to the questions asked regarding unemployment

Shrimati Renu Chakravartty: (a) Will the Minister of **Education** be pleased to state whether it is a fact that the Central Government will give to the West Bengal Government funds to engage 30,000 teachers to relieve educated unemployment there?

(b) What are the financial liabilities undertaken?

(c) Is this scheme to be a temporary or a permanent one?

(d) How many schools are to be opened?

The Minister of Education and Natural Resources and Scientific Research (Maulana Azad): (a) to (d) The subject of educated unemployment is under the consideration of the Government and an emergency scheme for absorbing 80,000 teachers all over the country during the period 1953-55 has been prepared in this behalf. A copy of the circular letter addressed to the State Government in this connection is placed on the Table of the House which gives the necessary information. [*See* Appendix V, Annexure No. 45.]

Shrimati Renu Chakravartty: The statement says that money is going to be spent for opening new schools and for expansion of existing schools. May we know whether any part of this money is going to rehabilitate those schools which are faced with financial collapse or gone out of existence due to lack of funds?

Maulana Azad: Yes, such schools can be opened with these funds.

Shrimati Renu Chakravartty: May I know, Sir, because certain State Governments do not allow girls to take part in educational institutions after the elementary stage, whether any part of this money is going to be spent for opening schools for girls in the rural areas?

Maulana Azad: No sex distinction will be there.

Shrimati Renu Chakravartty: Does it mean that in these schools there will be co-education?

Maulana Azad: It depends on the policy of each State Government which will not be required to follow any particular procedure so far as this scheme goes.

Shrimati Renu Chakravartty: The last date is the 10th September when the State Governments have to reply. May we know how many State Governments have accepted these proposals?

Maulana Azad: I cannot answer it just now.

Reply to the Suplementry question asked by S.Ajit Singh

Maulana Azad: At present no group of persons is being removed from service.

Mr. Deputy-Speaker: The hon. Member is giving information. The Minister says that it has not come to his notice that any persons have been removed.

Sardar Ajit Singh: Sir, I can well understand Urdu.

Mr. Deputy-Speaker: Let him pass on this information to the Minister.

Shri Sarangadhar Das: May I know. Sir, in view of the fact that certain States do not advocate co-education, if there will be girls schools of these categories in the rural areas?

Mr. Deputy-Speaker: He has already said that it is left to the State Governments.

Maulana Azad: It lies in the powers of the State Governments.

Clarification to question asked by Mr. Samant[1]

Maulana Azad: It is difficult for me to answer this question at this stage. There are many matters connected with the scheme which are under consideration. One thing, however, is clear. Whatever new schools are opened, they will be basic schools and mostly junior basic schools.

Reply to the Suplementry question asked by Mr. Prabhakar[2]

Maulana Azad: It is proposed to prepare such a scheme that those who are employed may be given two or three months' training.

Shrimati Renu Chakravartty: In the statement it is said that social education centres are going to be opened. What will be the curriculum of these centres and will they be opened in the existing schools or new schools will be opened?

1. Mr. S.C. Samant.
2. Mr. Naval Prabhakar.

Maulana Azad: All these questions are premature yet. We have an adult education scheme also which is known as Social Education and wherever necessary we will open schools for this purpose also. But it is not possible to have a complete picture of the details until important matters are decided with the State Governments.

Shri Kelappan: May I know the amount sanctioned for the scheme?

Maulana Azad: The exact amount has not been decided upon yet. Many things are to be considered. However, it has been decided that a minimum number of 80 thousand men will be taken and whatever expenditure it involves will be incurred.

Shri C. Bhatt: What is the amount sanctioned for Bombay?

Mr. Deputy-Speaker: This refers to Bengal.

Dr. M.M. Das: Out of the money earmarked by the Central Government for this purpose, may I know how much will be spent on paying the salaries of teachers and what part will be spent in the construction of buildings and other equipment?

Maulana Azad: Both items are included in it. The scheme of aid is this that the Centre will assist for three years. For the first year it will contribute 75 per cent. and the State Government 25 per cent; for the second year 50 per cent. each; and for the third year the contribution of the Centre will be 25 per cent. and that of the State Government 75 per cent. Thereafter the entire liability will be of the State Government.

Shri K.K. Basu: May I know how the average salary that is going to be paid to the teachers will compare with the existing rates?

Maulana Azad: The matter has not been decided yet.

Document No. 39

Replies of Maulana Azad dated 8-9-1953 in the House of People to questions asked, in connection with the method adopted for the Scholarship and Social sciences awards, by the Shri Radha Raman and others

Shri Radha Raman: (a) Will the Minister of **Education** be pleased to state whether it is a fact that an award was announced by a U.S.A. University in the name of Shrimati Vijyalakshmi Pandit to an Indian Student for the study of Social Sciences?

(b) If so, what are its full details?

(c) To whom the award will be given?

The Minister of Education and Natural Resources and Scientific Research (Maulana Azad): (a) and (b) A scholarship has been offered by the Fairleigh Dickinson College, Rutherford, New Jersey, U.S.A. to an Indian student but it is not reserved for the study of social sciences. The scholarship is worth $ 475 a year which covers tuition and fees only and can be applied to any course given by the College. The college offers courses leading to the Bachelor's degree only. The length of the course would be from one to four years. The minimum qualification is Matriculation. Board, lodging, travel expenses to and from the U.S.A. and other incidental expenses will have to be borne by the scholar.

(c) Not yet finalised.

Further clarification by Maulana Azad

Maulana Azad: Applications have been called and the Ministry will consider them.

Replies to the Suplementary questions asked by Mr. R. Singh[1], Mr. Bansal and Radha Raman

(A) **Maulana Azad:** Because a scholarship has been offered for an Indian, it is not necessary that India should also offer a scholarship associated with the name of an American.

---

1. Mr. Raghunath Singh.

(B) **Maulana Azad:** Applications have been called direct by the Ministry. When the Ministry learnt that the college wanted to call applications direct, we drew their attention to the fact that the action should be taken through the Government. Now the Government of India is calling applications and they will make the selection.]

(C) **Maulana Azad:** The applications have been called through the State Governments and the Universities.

(D) **Maulana Azad:** Yes.

Document No. 40

Maulana Azad's replies dated 8-9-1953 in the House of People to the questions asked about the Indian Museum in Calcutta (Staff)

Shri S.C. Samanta: Will the Minister of **Education** be pleased to state:

(a) the basis on which the scales of pay and allowances of the staff of the Indian Museum at Calcutta have been revised;

(b) whether class IV employees will also get benefit from it;

(c) the percentage of increment in general; and

(d) the number of staff employed in the Museum (grade-wise)?

The Minister of Education and Natural Resources and Scientific Research (Maulana Azad): (a) On the recommendations made by the Central Pay Commission in respect of Central Government servants residing at Calcutta.

(b) Yes, Sir.

(c) No general percentage can be indicated. It varies from post to post.

(d) Grade III–10

Grade IV–68.

Reply to Supplementary question asked by Mr. Samant.[1]

Maulana Azad: I have not calculated the total amount yet. There is a list with me from which I can tell you whose pay has been raised by how much, but I cannot just now say how much total increment has been effected. This list can be placed on the Table if the hon. Member so desires.

---

1. Mr. S.C. Samant.

Document No. 41

Replies dated 8-9-1953 of Maulana Azad to the questions asked in the House of People

WELFARE SCHEMES FOR WOMEN AND CHILDREN

Shri M.L. Dwivedi: Will the Minister of **Education** be pleased to state:

(a) the progress made in administering the fund of rupees four crores set apart by the Planning Commission for aiding welfare schemes for women and children;

(b) whether the schemes which were to be implemented through the Central Social Welfare Board have been formulated; and

(c) the work done so far either by the Social Services Division of the Planning Commission or any other institution?

The Minister of Education, Natural Resources and Scientific Research (Maulana Azad): (a) and (b) The Government have recently set up the Central Social Welfare Board whose functions are not confined to welfare schemes for women and children alone – to administer this fund. The Board has had one meeting already, has formulated its plans and methods of work and has called for applications from the voluntary agencies working in the field of social welfare.

(c) A statement is laid on the Table of the House. [*See* Appendix V, annexure No. 44.][1]

May I also state that a few days ago all details have been given in reply to a question.

Shri T.S.A. Chettiar: I understand the Board has made certain rules for their guidance. Will the hon. Minister please place them on the Table of the House?

Maulana Azad: The board is framing the rules which will later on be considered by the Ministries of Education and Finance. If the hon.

---

1. Not included.

Member so desires, they can be placed on the Table of the House after they are approved.

Shri T.S.A. Chettiar: Some rules were published in the newspapers. If they were not approved, how could they get into the newspapers? If they are published, they could well be placed on the Table of the House.

Maulana Azad: I do not know what rules the hon. Member is referring to. Possibly some preliminary talks which were held at the first meeting have appeared in the reports. So far as I know the rules are being framed and will be put before the Ministry after whose approval they will be considered as having been completed.

Shrimati Renu Chakravartty: May I know what special welfare schemes for women and children have been considered by this Social Welfare Board?

Maulana Azad: Details cannot be given as yet. The board will frame these schemes. All that can be said at present is that work will be done specially for the welfare of children and women, the disabled and the helpless.

Shrimati Tarkeshwari Sinha: May I know whether the Government of India have set up an Indian National Committee on early childhood education, and if so how many members are there in that committee, and what was the work done by them so far?

Maulan Azad: It has nothing to do with this board and I cannot answer this question at this time.

Shri Thanu Pillai: May I know the qualifications for membership of the Board, and who the members of the Board are?

Maulana Azad: I can read out the list of the members, but as for their qualifications, the hon. Member can himself judge them.

Shri Thamu Pillai: Can I have a translation?

Mr. Deputy-Speaker: The hon. Minister is prepared to give the names, and the hon. member may see their qualifications himself.

Shri Thanu Pillai: My question was whether any qualifications are attached to that membership, not what their qualifications are.

Maulana Azad: No.

Shri N.M. Lingam: May I know the number of social welfare organisations in the country, and how many of them have been recognised by Government as agencies for implementation of the schemes of social welfare?

Mr. Deputy-Speaker: That will be done hereafter by the Board. That is what the hon. Minister stated.

Shrimati A. Kale: Am I to understand that so far no help has been given to the social welfare institutions, and that no work has been started so far?

Maulana Azad: As far as I know, no agency has been given any special help so far. Preliminary work is being done as yet.

Shrimati Renu Chakravartty: What is the agency through which this social welfare work will be undertaken by the various States, and may I know whether direct communications may be made by the Social Welfare Board now?

Maulana Azad: This board has been set up so that work may be done through the existing private agencies who are doing this work now, and that they may be rendered help. The board has the full authority to hold direct communication in this regard and it is doing so.

Reply to the Suplementary question asked by Seth Govind Das

Maulana Azad: Yes. The board will consider this matter also.

Reply by Deputy-Speaker to question asked by Babu Ram Narayan Singh

The hon. Minister said there were no special qualifications imposed on or expected of these membes. No definite rule has been laid down.

Shri Kelappan: May I know whether any amount out of these Rs. 4 crores has already been spent?

Maulana Azad: No.

Shri Boovaraghasamy: How many social service divisions or institutions have been set up, and what are the names of the places where they have been set up all over the country?

Maulana Azad: I cannot say anything on this. The board has been set up not to establish new institutions but to help those private agencies which are already doing this work.

Mr. Deputy-Speaker: Private institutions will be taken advantage of, and through their agency, this will be done.

Shri Kelappan: Is any amount going to be spent during the plan period?

Mr. Deputy-Speaker: Nothing so far.

Shri Kelappan: In the next three years?

Mr. Deputy-Speaker: The hon. member may read the reply. Rs. 4 crores have been set apart for this purpose, to be spent within this period.

Mr. M.L. Dwivedi: May I ask another suplementary question?

Mr. Deputy-Speaker: I have allowed so many supplementaries.

Shri M.L. Dwivedi: But any for me?

Mr. Deputy-Speaker: I am sorry. The hon. member has got another question now.

Document No. 42

Maulana Azad's Answers to the questions asked in the House of People on 8-9-1953

EDUCATION MINISTERS' AND VICE-CHANCELLORS' CONFERENCE

Shri M.L. Dwivedi: (a) Will the Minister of **Education** be pleased to refer to the reply to starred question 1932 asked on the 7th May, 1953 and state the steps which Government have taken or are going to take to fulfil the assurance given by him on the occasion of the Education Ministers' and Vice-Chancellors' Conference held in Delhi on 18th and 19th April, 1953 *viz.*, that the Government of India would consider with the greatest sympathy the recommendations of the Conference of Education Ministers and Vice-Chancellors of Universities?

(b) Have the recommendations, submitted to Government by the Conference been accepted?

The Minister of Education and Natural Resources and Scientific Research (Maulana Azad): (a) and (b) The Government have accepted in principle the recommendations of the Conference to establish a University Grants Commission instead of two independent bodies like the Central Council of University Education and a University Grants Committee.

Reply to the suplementary question asked by Mr. M.L. Dwivedi

Maulana Azad: This is a question of reforming the entire educational system. The Government want that an agency should be first set up. Then they will be in a position to consider the question of introducing necessary reforms. The particular issue raised by the hon. Member is already before the Government and will soon be considered.

Shri A.M. Thomas: The hon. Minister remarked on prior occasions that in spite of the objections raised by the various Universities to the proposed Bill, the Government were not going back upon the introduction of that Bill. May I know when it will be introduced? Can it be expected during the next session?

Maulana Azad: The Bill is ready and the Government wanted to introduce it in this Session. But as the hon. Member is aware, it is a heavy Session and we have been compelled to postpone the introduction of the Bill to the next.

Reply to the suplementary question asked by Prof. Dr. C. Sharma

Maulana Azad: That Commission will be framed only when the Bill is passed.

Shri N.M. Lingman: May I know when the proposed University Grants Commission is likely to come into being?

Mr. Deputy-Speaker: Order, order. I am really sorry hon. members who are sitting in the front benches go on talking like this. I do not hear a word of what is being said on the one side or the other. How can I get along with the proceedings?

Shri K.K. Basu: They should be removed.

Mr. Deputy-Speaker: Shri N.M. Lingam. Will the hon. member repeat his question?

Shri N.M. Lingam: When is the proposed University Grants Commission likely to come into being?

Maulana Azad: When the Bill comes before the House and is passed.

Document No. 43

Maulana Abul Kalam Azad's replies dated 8-9-1953 to the questions asked in the House of the People

Educational Programme

Shri M.L. Dwivedi: (a) Will the Minister of **Education** be pleased to state whether any scheme has been prepared to encourage students to undertake manual work and social service as part of their educational programme at the University and Secondary education levels as recommended by the Conference of Education Ministers and Vice-Chancellors?

(b) If so, when is it likely to be implemented?

(c) If not, what is the stage of progress of the proposals?

The Minister of Education and Natural Resources and Scientific Research (Maulana Azad): (a) Yes. Detailed plans, envisaging participation of students in manual and social service work on a voluntary basis, are being drawn up in consultation with all interested in this special field.

(b) and (c) As soon as the information, which is being collected, is ready.

Replies to the Supplementary questions asked by Mr. Dwivedi[1] and Govind Das[2]

Maulana Azad: Correspondence with the Universities is going on. Some schemes have been received and it is hoped that those that are being awaited will not take long and the work can be started very soon.

Maulana Azad: The matter was considered, but it was found that if it was made compulsory the effect would not be good and that it would be much better if the work was done voluntarily. In fact, the scheme that is being prepared now is based on the principle of voluntary participation. As far as we could gather, we believe that people are prepared to participate voluntarily.

Shrimati Jayashri: May I know, Sir, whether the students who will be doing this work will be paid their expenses?

Mr. Deputy-Speaker: Will the students who are asked to do manual work be paid?

Maulana Azad: There is no such provision in the scheme.

Replies to the suppl. questions asked by Sinha[3], Dwivedi[4] and Mr. Singh[5]

A–**Maulana Azad:** Those camps were not opened under this scheme. This is a different scheme.

B–**Maulana Azad:** At this time I am not in a position to give the names of the Universities.

C–**Maulana Azad:** Of their free will. When they joined the colleges they joined of their own choice.

Shri T.S.A. Chettiar: The hon. Minister said that a draft scheme had been circulated to different Universities. I hope I have understood him correctly. How do they propose to encourage implementation of the scheme? Do they offer any monetary help for purchase of raw materials or do they propose to give any extra grants to Universities or do they propose to withhold grants from Universities which do not encourage the scheme?

Shri K.K. Basu: Everything is scheming.

Maulana Azad: This work will be done by the Universities which alone are the proper agency for it. But the Planning Commission has earmarked some funds out of which the expenditure for organising this work may be met.

Shri Veeraswamy: May I know, Sir, what kind of manual work and social services students are expected to do, and whether scavenging work is also one of the items?

Maulana Azad: It is difficult to give an account of all types of work. The aim is that they will be made to do manual work.

Mr. Deputy-Speaker: Next question.

---

1. Mr. M.L. Dwivedi.
2. Seth Govind Das.
3. Mrs. Tarkeshwari Sinha (A).
4. Mr. M.L. Dwivedi (B).
5. Babu Ram Narayan Singh (C).

Document No. 44

Joint replies dated 11-9-1953 in the House of People by Maulana Azad and Shri K.D. Malaviya to the questions asked in connection with the students studying abroad

Dr. Ram Subhag Singh: Will the Minister of **Education** be pleased to state:

(a) the number of Indian students sent abroad for study during the financial year 1953-54 on Government scholarship; and

(b) the number of Indian students who have been awarded fellowships by the U.S. Education Foundation in India for the academic year 1953-54?

The Deputy Minister of Natural Resources and Scientific Research (Shri K.D. Malaviya): (a) No Indian student has been sent abroad for study on a Government of India Scholarship during the current financial year.

(b) None. I may also be allowed to state here very briefly the various schemes in view of the fact that there are various enquiries made by hon. Members of the House about scholarship schemes. There are three main scholarship schemes under which people are sent abroad for study – academic and practical:

(1) Modified Overseas Scholarship Scheme.

(2) Central-State Scholarship Scheme.

(3) Indo-German Industrial Co-operation Scheme.

Besides, there are Technical Exchange Agreements such as the Fulbright Agreement. The United States Technical Foundation awards each year a number of travel grants to research scholars, professors, etc. These are the four schemes under which people go abroad for studies.

Dr. Ram Subhag Singh: May I know, Sir, whether the values of the various scholarships are the same?

Shri K.D. Malaviya: They are different. Conditions are not similar.

Dr. Ram Subhag Singh: What is the different in value between the various scholarships?

The Ministe of Education and Natural Resources and Scientific Research (Maulana Azad): The old scheme of Overseas Scholarship was suspended two years back. Under this new scheme the students generally do not get these scholarships; but those University teachers whom their respective universities want to send abroad, are selected. In such cases half the expenses are borne by the University and the other half by the Central Government. Those junior men in service who are desirous of adding to their ability are also selected. Therefore, the reply given was that no student was sent during the current year as there was no more any scheme for sending students abroad in that way.

Reply to the Sppl. question by Seth Govind Das

Maulana Azad: The Government have made full efforts to provide them with jobs. I cannot give exact figures at the moment; but I think, all of them have been provided with jobs.

Shri Nanadas: In view of the fact that the Central Scholarship Board for Scheduled Castes and Scheduled Tribes has discontinued sending scheduled caste people to foreign countries, may I know, Sir, what steps have Government taken to send such people for studies abroad in the general scheme?

Shri K.D. Malaviya: According to the recommendation of the Board, the scholarship for the scheduled castes and tribes is stopped, but they are again reconsidering the question as to whether it is possible to send scheduled castes and backward class people for studies abroad.

Document No. 45

Joint replies dated 11-9-1953 in the House of People by Maulana Azad and Shri K.D. Malaviya to the questions asked in connection with the Adult Blind Training Centre

Shri Radha Raman: (a) Will the Minister of **Education** be pleased to state the number of students getting training at present at the Adult Blind Training Centre, Dehradun?

(b) What are the different industries in which they are being trained?

The Deputy Minister of Natural Resources and Scientific Research (Shri K.D. Malaviya): (a) 136.

(b) Simple cottage-industry-type handicrafts like weaving of cotton and woollen textiles, spinning, chair-caning, etc.

Shri Radha Raman: May I know, Sir, if the Government of India has got any statistics about the number of adult blindmen in this country?

Shri K.D. Malaviya: We have no statistics, but from information that is available, it seems there are about two million blindmen in the country.

Shri Radha Raman: May I know, Sir, from which States the blindmen are admitted into this institution?

Shri K.D. Malaviya: There is no reservation for any States.

Shri S.N. Das: In view of the fact that the hon. Minister has stated that there is no reservation for any States, may I know, Sir, from which States the blind adults have come?

The Minister of Education and Natural Resources and Scientific Research (Maulana Azad): Nothing can be said at this stage.

Shri Muniswamy: May I know, Sir, whether only adults are admitted into the School or whether young boys are also admitted?

Shri K.D. Malaviya: Any blind person between the age of 18 and 40 is eligible for admission.

Shri Veeraswamy: May I know, Sir, whether there is any comprehensive scheme under the consideration of the Government to educate all the blind children in different avocations?

Mr. Deputy-Speaker: The question is "Is there a school for the blind children where they are educated in different avocations?"

Shri K.D. Malaviya: Yes, there are such schools for the blind.

Shri Radha Raman: May I know, Sir, what are the conditions for admission of students in this Institute?

Shri K.D. Malaviya: I am not aware of any other condition except that the blind should be between 18 and 40 years of age.

Shri Boovaraghasamy: Who bears the expenses of these students – Government or the students themselves?

Shri K.D. Malaviya: The expenses are borne by the Government.

Maulana Azad: The entire expenses of this Centre are borne by the Government of India.

Shri Boovaraghasamy: I am not able to follow this answer.

Mr. Deputy-Speaker: It is given in the proper language – the official language of the country. The hon. Member cannot cast aspersion at the language which has been accepted as the official language of the country. But I will give the information to his question – so far as this Centre is concerned, the expenditure is borne by the Central Government.

Shri Muniswamy: May I know, Sir, whether blind ladies are also admitted into the school?

Maulana Azad: There is no such condition that blind men only can be admitted.

Document No. 46

Oral Answers by Maulana Azad and Shri K.D. Malaviya in the Parliament dated 16-9-1953 to the questions raised regarding Delhi Polytechnic

Shri M.L. Dwivedi: Will the Minister of **Education** be pleased to state:

(a) whether it is a fact that important changes in the syllabus of the Delhi Polytechnic were made in the month of January 1953 and examinations held in March 1953;

(b) how many students appeared in such examinations who had taken up subjects in which changes had been made;

(c) how many of them passed; and

(d) why such important changes were made in the curriculum and syllabus towards the end of the school session?

The Deputy Minister of Natural Resources and Scientific Research (Shri K.D. Malaviya): (a) Certain changes were made in January 1953 in the syllabus for Degree courses in Engineering, Textile Technology, Chemical Engineering and Architecture. The annual examinations for these courses were, therefore, postponed to June 1953.

(b) and (c) A statement giving the desired information is placed on the Table of the House.

(d) The Delhi University Act came into effect in May 1952, and the Faculty of Technology, which, under that Act, had to draw up the syllabii and curricula for these courses could not be set up by the University before September, 1952.

Reply to the Supplementary questions asked by Mr. Dwivedi

1–**The Minister of Education and Natural Resources and Scientific Research (Maulana Azad):** I cannot say that just yet, but there will of course be a supplementary examination in November. This has been conceded by the University.

2– **Maulana Azad:** No, there has been no change. There has been a change only in the three subjects to which the question relates.

STATEMENT

Name of course		Number of Students			
		Appeared	Passed	Passed in compartment	Failed
(1)	Bachelor of Engineering	59	45	11	3
(2)	Bachelor of Chemical Engineering	30	14	11	5
(3)	Bachelor of Architecture	30	20	7	3
(4)	Bachelor of Textiles Technology	32	6	7	19

Document No. 47

Replies dated 16-9-1953 of Maulana Azad and Mr. K.D. Malaviya to the questions asked in Lok Sabha

Secondary Education Commission's Report

Shri A.M. Thomas: Will the Minister of **Education** be pleased to state:

(a) what steps the Central Government propose to take to implement the recommendations of the recent report of the Secondary Education Commission;

(b) whther any immediate steps are contemplated; and

(c) if so, what are they?

The Deputy Minister of Natural Resources and Scientific Research (Shri K.D. Malaviya): (a) to (c) The Report to the Secondary Education Commission will in the first instance be placed before the Central Advisory Board of Education at their next meeting to be held at New Delhi in November, 1953, for their consideration. The views expressed by the Board will then be considered by the Government of India and action will be taken on such recommendations of the Board as are finally accepted.

Shri A.M. Thomas: May I enquire whether a conference on the lines of the conference held to consider the University Commission Report is contemplated to consider the recommendations of the Secondary Education Commission?

Shri K.D. Malaviya: This suggestion will be considered.

Shri A.M. Thomas: Some steps are contemplated by the Government as part of the Five-Year Plan to relieve educated unemployment by the appointment of teachers, etc., by the Centre giving aid. May I enquire whether it is the intention of the Government to co-ordinate this deviation in the Plan with the recommendations of the Secondary Education Commission?

Shri K.D. Malaviya: The recent scheme which had been announced with regard to solving the problem of unemployment through the appointment of teachers has not so much relation with the report of the Secondary Education Commission which is before the Government.

Shri A.M. Thomas: One of the recommendations, for instance, of the Secondary Education Commission is to set up co-ordination committees both at ministerial and lower levels in the States and the Centre for the administration of secondary education, and set up a Board for teachers' training. Does the Centre propose to take any initiative in the matter?

Shri K.D. Malaviya: I shall read the report. Just now I take that information from the hon. Member.

Shri Punnoose: Has Government given any advice to the State Governments not to make any changes in the secondary education system before these recommendations are examined and finalised by the Central Government?

The Minister of Education and Natural Resources and Scientific Research (Maulana Azad): Yes.

Shri Syamnandan Sahaya: Is it proposed to circulate copies of the report of the Secondary Education Commission to the Members of this House?

Shri K.D. Malaviya: It is a priced publication. Hon. Members are invited to purchase copies.

Prof. D.C. Sharma: May I know what connection there is between the report of the Secondary Education Commission and the eight educationists, Indian as well as foreign, who are going to be sent out abroad to study the secondary school education system?

Mr. Deputy-Speaker: Is there a proposal to send 8 educationists? The hon. Member is assuming that there is a proposal to send 8 educationists to study the educational system abroad. What is the connection between their being sent and this report? Is it based upon any recommendation?

Maulana Azad: There is no connection between the two. The two are quite separate. The Commission was appointed to enquire into the system of secondary education. Its report has been received. This board consisting of eight members will do nothing about it. They would deliver lectures on new experiments in education for the benefit of secondary school teachers.

Prof. D.C. Sharma: May I know what action Government is going to take when there is such a great duplication of reports on the secondary education system: there is the Acharya Narendra Deva report, there is the Bombay report,.......

Mr. Deputy-Speaker: The hon. Member need not give a list.

Prof. D.C. Sharma: How is the Government going to co-ordinate all these reports?

Mr. Deputy-Speaker: They are considering all these things.

Shri K.D. Malaviya: Education is not a central subject. The States are perfectly at liberty to appoint their own committees to go into their own problems. We are only helping them by appointing this Commission. As soon as we reach certain decisions, we shall communicate our decisions as recommendations.

Shri Feroze Gandhi: I do not want to ask any question. I only want to make a suggestion.

Some Hon. Members: No suggestion.

Mr. Deputy-Speaker: I hope the hon. Member is not making any suggestion for action.

Shri Feroze Gandhi: It is only to the Chair: not to the Minister. I would like to suggest that the main question, as it is printed on paper, may be answered by the Deputy Minister. But, since Members are taking so much interest, the supplementaries may be answered by the Minister.

Maulana Azad: Why should I get up again and again unnecessarily? I give a reply whenever necessary.

Shri C. Bhatt: May I know whether the State Governments have sent their recommendations keeping in view the report of the Secondary Education Commission, for meeting the unemployment problem, in view of the recommendations made by the Planning Commission?

Shri K.D. Malaviya: I am afraid Government cannot commit themselves just now about anything which has been published in the report. I will advise the hon. Member to wait for a little time.

Shrimati A. Kale: May I know whether in the eight people that are going to be sent abroad for studying the secondary education systems you have included any women?

Maulana Azad: Yes.

Shri Syamnandan Sahaya: What will be the main functions of this new committee which has been set up not only to go abroad, but also round the different provinces and States in this country in connection with the recommendations of the Secondary Education Commission? There is a little confusion in our mind. We would like the matter to be clarified.

Maulana Azad: There is no connection between the two. It is the same party consisting of eight members. It includes four experts from abroad and four from India. They will be lecturing to teachers and headmasters of schools on new experiments in and new methods of education. They have nothing to do with the inquiry about secondary education.

Shri Syamnandan Sahaya: May I take it, Sir, that the recommendations of the Secondary Education Commission will be implemented without waiting for any suggestion by this new Committee?

Maulana Azad: Certainly, yes.

Mr. Deputy-Speaker: There is no question of waiting.

Reply to the Supplementary question asked by Mr. Dhulekar

Maulana Azad: There is no connection between the two. The Commission was appointed to survey the entire field of secondary education and to state whether or not it is in need of being changed in any way and if so, what the changes should be. This eight-member party would only be lecturing to the teachers on the system of education. As I have drawn the attention of the House to this fact twice already, this party has nothing to do with the enquiry into secondary education.

Shri A.M. Thomas: Some of the recommendations of this Commission are intimately connected with University education. May I enquire whether the Government intend to take these recommendations also into consideration in drafting the University Bill?

Maulana Azad: Yes, the Government will also take that into consideration.

Document No. 48

Answers of Maulana Azad and Mr. K.D. Malaviya in the House of People to the questions asked on 16-9-1953

UNITED STATES EDUCATIONAL FOUNDATION

Dr. Ram Subhag Singh: Will the Minister of **Education** be pleased to state:

(a) whether the Government of India have endorsed a programme of the United States Educational Foundation to offer advanced courses to trained teachers and headmasters of Indian Schools;

(b) whether some educationists and teachers of U.S.A. have arrived in India under the auspices of that Educational Foundation to offer training in those courses; and

(c) where those courses will be held and what would be their duration?

The Deputy Minister of Natural Resources and Scientific Research (Shri K.D. Malaviya): (a) Yes.

(b) Yes.

(c) (1) Patna Training College, Patna for the Eastern India region.

(2) Prantiya Shiksan Mahavidyalaya, Jabalpur for the Central and Northern India region.

(3) Teachers' Training College, Baroda for the Western and Northern India region.

(4) Teachers' College, Mysore, for the Southern India region.

The duration of the Course at each Centre is programmed for eight weeks.

Dr. Ram Subhag Singh: May I know, Sir, the obligations which the Government of India or the State Governments will have to undertake for running this scheme?

The Minister of Education and Natural Resources and Scientific Research (Maulana Azad): There is an educational foundation of the U.S. in India. This plan originated with them. When the idea was communicated to the State Governments they liked it. The burden of expenditure involved in working it will not fall on our shoulders, barring the minor expenses that may be incidental to their stay over there.

Kumari Annie Mascarene: May I know, Sir, whether Government has any idea of stopping the infiltration of foreigners into the country and of encouraging indigenous talent?

Shri K.D. Malaviya: I do not think this question is very relevant in so far as our attempts to get people from outside who can teach us something or from whom we can learn something are concerned.

Shrimati Renu Chakravartty: May I know, Sir, what is the special object of getting them? Are they going to teach us any particularly new subject on which research is being carried on? Otherwise, what is the object?

Shri K.D. Malaviya: As I said, the idea is to bring our teachers and school administrators in touch with the latest advancement in secondary education.

Shri K.K. Basu: May I know whether the syllabus is fianlised by our authorities or is left entirely to the Foundation?

Shri K.D. Malaviya: Naturally, the Foundation people have their say.

Maulana Azad: This is a mixed party, some of whose members are foreigners and some Indians.

Shri Punnoose: Can I know the common features in our educational system and that of the U.S.A., and also other conditions existing in India and the U.S.A. which would facilitate and make this course beneficial to us?

Mr. Deputy-Speaker: How can that be answered?

Shri Punnoose: What is the fun of inviting these experts here when our system is quite different, and our conditions are quite different?

Mr. Deputy-Speaker: Who is to decide about this matter? I am in difficulty here. Shall we go into the whole length of the syllabus? So long as the Government is in office, you must leave something to them. So, we need not go into details as to what is the exact position, what is the difference and so on. Generally if there is no discretion at all allowed to the Government, I think the Government may go out of office.

Shri Punnoose: No, Sir.

Mr. Deputy-Speaker: I am not worried. A general kind of discourse on education, what is the difference between this syllabus and that syllabus, why a person is brought in and so on – I do not think these will arise on a question of this nature.

Shri V.P. Nayar: It is not a question of money alone. It is also a question of policy. We are entitled to know.

Mr. Deputy-Speaker: I cannot allow policy matters. Hon. Members will read and re-read the Rules. I cannot allow discussion on policy matters to be taken up in the Question-hour on a question.

Shri Joachim Alva *rose* —

Mr. Deputy-Speaker: I have allowed so many questions. The hon. Member is a little late.

Shri Joachim Alva: I got up thrice, Sir.

Mr. Deputy-Speaker: All right.

Shri Joachim Alva: Before Government accepted this invitation, did Government realise that by sending our teachers or our Headmasters they would be liable for being indoctrinated with the American system of education, especially the campus life with its attendant evils?

Shri K.D. Malaviya: Under this scheme, we have not sent anyone abroad, instead experts are coming from abroad. . . .

Document No. 49

Maulana Azad's address dated 21-9-1953 at the laying Foundation Stone of the 12th National Institute, Pilani (Rajasthan)

We have met today to lay the foundation-stone of the 12th National Institute started under the auspices of the Council of Scientific and Industrial Research. Though the Council was set up in 1942, it is only since 1949 that its programme of expansion began in real earnest. In the five years since then, eleven National Laboratories have already been set up and are functioning in different parts of the country. The establishment of the 12th institute therefore means that the Council has been setting up more than two institutes a year. I am sure you will agree that this is a rate of progress which, judged by any standard, cannot be considered slow, especially if we remember that each of the National Laboratories has conformed to the highest standards and compares favourably with similar institutions in any other part of the world.

The Electronic Engineering Research Institute, which is being brought into being today, will fill a lacuna in one of the basic fields of modern scientific research in India. During the last two decases, and particularly during the last World War, electronic research progressed a rapid rate and there is no field of science or industry that has not been aided by electronic research. Electronics has played a notable part in the developments which took place during the war for the radio location of aircrafts and submarines. Electronic machines are employed to solve complicated equations and save much laborious calculations. Problems which would require a band of mathematicians years to solve are dealt with by these machines in hours. In industry, electronic equipment has been used to melt metals, case-harden them, heat plastics and control chemical processes. Elecronics is also responsible for rapid strides in the field of radio communication and television. In a word, the development of electronics has become of fundamental importance both from the point of view of theoretical research and the application of its results to practical affairs.

Against this background of developments in other countries, India unfortunately has little to show. Research in radio and electronics has been confined only a few centres like the Calcutta University Institute of Electronics, the National Physical Laboratory, New Delhi, and the Tata Institute of Fundamental Research, Bombay. These centres cannot, however, meet all our needs. There is not only scope but an urgent necessity to set up an institute specialising in this vast field. Notwithstanding the fact that certain investigations sponsored by the Council of Scientific and Industrial Research and other bodies have demonstrated the possibility of using indigenous material for the manufacture of component parts of the radio, it has been found that the necessary progress is not possible without a separate institution devoting itself entirely to this field.

The Council of Scientific and Industrial Research therefore appointed a committee with Sri Kasturbhai Lalbhai as Chairman and Drs. S.S. Bhatnagar, H.J. Bhabha, K.S. Krishnan and J.C. Ghosh to report on (a) the priority to be accorded to research in radio and electronic engineering; (b) the possibility of having one or more production centres for these materials; (c) the best location of the proposed industrial undertaking and other points; and (d) the financial provision, both of a capital and recurring nature, required for the Institute. The Committee have, after careful consideration, recommended that, for the present, a sum of Rs. 25 lakh should be provided towards capital expenditure for the Institute and Rs. 5 lakh per annum for recurring expenditure.

Dr. S.S. Bhatnagar, Director, Scientific and Industrial Research, with his characteristic energy discussed the proposal with Sri G.D. Birla and was able to secure a generous donation of Rs. 21 lakh non-recurring and Rs. 50,000 recurring from the Birla Education Trust towards the establishment of the Central Electronics Engineering Research Institute. The Trust have already acquired a plot of over 700 bighas at a cost of approximately Rs. 1,50,000 for the establishment of the Institute at Pilani. The Birla family is well known for its generosity and this fresh gift in a public cause will be appreciated throughout India.

Some of you may have wondered why Pilani was chosen for the location of the Institute. Now that you have visited the place and seen the many fine educational institutions that have been built up here, I am sure you will agree that the choice has been the right one. For the expeditious execution of the programme, a local Planning Committee has been constituted with the Director, Scientific and Industrial Research, as its Chairman, Sri G.D. Birla, Lala Sri Ram, Dr. K.S. Krishnan, Dr.

D.S. Kothari and Colonel S.D. Pande as its members, and the Planning Officer as its Secretary.

The object of the Institute will be to conduct research on the utilisation of indigenous raw materials and to evolve processes on a pilot-plant scale to see if they would make reliable and quality components. The Institute will also conduct investigations on the development and use of electronic circuits to facilitate and improve the efficiency of all indigenous industries, to build standard electronic instruments for test purposes, to develop special radio circuits, to develop electronic apparatus for medical profession, to conduct experiments on communications, radar and other equipment, to develop and build acoustic instruments, and to utilise electronics for industrial purposes. The Institute will undertake projects sponsored by industries or initiate investigations, depending on the urgency of the problem for the benefit of industries.

The Institute will ultimately have a number of divisions and sections dealing with:

(1) electronic circuits;

(2) communication equipment;

(3) industrial electronics;

(4) electronic components;

(5) thermionic valves;

(6) electronic instruments;

(7) medical apparatus;

(8) acoustic-audio equipment;

(9) theatre and studio equipment; and

(10) very high frequency equipment.

I now request the Prime Minister to lay the foundation-stone of the Central Electronics Engineering Research Institute.

Document No. 50

Maulana Azad's Broadcast dated 30-9-1953 from All India Radio

Of the problesm which claimed our special attention after independence, one of the most important was that of national education and what may be called its system or pattern. We hear today an almost universal cry that there is something wrong with our educational system, that it has failed to meet the demands of the situation and therefore needs to be reformed. But, in spirit of this feeling, there are very few people who have actually thought over the problem and are able to say what exactly is wrong with the system and in what manner it should be reformed.

An obvious defect, which should be evident to every one, is that the general education available to the common people is neither adequate, nor appropriate to their needs, and the privileged minority who are fortunate enough to receive higher education in the universities cannot be usefully employed. The result is that of the thousands of graduates who are turned out by our universities every year, a large proportion is unable to secure employment and is forced to join the ranks of the unemployed. There are at present about 3 to 3-½ lakhs of students receiving education in our universities. This is by no means a large number for a country with a population of about 35 crores, and yet there is somewhere so radical a defect in our system that even this small number cannot find useful employment.

Unfortunately, the main objective of those who seek higher education in our country is to secure government service. It is obvious that the Government cannot give jobs to all. The result is that our educational system, instead of enabling people to become useful members of society, makes them superfluous and turns what should be an asset into a liability. If many of these educated persons had received no education, they could at least have earned their livelihood by some kind of manual labour. As it is, they cannot do even that.

Let me now, in the few minutes that are available to me, tell you what I think about this matter.

Every individual has a right to an education that will enable him to develop his faculties and live a full human life. Such education is the birth right of every citizen. A state cannot claim to have discharged its duty till it has provided for every single individual the means to the acquisition of knowledge and self-betterment. For education up to this standard, the question of requirements of society does not arise, nor can we provide facilities only in accordance with the existing demands. Every individual, unconditionally and without qualifications, is entitled to education up to this stage. To my mind, the requisite standard for such education is the secondary stage and I am convinced that regardless of the question of employment, the State must make available to all citizens the facilities of education up to the secondary stage.

There are three stages in this secondary education – elementary, middle and higher. Of these, elementary and middle are the more important because the foundation of the entire edifice of national education is laid in these two early stages. If the foundation is weak or wrongly laid, the rest of the structure is insecure or faulty. For these two stages we have accepted the pattern of basic education which is of great importance to the whole structure of our national education. To the extent to which we are able to implement effectively this pattern, we shall succeed in reforming the entire structure.

Beyond this stage, the position is somewhat different. When we consider the facilities for higher education in a Sate, we must match of the facilities to the needs of society. Any maladjustment between demand and supply at this stage would create problems which the State must at all costs seek to avoid. Apart from any other reason, the provision of higher education is so expensive that no State can afford to increase the number of persons receiving such education beyond what it can absorb. In the field of economics, there is always a close correlation between demand and supply. Any deviation from such correlation leads to social crises. In the field of higher education, we must accept the same law and fashion the supply according to the demands of society. If the supply is less than the demand, the progress of society is impeded; if it is more, there is unemployment. A fundamental defect of our educational system is that this very obvious and important consideration is overlooked. A university degree has been made a necessary qualification for government service, with the result that everyone runs after a degree and, having secured it, is faced with the disillusionment that what he spent his years and money on is not of much value in the market.

If we wish to avoid these unfortunate consequences, we should so organise our system of education that the majority of our people, having passed through the secondary stage, are able to engage themselves in the various professions, industries, handicrafts, etc., and only a small number which is considered adequate to the needs of society, go on to the universities for higher education. It is obvious that we cannot forcibly prevent people from joining the universities, but we can certainly create such conditions as will eliminate the present unhealthy inducements which lure so many students into the universities, not for the sake of knowledge but for the sake of degrees. It is unnecessary for me, nor is there sufficient time, to discuss this point in more detail.

There is, however, in this connection one more question which naturally arises. Is the present exaggerated emphasis on university degrees as a qualification for government service justified? The fact that a university degree is a necessary condition for government service has led people to look upon university degrees as a passport to government service. Those who join universities do so not to cultivate talent but to secure this passport. This state of affairs has had its repercussions on our universities also. Consciously or unconsciously an atmosphere was created which inevitably brought their standards down. Gradually a mental attitude was developed which seemed to say: "Let us have as many students as we can get and let as many as possible be given degrees." The natural result was that the standards of education steadily declined and how low they have become can be easily judged by those who are in a position to test the merit of our present-day graduates.

We know that in other countries government servants are not recruited in this fashion. In England, for example, while degrees are a necessary qualification for certain posts requiring professional training, as in the case of doctors, professors, engineers and the like, for other appointments the only qualifications deemed necessary are of age and of particular ability for the post. A university degree as such is not an essential condition.

It is time that we too in India considered seriously the adoption of a similar procedure of recruitment. Why should we continue to regard the university degree as a passport to service? Our stress should be on ability and not on the possession of a degree. Our Public Service Commission should evolve methods of testing such ability. For example, in the case of jobs for which it is necessary today for a candidate to be a B.A., we may lay down that a candidate's general ability and knowledge should be equal to that of a graduate, so that while we ensure that we get the right people for right jobs, the present unhealthy emphasis on degrees will be replaced by that on ability. This alone will go a long way in changing the mentality of our students.

We have, of course, to bear in mind that, so far as professional services are concerned, the acquisition of a university degree will continue to be necessary. We should allow no relaxation in this matter. We cannot accept a doctor or an engineer or a professor except on the basis of his academic qualifications. It is only in the case of appointments of a general nature which require no special or technical qualifications that we have to change the procedure of recruitment.

There is no doubt that such a change would add considerably to the work of our Public Service Commissions who will have to hold examinations for appointments. It may be necessary for us to increase the number of Public Service Commissions, but whatever arrangements may prove to be necessary, the step is worth taking.

Let me briefly recapitulate what I have said:

(1) We have to remould our system of education and so organise it that a great majority of our people, after completing their secondary education, should be absorbed in the various professions, industries, handicrafts, etc. Only a small proportion should pursue higher education in the universities and their number should not exceed the capacity of the society to make good use of them.

(2) The most urgent and important changes needed are in our system of secondary education. Our present system of secondary education was conceived as a stepping stone to the universities. What we want now is a system of secondary education which will not be a mere means to something else but an end in itself.

(3) We have accepted the pattern of basic education, of which the main idea is that learning should be not merely through books but through some form of manual work. This principle should be given effect to throughout the secondary education stage and should, in fact, become the basic principle of our national education.

(4) Since we propose to change the shape of our secondary education, it is necessary that it should not be cast in a single rigid mould. It should have sufficient elasticity to meet the different needs of

different groups of people. The Secondary Education Commission has made some very valuable recommendations in this respect which need to be seriously considered.

(5) We have also to consider whether the present insistence on degrees as a necessary condition for government service should be continued or modified.

The problem of how best to improve the standards of our university education is no less important, but the limited time at my disposal prevents me from dwelling on it.

Document No. 51

Maulana Azad's Address at the 20th annual meeting of C.A.B.E, held in New Delhi On 9-11-1953

I am glad to welcome you again to this the twentieth meeting of the Central Advisory Board of Education. I regret that it has not been possible to call the meeting earlier. When it became clear that it could not be held before August or September, I decided that we should wait till the Report of the Secondary Education Commission had been published and made available to the members for consideration. This, as you know, was submitted at the end of August and the Board will therefore have an opportunity to consider it at this meeting. I have, however, directed that in future the meetings of the Central Advisory Board should be held every year in the third week of January.

All educationists today are concerned at the evident lack of adjustment between the educational system and the needs of the community. The problem has assumed gigantic proportions today but its origin must be traced to the beginning of modern education in India.

When the modern system of education was fashioned for the country, sufficient attention was not paid to our needs and ideals. There was no National Government and hence the system of education that was built up looked more to the needs of the Government than to the needs of the people of the country. Though the East India Company, on becoming the rulers of the country, accepted the need of providing education in the modern sciences, the main need of the Company was to train up a number of English-educated persons who could help it in carrying on the administration of the country. Education was therefore organised to ensure the supply of an adequate number of English-educated Indians, and the attention of the Government was concentrated on providing higher education needed for the training of such personnel. Since, however, it is impossible to have students at a higher stage unless they have gone through the stages of elementary and secondary education, the Company made some provision for education at these stages as well, but the emphasis was nevertheless on higher education and the other stages were subsidiary and subservient to it.

So long as the number of persons educated in English was not larger than that required by Government, there was no problem of the educated unemployed. This situation continued till the beginning of the 20th century. An English-educated Indian was then almost sure of a job but already a situation was developing when the supply of Indians with university education was tending to become larger than the demand. Government service could not absorb all educated Indians nor had there been any development of commerce and industry which could profitably use such personnel. In the last few decades, this problem had steadily become more acute. We therefore find a growing volume of criticism against the prevalent sytem of education and one cannot deny that this criticism is, to a large extent, justified. If the result of education is to create a situation where society is not able to utilise the services of the educated there is obviously some defect which must be remedied. Increasing stress is now being placed on technical education but the position has not eased as there is no clear picture of how the national industries would develop. The result is that there is growing unemployment among persons educated not only in the academic disciplines but also in various technical subjects. We find that the surplus over requirements is increasing every day. Since there is no alternative mode of utilising this body of educated personnel, the result is a growing volume of dissatisfaction in society and a sense of frustration among young men and women who have received the highest training available in the country.

It is, of course, true that if we consider India's total population, the number of persons who are receiving higher education is by no means large. If only 3.5 lakhs of students are in the universities in a population of over 350 millions, no one can say that the number of university students is too great. Since, however, the present state of the country's development in agriculture, industry and commerce does not enable us to provide gainful employment even for this small number, it has become a burden for society. Today, our universities are like factories which are turning out products that do not conform to the demands of the society in either number or quality. It is therefore necessary to carry out changes in higer education which will, by carrying out improvements in both directions, enable society to utilise the talent and training of the men and women who are receiving education beyond the school stage.

The need for educational reform has been voiced from every side but those who plead for such reform do not generally have any clear or concrete picture before them. There is a general desire that something should be done for the reform of education but few know what that "something" ought to be. It is therefore necessary to survey the whole field of education and prepare a comprehensive plan of positive reconstruction of education so that we can maintain, for the country, the progresss that has been envisaged after the attainment of independence.

I would in this context like to place before you my conception of the function of education in society. Every individual has a right to an education that will enable him to develop his faculties and live a full human life. Such education is the birthright of every citizen. A state cannot claim to have discharged its duty till it has provided for every single individual the means to knowledge and self-betterment. For education up to this standard, the question of requirements of society does not arise, nor can we provide facilities only in accordance with the existing demands. Every individual, unconditionally and without qualifications, is entitled to education up to this stage. To my mind, the requisite standard for such education is the secondary stage and I am convinced that regardless of the question of employment, the State must make available to all citizens the facilities of education up to the secondary stage.

Beyond this stage, the position is somewhat different. When we consider the facilities for higher education in a State, we must match the facilities to the needs of society. Any maladjustment between demand and supply at this stage would create problems which the State must at all costs seek to avoid. Apart from any other reason, the provision of higher education is so expensive that no State can afford to increase the number of persons receiving such education beyond what it can absorb. In the field of economics, there is always a close correlation between demand and supply. Any deviation from such correlation leads to social crises. In the field of higher education, we must accept the same law and regulate the supply according to the demands of society.

Since the attainment of independence, the Government of India have been conscious of the need of preparing a comprehensive blueprint for educational reconstruction. Some steps in that direction have already been taken. You are aware that during these five years we have appointed two high-power commissions to enquire into the problems of university and secondary education and make recommendations for their improvement and reform. The problem of elementary education has also been repeatedly considered, and there is a consensus of opinion that it should be of the basic pattern. The Government have already taken a decision in this behalf, and the time has come when similar decisions must be taken in the field of university and secondary education.

I have already said that the provision of secondary education must be universal and without any reference to any special needs of society. This, however, demands a reform of the system which will enable the vast majority of the people to find in it a satisfying and complete stage of education. The Commission whose report was recently published and which you are going to consider today has recommended that secondary education should be reorganised. It must be the completion of education for the vast majority of people. At present it is only a stepping stone to education in the universities. In future it must be for the majority the entrance to life in various industries, crafts and professions and serve as an entrance to higher education only for a select minority. For a proper and healthy development of society, it is necessary that the vast numbers who are in elementary and secondary schools accept the responsibility of various traditional occupations in accordance with their taste, aptitude and training. There must also be unambiguous recognition by society that all professions are socially valuable and a person is to be honoured if he performs the duties of his station with competence and sincerity. If we are to ensure equal respect for various professions and provide that the majority seek such professions at the end of secondary stage of education, it is necessary to reorganise secondary education to provide for a variety of diversified courses. I think that one of the most valuable recommendations of the Secondary Education Commission is the insistence that every student at the secondary level must learn some craft irrespective of the fact whether he or she aims at adopting it as a profession or not.

Such a reorganisation of secondary education presupposes and will be facilitated by a further expansion and improvement of basic education. I have already stated that it is an accepted policy of the Government that education at the elementary level shall be of the basic pattern. The real object of basic education is to train up children as members of a community and develop in them habits of co-operative action for the social good. While the ideals of basic education have been accepted by the Centre and the States, I regret to say that the implementation of the programme has not been as rapid as we would wish. Greater emphasis must be placed on the early conversion of all elementary education to the basic pattern, but we must, at the same time, remember that this can succeed only if basic education is conceived in an imaginative and creative way. One of the reasons for the inadequate response of the

State and the community to the appeal of basic education has been the rigidity of outlook of some of the advocates of this pattern of education. We have to recognise that all education is and must always be an experiment. Basic education is a great experiment and we have to recognise the fact that it has not yet been carried out on a sufficiently wide basis. We must be prepared to develop, modify and adapt it to meet the divergent needs of town and village, of industrial and agricultural areas and of the different parts of the country, some of which are coastal, some mountanous and some riparian and some arid or semi-arid. We must also recognise that there are differences in taste and aptitude of children and there are some who are more practical-minded while others have a greater predilection for abstract or artistic activities.

The most important consideration for the reform of university education appears to be to limit the number of students who enter their portals. I have already said that the present number of such students cannot be regarded as excessive but we have to ensure that with the expansion of elementary and secondary education there is no inordinance increase in these numbers till the necessary agricultural, industrial and commercial development has taken place to sustain a larger number of highly trained personnel. The chief aim of university education must therefore be consolidation and improvement.

One of the important measures for reform of university education is the need to dissociate the possession of a degree from the conditions of service. At present, nobody can hope to get a responsible post without a degree. The result is that everyone wants to enter a university, not for the pursuit of knowledge but in order to secure a passport to a job. The result of such insistence has been that instead of an emphasis on study and self-improvement, educational institutions have tended to emphasise the securing of a degree by some means or other. Not only have educational standards been lowered and all kinds of malpractices encouraged but students have missed the very purpose of education and concentrated on the acquisition of a degree without considering the means to it. It is not surprising that in this background students have continually pressed for an increase in the percentage of passes. The universities also have consciously or unconscioulsy fallen in line and without adequate attention to standards striven to increase the number of passes in various examinations. There has been, in consequence, a slackness both in admission to the universities and in examinations conducted by them.

After considering all aspects, it is today my considered judgement that, except for professional services, the possession of a degree should not be a pre-requisite for appointment to government service. I can understand that we may have to make an exception in the case of professional jobs. In the case of an engineer, a medical man, a technician or a teacher, it is not enough that the practitioner has merely the necessaty theoretical knowledge. In their case, the discipline of studying such subjects for a number of years under proper guidance and supervision is essential for the successful performance of their duties. Leaving aside such professional services, I do not see any justification for insisting on a degree for appointment to other posts, especially where such posts are filled by the Public Service Commission or the State Public Service Commissions, as constituted today, cannot cope adequately with the volume of work which will devolve on them if this proposal is implemented, but we can meet this difficulty by establishing two or more Boards for the recruitment of personnel at different levels. It appears to me almost self-evident that since such Boards do, in any case, conduct examinations for recruitment to the services, the demand for the possession of a degree is very largely unnecessary. For example, in the case of jobs for which it is necessary today for a candidate to be a B.A., we may lay down that a candidate's general ability and knowledge should be equal to that of a graduate, so that while we ensure that we get the right people for right jobs, the present unhealthy emphasis on degrees will be replaced by that on ability.

With the increase in the number of pupils at the elementary and secondary stage, this will mean that a smaller proportion will be provided with facilities for education at the higher stage. The corollary to this is that ability, and ability alone, must be the criterion for entry into the universities and other institutions of higher learning. Today very often it is the financial position of the family which decides whether a student is to go to the university or not. With limitation of numbers, we must ensure that poverty is not a ban on entering a university. This demands a much larger provision of stipends and scholarships for meritorious students. The additional expenditure will have to be met by the State and we must explore different alternatives to find the necessary resources. One suggestion which occurs to me is that the less meritorious but more affluent student may be required to pay higher fees. In any case for raising these fees provided the number of scholarships and stipends are simultaneously increased to ensure that poor but meritorious students are not shut out of the universities.

It appears to me that increasing emphasis will have to be placed on providing higher education in the field of agriculture, medicine, engineering, technology and science. This does not, however, mean that we can afford to neglect the humanities. No nation can survive if it neglects the discipline of the spirit. We must therefore ensure that the increasing emphasis on science and technology does not lead to any reduction in the facilities for education in the liberal arts. The Government of India are fully aware of the importance of encouraging higher education in all these fields, and a small beginning has been made by providing a number of scholarships to encourage research in science and industry, and you will be glad to hear that from the current year it is proposed to institute similar scholarships for research and further studies in the humanities also.

The educational picture I have is that of universal education of the basic pattern for all children of school age, followed by a diversified secondary education. Thereafter, we must have, for a select minority, facilities for higher education in all fields of arts and science and see that this is of the highest standard.

We have been stressing for years the need for educational reform, but so far no practical step could be taken in this direction. We can no longer afford to delay and must immediately set in motion an effective machinary for reform. The University Education Commission's Report has been with us for the last four years and we have recently received the Report of the Secondary Education Commission as well. We must now seriously consider how best to implement the recommendations of these two Commissions as soon as possible. I would like you to give first priority to this question in your discussions.

It was important in this connection to create an effective and permanent agency to supervise the standards of university education and to co-ordinate them. Accordingly, the Government of India are setting up a University Grants Commission of which the formal announcement will be made very soon. The Commission will be a statutory body. The necessary Bill will be presented in Parliament in the coming budget session. But since it is necessary that the Commission should begin to function without delay, the Government have decided to set it up immediately on the basis of a Resolution passed last year. After the Bill is passed, the Commission's scope and powers will be extended in conformity with it and its composition enlarged.

Document No. 52

Maulana's views expressed in the Parliament, dated 14-12-1953 by participating in discussion raised regarding the special Marriage Bill and his appeal to postpone the same for some time. His reply to the questions raised further in this connection

The Minister of Education and Natural Resources and Scientific Research (Maulana Azad): I think that in view of the trend the Debate has taken just now it will not be proper to carry it on any further. It would be better to postpone it for the present and to take up some other item, so that we might be in a position to consider the issue dispassionately at a later stage.

Dr. Lanka Sundaram: Long live the Speaker:

Mr. Deputy-Speaker: Order, order. The matter has been taken up. May I suggest to the Deputy Leader to make a formal motion that this matter do stand over to some other date or be adjourned to some other date? The House must approve of that.

Shri S.S. More: He can make a motion.

Mr. Deputy-Speaker: The Law Minister may make a motion.

Dr. N.B. Khare: On a point of information, Sir, if I want to shine your shoe, who can prevent me?

Shri Biswas: I do not quite follow the suggestion that was made by the hon. Deputy Leader. Unfortunately, I could not understand the language.

Maulana Azad: My proposal was that it should be postponed.

Shri Biswas: If the suggestion is, Sir, that we might sit round a Table and discuss the matter and that the motion may stand over for a day or two, that is one thing that I can appreciate; instead of letting off air on the floor of the House, it is much better if we could examine and come to a sensible decision. (*Interruption*). An I am confident that the principle which is found here in this Resolution represents a sensible decision.....

Some Hon. Members: No, no.

Shri Biswas: ......emulating the action of this very House in this respect. However, I have no objection to the matter being held over if it is to be discussed in a cool atmosphere, and in an absolutely dispassionate attitude. It is no use bringing your closed minds to a question on the plea of taking time to discuss it.

Sardar Hukam Singh: (Kapurthala-Bhatinda): Sir, I take objection to the implications of the statement of the hon. Law Minister. He has heard us say that this House takes strong objection to the Resolution passed by the other House. At the same time, it has been stressed that that Resolution expresses a sensible decision which means that our objection is something else than sensible. I do not think it should be allowed to be stated here in regard to a discussion that has taken place.

Some Hon. Members: Withdraw.

Shri Biswas: I have said that what I have done, I have done as a sensible sentient being. *(Interruption)*

Shri K.C. Sodhia (Sagar): Is this not sensible?

Mr. Deputy-Speaker: Order, order.

Maulana Azad: I beg to move:

"That the debate on the motion may be adjourned."

Shri M.L. Dwivedi (Hamirpur Distt.): On a point of order, Sir....

Mr. Deputy-Speaker: Order, order. Here is a motion for adjournment of this debate.

Shri M.L. Dwivedi: I have a point of order.

Mr. Deputy-Speaker: I have heard that point of order relating to the Resolution as sensible. I shall put this motion to the House first. Then, I shall come to the point of order later.

Maulana Azad: Till tomorrow or for two days.

Mr. Deputy-Speaker: Today is the 14th. Until the 16th. All right.

Document No. 53

Homage paid to Shri H.N. Shastri dated 14-12-1953

Maulana Azad: Our hearts just now are borne down by a fresh grief. The air accident that occurred at Nagpur two days ago resulted in the loss of 13 lives and it is a matter of deep sorrow that one of our dear comrades, an active member of this House, Shri Harihar Nath Shastri was also a victim of this accident. The deceased had been a valiant soldier in the country's fight for freedom. He was still engaged in his studies when the movement started under the leadership of Mahatma Gandhi. He gave up his education and jumped into the field. He came into that field a number of times and courted imprisonment on a number of occasions. Then he completed his studies at Benaras. Thereafter, instead of worrying about himself or about his family and engaging in some service or business, as might have been expected, he dedicated his life to the service of the country and for that too he chose a field that was best with difficulties. He devoted himself to the service of labour. He made the good and the welfare of the workers his goal in life. For years he had been engaged in this work not only in this country but also abroad, where he participated in the work of international organisations as India's representative. Although he certainly had the good of the workers at heart he was not one of those people who allowed themselves to be swayed over to any one side. He was also conscious of the difficulties of the Government, of the factories and of the industry and it was his constant endeavour, while keeping the good of the workers in view, to adopt the course of moderation and to see things in their right perspective.

I am sure we are all equally feeling the sorrow caused by his separation from us and that every member of the House has heartfelt sympathy for his survivors.

Document No. 54

Maulana Azad's clarification dated 16-12-1953 in Parliament regaridng his motion, made in connection with the postponement of the Debate on the Special Marriage Bill

The Minister of Education and Natural Resources and Scientific Research (Maulana Azad): Sir, the motion that I made that day was simply to the effect that the issue might be put off for the present and that it should come up on the 16th. If the hon. lady Member had some other plan in view I cannot be held responsible for that.

Document No. 55

Maulana Azad's Address dated 28-12-1953 at the first meeting of the University Grants Commission, held in New Delhi

I am glad to welcome you to the first meeting of the University Grants Commission.

In accordance with one of the recommendations of the Central Advisory Board of Education, the Government of India decided in 1945 to set up a University Grants Committee. The functions of this Committee were confined to the three Central Universities and it was only an advisory body. There were several non-officials who were members but they acted on a part-time basis and there was only one whole-time officer who acted as Secretary for the Committee. With this limited personnel and the circumscribed powers, it was not surprising that the University Grants Committee was not able to make any effective contribution to the development of University education. In 1947, the Committee was reconstituted with somewhat enlarged membership but since the functions and the official assistance remained more or less the same, this Committee also did not prove effective.

In 1952, the Government of India therefore decided to set up a reconstituted University Grants Commission with a full-time Chairman and full-time Secretary and with enlarged membership. It was intended that this Commission should look mainly after the four Central Universities and be entrusted with the following functions:

(1) to advise the Government on the allocation of grants-in-aid from public funds to the Central Universities;

(2) to advise the Government on the allocation of grants-in-aid to other universities and institutions of higher learning whose case for such grants may be referred to the Commission by the Government; and

(3) to advise the universities and other institutions of higher learning in respect of any question referred by the Government to the Commission.

After the passing of the Constitution, the Central Government was entrusted with an important responsibility in higher education in respect of the co-ordination of facilities and the maintenance of standards in the universities. The Government considered various measures for the discharge of this responsibility and came to the conclusion that it could be best fulfilled by the establishment of a Council of University Education by an Act of Parliament. A draft Bill to set up a Council of University Education was accordingly prepared and circulated to the universities in order to secure the largest possible support and co-operation from them. The draft Bill was considered by the Inter-University Board which agreed with the objects of the Bill but felt that its provisions might not lead to the desired end. Since the Government of India wanted to carry out the reforms with the greatest possible support and co-operation of the universities, it took note of these objections and convened, in April 1953, a conference of the State Education Ministers and Vice-Chancellors to consider the matter and suggest suitable measures for the purpose. This conference recommended unanimously that instead of setting up a separate body for the co-ordination of facilities and maintenance of standards, the Government should establish a University Grants Commission in terms of the University Education Commission's recommendations and allot to it the functions proposed to be delegated to the Council of University Education. The conference held that the University Grants Commission with enlarged powers and functions would be better able to co-ordinate the facilities and suggest proper measures of reform as it would be in constant touch with the various universities and be sensitive to their requirements and needs.

The Government accepted this recommendation as it itself felt that a properly constituted University Grants Commission with enlarged powers and functions could discharge these duties more effectively.

This also appeared to be in consonance with the recommendations of the University Education Commission. In its Report, the Commission had recommended that a University Grants Commission on the lines of the University Grants Committee in Great Britain should be set up as early as possible. The Scientific Manpower Committee had also recommended the provision of generous grants for the development of post-graduate facilities in the universities. The Government had accepted these recommendations in principle, but on account of financial stringency no action could be taken on them at the time. After the acceptance of the Five Year Plan, it was known that some funds had been provided for the improvement of university education, and the Ministry of Education considered the time appropriate for the establishment of a University Grants Commission. Further discussions have been held by the Government to increase the quantum of these funds, particularly in view of the fact that the University Grants Commission would have to deal not merely with the four Central Universities but all the universities of India. I am happy to announce that we are now in a position to establish a statutory University Grants Commission with larger funds to look after all universities, and this Commission will also serve as an instrument of university reform. A draft Bill has been prepared, and it is hoped that this will be presented to Parliament at an early date.

The consideration of the Bill by Parliament and its enactment is likely to take some time. The Government, however, felt that in view of the growing problems of the universities, immediate action was needed. It has therefore considered it desirable to set up a University Grants Commission in accordance with the resolution of November last and allow it to start functioning immediately. This Commission will consist of five members and have as its Chairman Dr. S.S. Bhatnagar. In order to ensure that the universities do not look upon it as an external body, it has been decided to associate a number of Vice-Chancellors with it.

I am sure you will all agree that this is a momentous decision and will have far-reaching influence on the development of university education in India. I therefore want that the importance of this step and the results which we hope to attain through this Commission should be properly appreciated by the people at large. The first thing I want to make clear is that while the choice of the Chairman and the members had necessarily to be made by the Government, the Commission will be fully free and will have no interfence in its day-to-day work from the Government. The second thing is that even though its findings may be in the nature of recommendations, the Government will treat these recommendations as binding and will be guided by the Commission's advice. Once the budget for the year has been approved by the Government, the Commission will be informed of the amount available for university education. Within the limits thus fixed, the Commission will be free to allocate amounts among the universities, and the Government will be guided by such advice. Further, the Government of India will not consider the establishment of any new university or the grant of assistance to any such university established otherwise except on the recommendation of the Commission.

In order to enable the Commission to discharge its responsibilities satisfactory, it must have full access to information, and the universities must freely supply it with any data that it requires. The Commission will examine such data and frame its recommendations which it will send to the universities or the Government in accordance with the needs of the case. Both the Government and the universities will give full consideration to its advice. The Commission will thus help, among other things, in avoiding unnecessary duplication and allow the full utilisation of our limited resources in money and personnel. It will also help the Government in realising its objective of achieving co-ordination of facilities and maintenance of standards in university education. All these, of course, greatly enhance the responsibility of the Commission, and I have no doubt it will discharge its duties to the full satisfaction of the Government and the universities.

I am happy that the Prime Minister has taken much interest in the proposal to set up the University Grants Commission and agreed to participate in its first meeting. I will now invite him to address the Commission and give it the benefit of his views.

Document No. 56

Maulana Azad's Presidential speech dated 19-1-1954 at the Conference of the Indian National Commission for Co-operation with Unesco

I am very happy to welcome all of you to this conference of the Indian National Commission for Co-operation with Unesco. My pleasure is the greater because fraternal delegates from many sister nations of Asia and Africa have accepted our invitation to attend the conference and share in its deliberations. Since the aims of Unesco can be realised only through mutual understanding and co-operation, their participation is particularly valuable. It will help them to understand the problems with which we are grappling and gives us a clearer idea of the programmes we must recommend to Unesco.

It also gives me great pleasure that on the occasion of this conference, we have, among us, the Director General of Unesco and the Chairman and a Member of the Executive Board. Their participation will enable them to appreciate the problems and aspirations of a region where more than half of mankind lives. It will also give the new Director General a deeper insight into the tasks which await the organisation in this part of the world.

The proposal to set up National Commissions in member-States is to be commended for many reasons. This has resulted in the establishment of a permanent agency for the working out of Unesco's ideas at many levels. While the membership of Unesco is confined only to States, it is obvious that its work must be carried out among the people. The National Commission with its close association with various non-official agencies provides a platform to disseminate Unesco's programmes in many ways. One may, in fact, say that Unesco's work is delegated to these National Commissions. To my mind, the main purpose of setting up the National Commissions was, on the one hand, to make Unesco conscious of the people's needs, and, on the other, to make the people conscious of Unesco's functions and purposes. The National Commissions are therefore the proper agencies to spread Unesco's ideas and objectives among the people. One may, in fact, go so far as to say that Unesco is active only if the National Commissions are active. Similarly the National Commissions can function properly only if Unesco is active.

If we keep this test before us, we have to admit that the National Commissions have not always been as effective as we would wish them to be. I am not referring to the United States or some of the European countries, for I have no direct knowledge of the activities of the National Commissions in these areas. So far as the Eastern countries are concerned, by and large, they have not yet fulfilled what we expected of them. The Commissions have been set up, offices opened and staff employed, but they have not yet made their influence felt in their own countries; nor have they reflected adequately their points of view in framing Unesco's general programme. This is the feeling I have in respect of the Indian National Commission; though I am aware that our foreign friends feel that our Commission is very active. I have a feeling that many of our fraternal delegates will share this view in respect of their own National Commissions.

It is therefore necessary for us to devise methods by which National Commissions may be activised. Apart from the desire to have representatives of neighbouring countries among us, this is one of the main reason why we have invited fraternal delegates from sister nations. It is our purpose and hope that their association may create an opportunity where representatives of the Asian and African National Commissions may meet and consider why more progress was not achieved. Such discussions will also help all of us to define more sharply the main objectives of Unesco and advise it on the programmes which are necessary to fulfil these objectives in the context of the East.

I wish, in this connection, to place before the Conference some important issues which, to my mind, have prevented a more effective implementation of Unesco's ideals and programmes. My purpose is to express the feelings of my country and other countries in the East fully and frankly. There is no suggestion of complaint in what I am going to say. In the brotherhood of Unesco, there must not be any occasion for mutual recrimination. It is, however, necessary that we understand one another clearly and fully, for without such understanding we cannot co-operate in the achievement of our common goal.

The first thing I want to say is that there is a feeling throughout the East that the U.N. and its specialised agencies have not yet given to the East, the attention which it can rightfully claim. The Eastern nations feel that while in theory they are recognised as equal partners in the

United Nations, the practice does not always conform to the theory. They feel that the central offices of the U.N. and allied agencies do not fully understand their problems and needs. So long as there is this feeling, it will be difficult to create whole-hearted enthusiasm for the U.N. and Unesco in these regions.

One of the reasons for such a feeling in the East is its recollection of the attitude which developed in the West in the 18th century. Two things happened simultaneously in that period. On the one hand, the Eastern countries reached the lowest depths of depression and,on the other, a new impulse to progress and advancement swept throughout Europe and America. The inevitable result of these developments was that the Western nations divided the world into two categories. There was, on one side, the free and superior world of the Western peoples and, on the other, the world of inferior and subject nations in Asia and Africa. Whenever the Western nations talked of human rights, they were thinking only of individuals and nations in the West. For them, such a concept had hardly any reference to Asia or Africa. In the latter half of the 18th century, first the U.S.A., and later France, promulgated the doctrine of the rights of man, but in the United States this doctrine did not apply to the negroes nor in France to the people under colonial rule. It is true that a humanitarian like Jefferson was conscious of the implications of these declarations. He referred explicitly to the plight of the slaves but the climate of opinion was such that even a Jefferson could not carry his people in this respect. The 19th century and especially its latter half saw the spread of European colonialism in Asia and Africa and an increasing awareness of human rights and dignity. This period also saw a beginning of the change in the world situation. The Eastern countries shook off their age long torpor and began to share in a new awakening. A profound revolution has since taken place in their minds, and they are claiming equality with the Western people. With the progress of the twentieth century, there has been a further change of far-reaching import. A situation has developed where, with one or two unfortunate exceptions, the Western nations have recognised that the days of colonialism and domination are over. Today the Eastern peoples are not prepared to co-operate except on one term, *viz.*, on the basis of complete equality with the West. Superiority and inferiority between nations have no place in the modern world.

The recognition of equality is the basis of the United Nations. The U.N. has brought all nations on the same platform without regard to East or West. Unesco, which is one of its specialised agencies, is also working in the same spirit. I hope, I shall not be misunderstood if I say that there is, nevertheless, still a feeling among the peoples of Asia and Africa that the old ideas of superiority have not yet been completely eradicated from the Western minds. So long as there is such a feeling in Asia or Africa, Unesco's objectives cannot be fully realised. The first step should therefore be for the U.N. and Unesco to recognise the existence of such feelings in the Eastern minds and to adopt an attitude and procedure which will convince the Asian and African people that a true spirit of brotherhood, equality and co-operation has dawned on the world.

The U.N. and Unesco were set up after World War II. It was necessary in the conditions then prevailing that immediate steps should be taken for the rehabilitation of Europe. Though the war damages were not confined only to Europe, the higher priority placed on Europe was justified and could be understood. No Asian or African could object with reason to the programmes then adopted for the rehabilitation of war-devastated Europe. The position is, however, different today. European reconstruction has been largely achieved, while Asia and Africa are still waiting for effective programmes of rehabilitation and development. Asia and Africa are thereore waiting to see if Unesco will place today the same priority on work in these areas as it did on work in Europe immediately after the war.

I have already said that I am happy that the new Director General has taken this early opportunity of visiting Asia. I would like to impress upon him that there is a feeling in Asia and Africa that their needs are not considered as carefully as they have a right to expect. Even today in most of the programmes of the U.N. and Unesco, a greater importance seems to attach to the problems of Europe and South America. Unesco cannot succeed in its object so long as all parts of the world do not feel equally treated by it. We have also to consider what parts of the world are in greater need of Unesco's aid. There can be no doubt that in respect of education, culture, scientific progress and economic prosperity, Asia and Africa are far behind Europe and America. Millions are without access to literacy and education. Science has opened out prospects of immense advancement, but not for them. Their standard of life is so low that people of the Western world can hardly imagine it. In such a situation, if Asia and Africa find that more stress is laid not on their problems but on those of others, it is not surprising that there should be lack of enthusiasm for the U.N. and Unesco in these regions.

Unesco aims at the propagation of education, science and culture. If we look at the programmes of Unesco in the last six years, it becomes clear how much still has to be achieved. Some years ago Unesco accepted a most important programme in the field of fundamental education. The Asian and African countries were hopeful that this would help to spread literacy and raise the standard of life in the less developed regions of the world. It is a matter for regret that after the establishment of only two centres, one in South America and the other in Egypt, the programme was abandoned. I feel that one of the first priorities in Unesco's programme should be the establishment of more fundamental education centres in Asia and Africa. It is, however, necessary to emphasise that such centres must not be too elaborate and expensive. They must be in conformity with the requirements and resources of these regions, for only then can they serve the purpose in view.

I have referred to one reason why the Asian and African nations feel that Unesco has paid less attention to their needs. Another reason for this feeling is to be found in Unesco's attitude towards so-called international organisations. The multiplication of such organisations seems, at times, to be without sufficient justification, for they do not always seem to be concerned with the basic problems of Unesco and may be regarded more as frills on the margin. Nor do they seem to be international in the true sense. Very often their activities are confined to Europe and sometimes to only one or two countries of that continent. We, however, find that they are not only given accommodation in Unesco House but Unesco's meagre resources are dissipated in giving subsidies to them. We have to recognise that the days when Europe was equated with the world are gone for ever. Today, no organisation can be regarded as truly international unless it functions in both the East and the West. India has already suggested that no organisation should be recognised by Unesco as international unless it operates in at least three continents and has at least five member-States in each continent. This view has not yet been accepted, and the result is that a number of organisations, which call themselves international but have no right to do so, eat up a substantial portion of Unesco's funds. In view of the shortage of funds and the many claims on it, Unesco must in fact make a selection out of organisations which can satisfy the conditions mentioned above. We must therefore both decide an order of priority and lay down criteria to determine the international character of organisations before Unesco gives them any aid.

Unesco should also consider whether there is room for economy in the administration budget of the Headquarters. I recognise that the execution of programmes cannot be carried out without adequate staff. The staff is, however, only a means to an end and cannot itself be the end. Unesco would therefore defeat its own purposes if administration ate up so much of its resources as not to leave enough for the execution of its programmes.

I understand that Unesco's budget for this year is approximately nine million dollars. Of this amount, more than two-thirds, *viz*., 6.3 million dollars is shown as provision for administration while only 2 million dollars are for the execution of programmes and 4,88,650 dollars for subventions to international organisations. I am aware that the charges for administration include some items connected with programmes, but even then the allocation of two-thirds of the fund to administration appears to be too glaring to escape public criticism. I am sure the new Director General is aware of this disproportion and will take early steps to ensure that a greater proportion of Unesco's limited resources are diverted from the provision of means to the achievement of ends.

Closely connected with this is the problem of concentration of programmes. It is generally agreed that today Unesco's programme is spread over a vast field and contains items, at least some of which cannot be regarded as basic. I, of course, concede that an international organisation with many member-States must seek within its means to satisfy all their demands. I, nevertheless, feel that the time has come to concentrate on three or four basic programmes and devote all our funds and energy to their execution. It is surely better to accomplish one or two important projects than to attempt a dozen programmes of varying importance and leave all of them half complete. I hope that this conference will pay attention to this issue and frame a programme for the consideration of Unesco by which an order of priorities among programmes may be settled.

What I have said so far is largely negative. We should now consider what positive measures can be adopted to make the work of Unesco more effective throughout the world. I have said that Unesco should pay more attention to the feelings and needs of Asia and Africa. I will now add that Unesco must have greater access to such feelings and needs. One suggestion which occurs to me is the decentralisation of the work of Unesco and the establishment of regional centres in Asia and Africa. Just as W.H.O. has set up regional organisations which both reflect and respond to local feelings and needs, Unesco should also set up regional offices. These should be manned mainly by the people of the region, for only they can have adequate knowledge and sympathy with its problems and be able to interpret Unesco to them.

The execution of these programmes depends ultimately on the interests and the will of the member-States. Sometimes it is said that the limiting factor of Unesco programmes is funds. I do not fully agree. The funds themselves depend upon the interest and will of the member-States. If the member-States give greater priority to education and the programmes of peace, they can place much larger funds at Unesco's disposal.

In this context, I wish to draw your attention to an issue of paramount importance in the modern world. This is the question of the use of atomic power for the purposes of peace. One of the most hopeful developments in recent times has been the statement of President Eisenhower before the General Assembly of the United Nations. If the line of thought suggestsed by him is developed and all atomic energy placed at the disposal of the United Nations, the nightmare in which the modern world lives can come to an end. The peaceful use of atomic power would relieve the budgets of nations from the crushing burden of armaments. You are all aware that if one per cent of what is being spent on armaments today is placed at the disposal of Unesco, startling developments will take place all over the world. Peaceful use of atomic power would not only release existing funds for purposes of education, science and culture but also enormously enhance such resources. We have also to consider which organ of the U.N. is best suited for the peaceful exploitation of atomic power. To my mind , this can be none other than Unesco. By its very constitution it is pledged to the application of scientific research for human advancement. In part fulfilment of this purpose, it has already decided to set up a European centre for nuclear research. Its concern with education, science and culture also makes it comparatively immune from political influence. For all these considerations, Unesco would be the agency most suited to carry out researches for the peaceful use of atomic energy.

I would also like to refer to what the Eastern countries can give to the West. The East needs from the West science and technique but it need not only a receiver. It can also offer the West help in one very important respect. This is by the dissemination of the abiding values of Eastern culture in the West. In the West culture has often meant painting, music, literature and science. In the East it means something more. No Eastern concept of culture is complete unless it includes the values of the spirit. It is generally recognised that the West is in great need of these values. I am aware that Unesco has a programme of translation of the Eastern classics, but what I feel is that if this is done on a sufficiently wide scale, it may provide the West with just those values it lacks and needs. Unesco may thus well serve as the agency through which science and technique are brought to the East, while the values of the spirit are made available to the West.

Before I conclude I would like to mention one other issue which India has raised on several occasions and to which I myself referred when I addressed the General Conference of Unesco in 1951. This is the issue of throwing open the doors of Unesco to all countries without regard to their economic or political belief or status. Economic or political differences may divide the world into rival camps, but there is no reason why the cultural unity of mankind should not triumph over such divisions. Human culture in its real sense is one and indivisible and, as the agency for education, science and culture, Unesco must be global in its approach and compass. I feel that Unesco cannot really fulfil its function until nations which now stand outside its portals join its brotherhood. The U.S.S.R., and the Chinese People's Republic are not members of Unesco and yet a large section of the world's people live in their territories. How can Unesco's role be fulfilled till these people can also share in its message of education, science and culture? It does not matter whether these countries have applied for membership to Unesco or not. It is Unesco's duty to extend to them an invitation to join its brotherhood. If they refuse, the responsibility will be theirs.

I am sorry that an accident keeps me confined to my bed and prevent me from participating in your deliberations. My thoughts are, however, with you. I have therefore placed before you in writing what I would have liked to say to you in person. I hope you will consider what I have said and formulate proposals that will advance the cause of Unesco in this region of the world.

I am happy that in spite of the many calls upon his time, the Prime Minister has been able to participate in our conference. I now request him to inaugurate this conference and share with us his thoughts for the peace, progress and welfare of man.

Document No. 57

Maulana Azad's address at the 21st session of C.A.B.E. held in New Delhi on 7-2-1954

I expressed my regret at the last meeting that the Central Advisory Board of Education could not hold its annual session until November, but this has also had one advantage that we are meeting within three months to consider measures for the reconstruction of education in India. In the last meeting of the Board I drew your attention to some of our most important and pressing problems. What I would like the Board to do at the present meeting is to draw up a programme of reform and suggest measures which will bring them into effect without delay.

I think you will agree that reform has become urgent in two spheres of education in India. The first is the field of university education and the other of school education. So far as the reform of university education is concerned, we will have to depend mainly on the activities of the University Grants Commission which, as you know, has been functioning since December last. The Commission will be the agency through which we propose to carry out all our programmes of university reform. It consists of well-known and experienced educationists and is fully aware both of the problems the universities have to face and of its own responsibility in the matter. I am glad that the Commission has, at its very inception, started its work with despatch and taken one decision which I consider to be of basic importance.

You will agree that there can be no adequate improvement of university education till there are better qualified and satisfied professors. Until university teachers are recognised for their standard of scholarship and character, they cannot offer to the students the leadership which we expect from them. No real improvement of university education is possible nor can the universities give what we expect from them till this condition is satisfied. The Commission has therefore taken up as its very first task the question of improving the conditions of service of university teachers, and I have accepted its recommendations in this behalf.

In the last meeting of the Board it was pointed out that, though the Board had accepted generally the recommendations of the University Education Commission nearly four years ago, hardly any steps had been taken for their implementation except in the case of the Central Universities. The Board therefore decided to appoint a Committee to survey the position and suggest measures for the speedy implementation of these recommendations. This Committee has submitted its report which will be one of the items for your discussion. Briefly, the Committee has recommended that immediate steps must be taken to amend various University Acts in order to reconstitute University Senates, Syndicates and Academic Councils so as to free them from intrigues and political influence. The Committee has, in this connection, placed the greatest emphasis on the method of appointment of the Vice-Chancellor and suggested that immediate steps be taken to adopt a procedure more or less in conformity with that followed by Delhi University. The Committee has also recommended (a) an improvement in the scales of salaries of university teachers, (b) the provision of Government loans to enable the universities to build students' hostels and teachers' quarters, (c) a greater emphasis on tutorial, as opposed to the lecture, method of instruction, and (d) the provision of merit scholarships to enable poor but deserving students to pursue their studies. After the Board has considered the report and made its recommendations, they will be forwarded to the University Grants Commission for necessary action.

The reform of university education is important and urgent, but from the point of view of the present needs of the country, the reform of school education is even more important and urgent. Until schools improve, university education cannot but remain unsatisfactory. Of the various stages of school education, the one which is in most urgent need of reform is that of secondary education. You will remember that the Secondary Education Commission has already surveyed this field, and you have appointed a Committee to study its recommendations and select those which ought to be put into effect immediately. The Committee has submitted its report, and it is for you to approve it with such modifications as you may consider necessary. Since the Board is the highest educational body in the country and includes among its members representatives of both the Central and the State Governments, I am confident that any recommendations you may make will be implemented without delay. In so far as it concerns the Government of India, I can assure you that we will take immediate steps for their implementation.

As I told you at the last meeting of the Board, secondary education cannot meet the needs of the country till it is reorganised. In this connection, three things appear to me to be of great importance:

(*i*) Secondary education must be so fashioned that it will be the completion of education for the majority of the people. It must not be a mere entrance to the university but be a stage complete in itself.

(*ii*) Its pattern and content should be such that it may serve the needs of different groups of people with different aptitudes. It must not be cast in a rigid and cast-iron frame.

(*iii*) We have accepted basic education as the pattern of education at the elementary level. Secondary education should be so modelled as to complete the process of instruction initiated at the elementary stage and train up citizens who are able to discharge their responsibilities of citizenship. The emphasis on some one craft in the Secondary Education Commission's report appears to me to be valuable from this point of view.

I am glad that the Secondary Education Commission has paid due attention to these points and they have been stressed by the Committee you appointed. I am sure that you will also consider them with the care that they deserve.

One of the major recommendations of the Committee you appointed is that the educational structure in the country should eventually consist of eight years' integrated elementary (basic) education, four years of secondary education and three years of university education. This will mean that normally a child will be in the basic (junior and senior) school till he is fourteen, and will then have four years of high school followed by a three years' course at the university leading to the Bachelor's degree. The Committee has drawn special attention to the Commission's recommendation that languages, general science, social studies and a craft should form the core subjects of secondary education for all. In addition, the Committee has given the highest priority to the introduction of diversified courses in the following main groups:

(1) Humanities
(2) Sciences
(3) Technical Subjects
(4) Commercial Subjects
(5) Agricultural Subjects
(6) Fine Arts
(7) Home Sciences

The Committee has also reported that there should be one examination at the end of the secondary course. Greater emphasis should, however, be placed on periodical tests and the regular progress report of students in the curricular and co-curricular activities. The Training Colleges should not charge any tuition fees and teachers under training should be given their full salaries or stipends that will meet their expenses. Finally, the Committee has reiterated the Commission's recommendation that the higher secondary examination should be made the normal qualification for most government services.

If we accept these recommendations, as I hope you will, we must try to fix some targets, for without such targets our programmes of reform are bound to remain vague and indefinite. The Committee has reported that about five per cent of the existing secondary schools should be converted into multi-purpose schools in the course of the next two years and another ten per cent in the next five years. To me it appears that this programme of reform is slow and must be accelerated.

I agree that in any measure of educational reform, progress is bound to be slow in the beginning. The pace must, however, be steadily quickened and in the later stage we must achieve really rapid progress. I consider that the first task in the context is to define a target date for the complete reorganisation of secondary education. My own idea is that this task must be accomplished within ten years. I confess that even ten years appear to me too long and would be happy if the period could be shortened still. I hope the Board will consider the question carefully and suggest measures which may contribute to this end.

Once this general target has been set, we have to consider specific items. I have already said that I consider the target set by the Committee regarding the conversion of existing schools into multi-purpose ones to be slow. I am of the view that at least 25 per cent of the existing schools must be so converted as early as possible. The Board may consider the suggestion and define the period in which this should be done.

The Committee has drawn our attention to the difficulty of transforming existing schools to the new pattern, and rightly pointed out that it is bound to take time. This may be true in some respects, but there are some changes like those in the curriculum and reform in examinations, where the process of reform can begin without delay. Our programme therefore ought to be that during the next two years programmes for reconstruction of curriculums and reform in examinations should be carried out on as wide a range as possible.

I would now like to draw your attention to another problem of the greatest importance to the future of our education. This is the problem of students' unrest. Since the attainment of independence, there has been a marked deterioration in order and discipline among students. In the last two years, there has been one incident after another in which students have been involved. This has become a cause of national concern, and everyone who has any sense of responsibility is troubled by these developments.

What worries me most is that the extent and magnitude of students' unrest is very often without any relation whatever to its supposed cause. In recent months we have witnessed ugly developments in Lucknow and Allahabad. The trouble arose out of the question as to whether or not the membership of the University authorities were of the view that students should not be compelled to become members of the University Union. The students held the opposite view. The authorities at Lucknow later accepted the demand of the students, but there arose a new question about the constitution of the Union. I do not wish to enter here into the controversy as to the merits of the question. What grieves and surprises me is that there should be such turmoil over the question of the constitution of a students' union. It suddenly appeared as if it was not a matter between the authorities and students of a university but a conflict between two enemies who were ready to fight against each other at the slightest provocation. The students set up an Action Committee which drew up a programme of struggle. Procedures which belong to belligerents were thus imported into university affairs. What happened later is well known to you and cannot but be a cause of the greatest sorrow to everyone who has the welfare of the country at heart.

This issue of students' unrest has now reached a stage where the Board must pay the greatest attention to it, explore its causes and suggest measures of remedy. While these events were happening in Lucknow, I called a conference which was attended by some eminent educationists and the Prime Minister. We considered the issue as carefully as we could and the conclusion to which we reached was later placed before the Congress Working Committee, which has passed a well-considered resolution in the matter. You are, no doubt, aware of this resolution, but I want the Board to give further thought to it and consider it more in its educational implications. A note on the subject has been prepared by Sri Humayun Kabir which is down for discussion in your agenda. I want you to consider this note in its different aspects and advise the Governments at the Centre and the States on the steps which must be taken if we are to check the growing indiscipline and unrest among our students. Unless this is done in time, it will threaten the foundations of our educational structure.

I will in fact go further and say that such unrest among the students strikes at the root of our national future. The student of today is the potential leader of tomorrow. He will have to sustain the social, political and economic activities of the community. If he is not properly trained and does not develop the necessary resources of character and knowledge, he cannot supply the leadership which the nation will need. We must therefore adopt measures which will eradicate the causes of students' unrest and make the universities creative centres of learning and leadership.

Document No. 58

Maulana Azad's Address at the first session of N. A. L. held in New Delhi on 12-3-1954

I have pleasure in welcoming you to this first meeting of the National Academy of Letters.

In 1944, the Government of India accepted, in principle, a proposal of the Royal Asiatic Society of Bengal (as it was then called) that a National Cultural Trust should be set up to encourage cultural activities in all fields. The Trust should include three academies – one in letters, one in the visual arts and one for dance, drama and music. After the National Government was established in 1947, three conferences were convened to work out in detail the implications of this proposal. The conferences agreed about the need for the academies but felt that since a National Government had been established, it was not necessary to set up a National Trust. It was, however, recommended that steps should be taken to set up the academies as autonomous bodies and provide them with the funds necessary for their work. The Government of India has accepted that recommendation.

The Government's function in this process is mainly that of a curtain-raiser. Someone has to set up the academies, and the Government has decided to do so. Once they are set up, the Government will refrain from exercising any control and leave the academies to perform their functions as autonomous institutions. The Sangeet Natak Akademi has already been established in accordance with this decision of the Government. The Academy of Fine Arts is in process of formation, and today we have met to set up what is perhaps the most important of the three.

There are some – and the Prime Minister was one of them at one stage – who expressed the view that the academies should not have been established in this fashion. They regard it as an imposition from above. They hold that the growth of the academies should have been encouraged from below. Instead of establishing an academy, the

Government should have waited till there grew up in the country societies or individuals who had the necessary authority to establish the academies. Once such academies had been set up, the Government's function should have been merely to recognise them.

I am afraid I cannot agree with this approach. Since the Renaissance, many academies have been established in Europe. Today there is hardly any country in the Western world which does not have one or more national academies. All these academies were established by the Governments under letters-patent of the Sovereigns or by legislation. There was therefore no reason why the Government of India should not take the imitiative for the establishment of the academies. In fact, if we had waited for the academy to grow from below we might have had to wait till the Greek Kalends.

I should like to dwell for a moment on the meaning of the term 'academy'. We are all aware that this term was first used for the school that Plato had established. The garden in which the school was set up was named after an ancient hero 'Akademus,' and it was after him that the school came to be known as the Academy. Whatever the origin of the name, it has, in course of time, acquired a connotation of its own which, as far as we are aware, cannot be expressed by any other single word. What do we mean by an academy? Is it a school? The answer is 'No.' Is it a research institute? Again the answer is 'No.' Is it then an association of writers and authors? Still the answer is in the negative. If, however, it be asked whether it possesses the attributes of all of them, the answer must be an emphatic 'Yes.' By calling it an academy, we refer to all these facets and signify that it is at the same time a school, an institute and an association. If we were to call it a school or an institute or association only, the full significance of what we intend would remain unexpressed. An academy is, in fact, something more than any or all of them.

The academies flourished in Greece for almost 900 years until Justinian ended them by a special decree. During this period, the term 'Academy' acquired its special significance. There is no other word in any Eastern or Western language which can convey the full flavour of the academy. That is why we have resisted the temptation of a vain search for a new term and have kept the original word in its adapted form as 'Akadami,' in conformity with the requirements of Hindi pronunciation.

Today is the first in the life of the Indian Academy of Letters. It is necessary that we should have a clear idea of the work which it is intended to perform and the standards it will place before the world.

The question of standard is, to my mind, fundamental in the concept of the academy. The Academy must lay down a standard for those who seek to be recognised as distinguished men of letters. The Academy would serve its purpose only if its standard is set as high as possible. If the standard is lowered, the very purpose of establishing the Academy is lost.

The object of the Academy is to educate public taste and advance the cause of literature. This can be done only if we maintain the highest standard. Then alone will writers aim at giving their best and create works of art which will add to the heritage of man. On this question of standard, we should, I feel, be guided by the example of the French Academy. Established by Louis XIV in 1635 with only 40 members, it has to this day refused to increase this number. The number of men in the whole of France who can achieve the status of Academician is thus only 40. Even the most distinguished men have to wait for a place in the Academy till there is a vacancy.

The result of this insistence on standard is that France regards the membership of the Academy as an earnest immoratality. To be elected to the Academy was held to be a guarantee of permanent fame. The Academy has been so exclusive that we find that even the greatest men of letters have sometimes been denied the status of members. Descartes, Pascal, Moliere are all men whose distinction as men of letters is beyond dispute, but they never found a place among the Academicians. Montesquieu and Voltaire were fortunate in this respect but Rousseau never achieved the distinction. We all know the high position occupied by Encyclopaedists in the world of French letters but among them only D' Alembert and Marmontel were able to become members. Even Diderot and Helvetius found no place in the Academy.

Coming to modern times, we find that some of the greatest figures of French literature waited long and sometimes in vain to achieve the distinction. The nineteenth century is perhaps the most glorious period of modern French literature. There were, in this period, writers whose works have become classics, but, even among them, there were many who never achieved the membership of the Academy. Neither Daudet nor Maupassant nor Zola were members. Lamartine regarded himself fortunate that he was elected a member after some years' waiting. Even the author of *Les Miserables* had to wait for ten years before he could become a member. In recent times, Andre Gide, who is a French writer of world-wide reputation and had received the Nobel Prize in 1947, was never a member of the Academy. If the Indian Academy of Letters does not maintain similar standards and reserve its honours only for the immortals of literature, the Academy will not be able to serve the object for which it is being established.

In framing the constitution of the Academy, these considerations were constantly before us. We saw that if we prescribed the membership of the Academy on the same basis as in the French Academy, it would have been difficult to set it up at all. We must admit that the literatures of India today have not reached a stage where 30 or 40 persons could be selected straight-away and be regarded as immortals. We have accordingly made a distinction between Members and Fellows. For membership, we have not laid down the standards prescribed for the French Academy and have considered it enough that a person should have helped in the development of literature or established his position as a man of letters. In order, however, to create the same standards as in the French Academy, we have created a separate class called 'Fellows of the Academy.' Here, as in the French Academy, only the selected will be admitted.

We considered carefully the question as to what should be the number of Fellows. We finally decided that the number of Fellows in the Sahitya Akademi must not exceed 21. This does not, however, mean that there will be necessarily 21 in the Academy. It only means that there will never be more than 20 fellows. In the Sangeet Natak Akadami, where the limit is higher, namely 30, there are at present only seven Fellows. For the Academy of Letters, my feeling is that the number will perhaps be less, for, the selection is to be done with even greater care.

So far as the constitution of the Academy is concerned, it may be briefly described as follows. All the fourteen languages enumerated in the Constitution of India have their representatives on the Academy. There are also representatives of the States, the universities and of the Government of India. In addition, there are eight persons nominated by the Minister for Education for their services to the cause of literature. All the three academies have a constitution more or less on this pattern.

You will find that while all the languages named in the Indian Constitution are represented in the Academy, English does not find a place there. You will agree that the Academy would have remained incomplete if some distinguished writers of English had not been included. We have to admit that for the last 100 or 150 years, English has served not only as a vehicle of knowledge and learning but also as the medium of expression for many of our finest writers. This was inevitable, for English had achieved such a pre-eminence that the status of an author was not assured till he had expressed himself through its medium. Tagore, who is the greatest poet of modern India, had been writing in Bengali ever since his childhood but his fame was not fully recognised even in his own province till the English version of *Gitanjali* declared him as one of the greatest poets of the world. Mahatma Gandhi's contribution to national awakening and the achievement of independence is acknowledged universally. His writings in Gujarati are, however, known only to the people in Gujarat. It was his writings in English that enabled him to evoke a new political consciousness and give a revolutionary turn to Indian life. Similarly, Aurobindo Ghosh's claim to distinction rests upon the quality of his writings in English.

I have, for some time, been thinking how best to encourage the development of creative literature in the different Indian languages. Some of the State Governments are no doubt working to this end, but I felt that it was necessary to take measures which would secure an all-India recognition for writers in different languages. I asked the Ministry to examine the issue, and it has been suggested that one way of such encouragement is to award prizes or other distinction to writers of merit. A scheme which has been accepted by the Government is to give prizes of Rs. 5,000 every year for the best work in each of the 14 languages mentioned in the Schedule to the Constitution. Every year, the work of the three preceding years will be surveyed and a prize given to the writer of the best work. No author will be entitled to get a prize a second time, for I am sure you will agree that such a scheme should benefit as many people as possible. The awards will be made on the recommendations of the Academy of Letters.

One thing I would like to make clear is that these prizes will be given for recognised merit, and no one should apply for them. It is my hope that the first prizes will be announced before the end of the calender year.

I have already said that the Government's function in establishing the Academy is that of a curtain-raiser only. This also applies to the appointment of its first Chairman. The Government of India have accordingly selected its first Chairman but hereafter it will be the Academy which will appoint its own office-bearers.

I am glad that Sri Jawaharlal Nehru has agreed to serve as the first Chairman of the Academy. He has been appointed not because he is the Prime Minister but because he has carved out for himself a distinctive place as a writer and author. The Committee which framed the constitution of the Academy submitted three names, of which the first was that of Pandit Nehru. The Ministry of Education offered the Chairmanship to him, as it was beyond dispute that from every point of view he is the best man we could have selected for the first Chairmanship of India's National Academy of Letters.

Document No. 59

Answers dated 15-3-1954 in the House of People by Maulana Azad and Dr. M.M. Das, to questions asked[1] about the Hindi Shabda Kosh

The Parliamentary Secretary to the Minister of Education (Dr. M.M. Das): (a) Ten.

(b) Eight. Out of ten Research Assistants, eight are familiar with the Sanskrit language.

(c) Yes, in a large measure.

The Minister of Education and Natural Resources and Scientific Research (Maulana Azad): Yes, it is so.

Mr. Speaker: Perhaps the question was not understood. The hon. Member means whether the article in the Constitution is disregarded.

Maulana Azad: That is not correct. I am sorry I had not earlier heard one part of the question.

Further Clarification

Maulana Azad: Yes, this matter has also been placed before the Board and if the Board likes, it can consider it.

Answer to the supplementary questions: No. 1

Maulana Azad: That is right, but it is a delicate and important matter and we cannot treat it as closed. The Board can consider this also if it so likes.

Mr. Speaker: The hon. Member is entering into arguments about the question.

No. 2

Maulana Azad: I cannot at this time say what expenditure has been incurred. It is, however, a fact that this kind of work is going on in the

---

1. By Seth Govind Das.

States also. When the Cabinet decided that a Central body be set up, at that time it was also decided that other Central Ministries and the State Governments be asked to stop this work and to send on to this Board whatever they had already done. The Central Ministries did so, but in some States this work is still continuing and I do not think it is so objectionable. Let them also coin terms. Their terms will also appear before the people and give them an opportunity for comparative study.

Mr. Speaker: The hon. Member is carrying on arguments in favour of having Sanskrit words.

Shri Gadgil: I only want to seek some information.

Mr. Speaker: I am going to the next question.

Document No. 60

Replies dated 18-3-1954 by Mr. Das[1] and Maulana Azad in the House of People to the questions asked about E.U.P.

Shri Bibhuti Mishra: Will the Minister of **Education** be pleased to state whether under the Educational Scheme for relieving educated unemployment any progress report is being received by the Central Government from the Bihar State in connection with the employment of rural teachers and basic education workers?

The Parliamentary Secretary to the Ministry of Education (Dr. M.M. Das): According to the information received from the State Government of Bihar, 2500 Primary (including 500 Basic) Schools and 250 Social Education Centres are being opened in connection with the scheme to relieve educated unemployment in that State.

The Minister of Education and Natural Resources and Scientific Research (Maulana Azad): Nobody has made such a claim.

Replies to the Supplementary questions

Dr. M.M. Das: Government is contemplating...

Mr. Speaker: The hon. Minister may address the Chair.

Dr. M.M. Das: Two Commissions have already submitted their reports, which contemplate some far-reaching changes in the education system of the country.

Shri L.N. Mishra: Are Government aware of the fact that not even 10 per cent. of the proposed educational centres have been opened in Bihar so far? If so, may I know the difficulties in the way?

Dr. M.M. Das: The Bihar Government may be able to give the reasons, but so far as we are concerned, we have not got the reasons with us.

Shri K.K. Basu: May I know the proportion of the educated people in Bihar that are going to get jobs?

Dr. M.M. Das: I beg to ask for notice of the question.

---

1. Dr. M.M. Das.

Document No. 61

Joint Answers dated 18-3-1954, of Maulana Aazd and Dr. M.M. Das to the questions asked in the House of People regarding the Teaching Facilities in Hindi for Government Employees

The Parliamentary Secretary to the Minister of Education (Dr. M.M. Das): (a) Ten part-time teachers were teaching Hindi to Central Government employees in September, 1953. Their present number is 8.

(b) and (c) The services of two teachers were dispensed with as there was not enough work due to fall in the number of students.

Mr. Speaker: I do not know whether the hon. Minister is prepared with the answer to this particular question.

The Minister of Education and Natural Resources and Scientific Research (Maulana Azad): You can put the question in Hindi. I will be glad to reply.

Reply to the supplementary questions: No. 1

Maulana Azad: The employees very well understand that if they learn Hindi their future will be secure and better. But for various considerations it is not proper to lay any such conditions. The Government are, however, thinking of taking some steps in this connection.

No. 2

Maulana Azad: The standard of Hindi is the same as in Junior Basic Schools.

Document No. 62

Demand for Grants of Education Ministry and Maulana Azad

The House of People
27-3-1954

Mr. Deputy-Speaker: The time allotted for this Ministry is from 3 P.M. to 5 P.M.– two hours. How long does the hon. Minister propose to take?

The Minister of Education and Natural Resources and Scientific Research (Maulana Azad): I require very little time because I had decided that I on my behalf will not like to review the activities of the Ministry. It is not necessary to do so. Last year I had placed before the House an outline of the activities, the Report has also been published. This year if during the discussion any such points came up that require clarification then I will try to clarify them. I think 15 or 20 minutes would be sufficient for me.

Document No. 63

Some clarifications made by Maulana Azad dated 27-3-1954 in the House of People in connection with the questions asked by the members about the Demands for Grants of Education Ministry

(1) **Maulana Azad**: I am not yet in a position to say that they have given advice in the case of even one such word. Now I have enquired from the Chairman. As yet I do not know that they have given advice in respect of even one word.

(2) **Maulana Azad**: I had only said that a Board has been set up for this purpose. It can take into consideration all sorts of terms. But in the terms of reference of this Board it is nowhere mentioned that it may discuss afresh these words also that have previously been decided upon.

(3) **Maulana Azad:** Government. After taking into consideration the advice tendered by them the Government would take a decision.

(4) **Maulana Azad:** I want to submit that in the terms of reference there is not a single word like this. The other day what I had said was that we have not debarred them. If they like they can give their advice.

(5) **Maulana Azad:** Do you not remember that grant has been sanctioned to Nagri Pracharni Sabha for this work?

---

(1) to (5): For more details see Parliamentary Debates.

Document No. 64

Clarification, dated 27-3-1954, of Maulana Azad in the House of People to some points, raised by Dr. R. Singh regarding the education

Dr. Ram Subhag Singh: On a point of order, Sir, what has that to do with education?

Dr. M.M. Das: Education and language.

Mr. Deputy-Speaker: The hon. Minister must leave it to the Deputy-Speaker and not arrogate this to himself.

Dr. Ram Subhag Singh: The Parliamentary Secretary is a Bengali. That is the difficulty.

Shri Tyagi: He is a Bihari.

Mr. Deputy-Speaker: The point is about the language of the minorities; that is a fundamental right provided in the Constitution and it is sought to be denied according to the allegation. The hon. Member raises a point of order. It is open to the Government to enlighten the Chair.

Dr. Ram Subhag Singh: He is not the 'Government'. The 'Government' is the Education Minister. The Parliamentary Secretary is nothing.

Maulana Azad: I think that the question can certainly be raised in respect of education. There is no reason why it should be stopped.

Document No. 65

Maulana Azad's remark to the speech, delivered by a Member in the House of People dated 27-3-1954 in connection with the Demands for Grants for 1954-55

Sir, I have heard with utmost attention the speeches of my hon. friends. As there is no time left now, I think that it would be better if you give me time day after tomorrow after the question hour. I will try to finish my speech in 20 minutes time.

Document No. 66

Speech etc. delivered by Maulana Azad dated 29-3-1954 in the House of People regarding the Demands for Grants of Education Ministry

Minister of Education, Natural Resources and Scientific Research (Maulana Azad): Sir, my hon. friend Acharya Kripalani began the discussion day before yesterday. He emphasised in his speech that the present system of education was entirely defective and that it must be reformed. It occurred to me, when he took up the argument, that perhaps he would discuss the measures of reform suggested by the Education Ministry recently and the steps taken by the Central Advisory Board of Education in January last. I thought that perhaps he was going to offer some suggestions of his own in that behalf. But I was surprised to hear him say that we appointed a Commission for Secondary Education and now perhaps after a few days we might appoint a Commission for Primary Education. This shows that he has no idea of the way the Government is doing the work of education. Either he does not get the time to read these things or his remarks that now a commission would be appointed to examine Primary Education is entirely meaningless, because so far as Primary Education is concerned it was decided by the Government, not to-day but five years before, that it would follow the basic pattern. All the State Governments have accepted this and are acting accordingly. Now the question, that remained, related to University Education and Secondary Education. The question of Secondary Education was even more important than that of University Education because, as a matter of fact, the real defect that lies in our system is to be sought therein. The British Government evolved this system not to give education to the people of our country but for the reason that they needed English-knowing persons of a special type for carrying on the work in their offices. It was for this reason that they established Universities. University Education could not exist without the co-existence of Secondary Education and Primary Education. Secondary Education was evolved only as a means of University Education. No consideration was given to the fact that for thousands and millions of persons who cannot reach upto the stage of University Education, Secondary Education will not be the 'means' but the 'end'. Secondary Education, therefore, should be of that type and contain that element which can serve as an 'end' in the education of ninety per cent of our people rather than remian a mere 'means'. The result was that the whole system of our education was misshapen. However, the most important thing was to hold an inquiry in regard to the Secondary Education and then to recognise it anew. Therefore, a commission was appointed. It submitted its report in nine months. Now the report came up before the Central Advisory Board. The Central Advisory Board appointed a committee in November to examine this report and to submit its recommendations in January to the Board at the time it holds its meeting. A meeting of the Board was held again in January. The recommendations came up before the Board. The Board accepted them and then chalked out a programme. To say that nothing is being done by way of reforms in the system of education is entirely meanigless and wrong. It has become a fashion today for any and every man to stand up and give expression to the platitude that the education system is defective. There should be reform no doubt, but tall talk leads us nowhere. What needs to be considered is that if there be reform what should be the mode thereof. The Education Ministry considered this and it can be claimed that the programme of reform that it has chalked out for itself at present, is the only correct programme. Given full co-operation of the State Governments we will reorganise Secondary Education within a short time. So far as University Education is concerned, there was for that too the need to have some such agency by which the necessary reform could be carried out. It is known to the Honourable Members that a University Grants Commission has been appointed for this very purpose. The work has been started and it is hoped, so far as University Education is concerned, that steps will be taken speedily in that direction.

After this Shri Purushottamdas Tandon began his speech. As the discussion on education reform had already begun he too said a few words about it. But since this did not form the main burden of his speech I am also not paying much attention to it. I will urge upon him as well not to worry himself so far as education reform is concerned but to leave it to others. . . .

Mr. Tandon.. . . .

Maulana Azad: That too, you should leave to others. There are others who will detect the errors. You are not the man for the job.

Mr. Algu Rai Sastri.......

Maulana Azad: He was, however determined to take up the issue of Hindi; he had in fact come prepared for this. I do admit it is an important issue. It has been assured in the Constitution that English will go after fifteen years and that its place will be taken by Hindi in Devnagari script. It is accordingly our duty to give our keenest thoughts to it. I would have been immensely pleased had Shri Tandon given expression to his reactions to the programme which the Education Ministry has set for itself and to the plan of action which it has prepared and then formulated some of his suggestions. But I am constrained to say with regret that the way he began his speech made it evident from the very beginning that he had no mind to give any constructive suggestions. First, he made out a plan in his imagination, against the Education Ministry. Having prepared the plan he now wants to prepare his case for which he is collecting the material be it right or wrong. I will therefore let you know the plan he has formulated. His plan is to emphasise that we all know about this Education Minister that at the time the discussion started in the Constitutent Assembly he was in favour of Hindustani. Therefore even now whatever work is being done by the Education Minister or whatever help is being given by him is not for Hindi but Hindustani. This was the case that he formulated.

Mr. Tandon......

Maulana Azad: My anger need not worry you.

Mr. Deputy-Speaker: I would only appeal to both hon. Members to address me, and not address each other.

Maulana Azad: Tandonji just now said, "I did not say this. I never meant that the Education Ministry was not doing anything for Hindi and that all that was being done by it was for Hindustani. What I meant was that the greater inclimination of Education Ministry was towards Hindustani." Be it as it may, I want to point out to you that this is utterly incorrect. What was the argument that he gave for this? Kindly look at the measure of honesty with which he formulated his plan. The first thing that he presented as an argument was that the Education Ministry was helping the Hindustani Prachar Sabha of Wardha. Now it is evident that the name Hindustani Prachar Sabha does not include the word 'Hindi' in it. The word that finds place in it is 'Hindustani'. It is to such an organisation that the Education Ministry is giving help. In this way he expected that the effect on the hearers will be that the Education Ministry was in fact inclined towards Hindustani as it was helping the

Hindustani Prachar Sabha, Wardha. I want to tell you that this line of argument is based on 'deceptive reasoning'. I shall narrate the facts as they are 'deceptive' (*purfareb*).

Mr. Tandon......

Shri S.S. More (Sholapur): What is the meaning of that word? We are not able to follow.

Mr. Deputy-Speaker: What is the complaint of the hon. Member?

Maulana Azad: To utter the word 'deceptive' (*purfareb*) during a discussion is certainly not unparliamentary. A member can say during the course of discussion that the way another honourable Member has put or presented something is not clear, that it is deceptive, that it is not straightforward enough. I do not concede the contention that the use of this word is unparliamentary. In any case, I do not insist upon this word. I want to say that the way he has presented it is not proper according to my thinking. I want to tell you that the Hindustani Prachar Sabha Wardha... (*Interruptions*).

Mr. Deputy Speaker: All that I am appealing to hon. Members is that there should be no interruptions in the middle. If the hon. Member who was on his legs takes exception to any particular word or phrase, as unparliamentary, I would like to know what exactly it is. If there is nothing of that kind, I shall ask the hon. Minister to proceed.

Shri S.S. More: Our difficulty is that we cannot follow that word. (*Interruptions*).

Shri Tandon: Ask the Prime Minister what the meaning of that word is.

Shri V.G. Deshpande (Guna): On a point of order. Neither has the Chair nor have we understood the meaning of that word. No decision should be given without knowing the exact meaning of that word. The hon. Minister is speaking in Urdu, though Hindi is the National language. The Chair and the House should know the meaning of that word. (*Interruptions*).

Mr. Algu Rai Sastri......

Maulana Azad: I think every member is entitled to say about any discussion that it has been done in a certain way or that something has not been put in the right perspective. He may also say that it has not been presented honestly. It ought to be said in reply that it has in fact been presented honestly.

Dr. Ram Subhag Singh: Withdraw, (*Interruptions*).

Several Hon. Members *rose* —

Mr. Deputy-Speaker: Order, order. Let me hear the hon. Minister.

Shri Tandon: My speech consisted only of arguments not of abusive epithets against anyone.

Maulana Azad: In any case, I do not insist upon any particular word. If you object to the use of these words I do not insist on their use.

Pandit Thakur Das Bhargava (Gurgaon): May I say a word?

Maulana Azad: I want to say.....

Pandit Thakur Das Bhargava: It means dishonestly and fraudulently.

Mr. Deputy Speaker: The hon. Minister did not mean anything had against Mr. Tandon. Further, if the words import any such meaning, he has withdrawn them.

Maulana Azad: Yes, now I want to tell you that....

Shri C.K. Nair (Outer Delhi): It does not mean anything more than 'misleading'.

Mr. Deputy-Speaker: Let the hon. Minister proceed.

Maulana Azad: Now, kindly see the manner in which the case of the Hindustani Prachar Sabha came up before the Ministry. This organisation was in fact founded by Gandhiji. As Shri Tandon explained the other day, when Gandhiji came in conflict with the Hindi Sahitya Sammelan he drew himself away from it and founded the Sabha. Dr. Rajendra Prasad became its Chairman and Kakasaheb Kalelkar and many others became its members. In the very life-time of Gandhiji a majority of those who looked towards him were its members. When Gandhiji died Dr. Rajendra Prasad called a meeting of this Sabha. The one question that came up was whether or not to continue it and it was decided that it should not be discontinued. Dr. Rajendra Prasad and other members were of the opinion that it was a memorial of Gandhiji and that it ought to be maintained. Hence it was maintained. Then question that arose on that occasion was that the source that gave it its income existed no longer and that if it was to be kept alive it ought to be given some help. Accordingly, Dr. Rajendra Prasad invited the attention of the Government to this. I enquired as to what was the scheme and the amount of money that was required for it. A scheme was formulated and presented which required a very huge sum. It was suggested that its office be brought to Delhi and that it should have its own press. All this meant that it should be given the help of many lacs of rupees as a non-recurring and about one lac of rupepes as a recurring grant. The Education Ministry declined to do so but it agreed that the Government of India would be prepared to grant it as much as would be necessary for its maintenance. Hence a sum was granted. It is also to be borne in mind that although it is still known as the Hindustani Prachar Sabha, whatever is being done by it in practice is for Hindi. Hence, the grant was sanctioned. Now I want to ask my friend as to what does he think of Dr. Rajendra Prasad. Is he opposed to Hindi or is he one of its supporters? He is its chairman. Similarly what does he think of its other members?

Dr. S.N. Sinha: On a point of order, Sir. . . .

Maulana Azad : The day this question came up he was not the President. He was merely a chairman of the Sabha. He still continues to be its chairman. But when the issue came up he was not the President. That is why I have narrated the past events. These are the facts. There is no question of not relating them.

Mr. Deputy-Speaker : Does the grant refer to a period when Dr. Rajeindra Prasad was not the President.

Maulana Azad: Yes, When the recommendation was made he was not the President.

Shri Tandon: The question that I raised referred to the period when he was President. Yesterday it was said by the Education Minister that it was on the recommendation of the President that the sum was allotted in the Budget.

Mr. Deputy-Speaker: I have understoood the point of order. The house cannot be influenced by the mention of the name of the President or his association, either on the one side or the other. But, in this case, it so happens that he was the Chairman and made a recommendation at a time and it does not seem to be influenced merely because he is President today. The hon. Minister may refer to Dr. Rajendra Prasad.

Maulana Azad : Yesterday, also I did not refer to the President, I referred to Dr. Rajendra Prasad. Anyway, I want to draw your attention to the fact that in regard to the aid given to the Hindi Prachar Sabha it is not right to draw the conclusion that the Education Ministry favours Hindustani and not Hindi. This body was set up in special circumstances. It was regarded as a memorial to Gandhiji. He had declared that he would keep this body functioning even if he were to do so all alone. Therefore, it was not considered proper to abolish it. And the organisation does work for Hindi, There is no question of Hindustani. I, therefore, wanted to point out that to draw any conclusions that the Education Ministry favours Hindustani is not correct.

Mr. Deputy-Speaker: The hon. Minister has heard every word that was uttered by the hon. Members the other day here. He is trying to explain. Let there be no misapprehension.

Shri A.P. Sinha (Muzaffarpur East): We listened to the speeches of Tandonji and Seth Govind Das, bad as they were silently. Why don't they let us listen to the speech of the hon. Minister? Sir, it is for you to ensure this to the House.

Maulana Azad: Tandonji next referred to this year's non-recurring grant of 60,000 rupees to the Shibli Academy. This Academy continues to function for the last 30 or 40 years. It is true that all the books published by the Academy are in Urdu and that Gandhiji liked their books, patronised the Academy and wrote many articles about it. Anyway, the Academy has done useful and valuable work in Urdu. As the people working in this Academy are those who took part in the Congress movement, they have contacts with Congressmen. About eight months ago, these people waited upon Pt. Jawaharlal Nehru in a deputation and explained to him the condition of the Academy. They said that prior to the partition their books were largely in demand in the Punjab and Sind but now they had lost this market and owing to differences in the value of the rupee also much complicacy had been created. They stated that the condition of the Academy was so precarious that in the absence of an emergency grant of Rs. 60,000 they would be compelled to close it down. They did not ask for a recurring grant but on the basis of their figures demanded only an aid of Rs. 60,000 which would enable them to make necessary adjustments and the society could continue to function. The Prime Minister wrote a letter to the Finance Ministry and one to the Education Ministry expressing the view that this society should continue to function and that it would be undesirable that for want of such a small fund it should be compelled to close down and suggested that the matter should be considered. The Ministry also felt that it would not be desirable if this society was not given a small fund and had to close down, and that Pakistan could exploit the fact for propaganda purposes and say that after the partition the conditions in India are such that a society of this type cannot exist there. So, I also agreed that a lumpsum, non-recurring grant of Rs. 60,000 be given to this society.

I want to draw your attention to one point and I want that we should think over it in a calm and cool manner. We should once for all try to see how our mind is working. The Central Education Ministry spends about fourteen crore rupees annually and if out of this amount a sum of Rs. 60,000 is for once given to a society that works for Urdu, is it anything against which there should have been such severe complaints and such strong opposition? We should try to see in what narrow grooves our mind is working. A sum of Rs. 60,000 has been granted for another language of the country, and we cannot tolerate it and we complain of it.

Urdu is not the language of any religious group. Hindus, Muslims, Christians and others speak this language. Even if it were only Muslims who spoke Urdu – though that is not the truth – do we not have four and a half crore Muslims in India? And if a society that renders valuable service to Urdu is once given a sum of 60,000 rupees, is it anything that should be opposed and criticised as being a step for the progress of Muslim culture. Did they criticise it because they have love for Hindi? No.

Who is opposed to Hindi? All are of one mind so far as the progresss of Hindi is concerned. They do not voice this criticism because they have love for Hindi but because they do not want to see any other language make progress. That is the motive behind it. If you want to rise to great heights, you are welcome to it; but in doing so do not try to dwarf others. That is not the right way. So far as Hindi is concerned, I can assure you that there is not a single individual in the whole of North India who does not want this language to progress or who is opposed to it. In North India even those people who do not themselves know Hindi ask their children to study this languge. If anything stands in the way of the progress of Hindi, I should say it is this mental attitude. Only in 1949 a society in Madras was working on the compilation of an encyclopaedia in Tamil and it requested Government of India for help. The Government thought that they were doing a good and useful work and granted Rs. 80,000 for the society. I remember how people protested and what was said at that time. The fact that we had granted Rs. 80,000 for the preparation of an encyclopaedia in Tamil was not a thing that should have disturbed anybody. But at that time also the same strong feeling was at work. It was not love for Hindi that motivated all the criticism. The feeling was: why should another language be given an opportunity to make progress? There is a desire that no other language should continue to exist. This means that you do not want the progress of Hindi but the fall of other languages. This is a wrong attitude. It is because of this attitude that Hindi does not make progress as speedily as it ought to. What is behind the opposition that Hindi has to face in the South? We should see that we do not oppose any other language of India. We want to see every language prosper. But all the same, we must remember that Hindi is the national language of India and it is our duty, it is the duty of every Indian to be firm on this issue and make every sincere effort to develop Hindi. But a different attitude is adopted here – an attitude that my friend showed the other day when he said that a grant of 60,000 rupees to a society meant that this was done in the interest of Islamic culture. This is absolutely incorrect. No question of Islamic culture is involved in it.

I want to tell you that you should not expect me to talk in a tone of flattery. Only that man indulges in flattery who has his axe to grind and who wants that everybody should be pleased with him and that he should not lose the office of a Minister. I have no self-interest. Forty years ago, when nobody had even heard of my friends sitting around here, I decided to dedicate my life to the service of the country. I am talking of 1907 when I was 18 or 19 years of age and joined the Revolutionary Party of Bengal. Since then my whole life has been an open book before the world. There is no desire left in me now. The larger part of my life is over. Whatever little remains will also end one day. I have no desire and no ambition now. I may tell you that when a man has no personal motive left in him, he loses his identiy. I meant that such a man is immune from wordly set-backs. Such a man is unassailable by weapons because this body is assailable so long as there is self-interest in a man. Once this weakness for the self disappears nothing can harm or injure a man. I may tell you frankly that for the misfortune that befell this country as a result of the two-nation theory and the establishment of Pakistan this sort of mentality, this sort of attitude has been as much responsible as the msiguided Muslims and the Muslim League.

An Hon. Member: That is true.

Shri V.G. Desapande (Guna): The hon. Minister should take back those remarks.

Several Hon. Members: No, no. (*Interruptions*).

Maulana Azad: This responsibility falls on people of such mentality also because you are treading the path of narrow-mindedness when you say that there is no place for any other language, there is no place for another community or for others' rights. It is but natural that people who want to be separate will get an opportunity which they will exploit. They will say. "How can we leave our Government in the hands of such people?"

You know that I resisted such forces. I said that the Hindu intellect in India, the Hindu mind in India is not represented by this mentality. The Hindu mind and outlook are represented by Gandhiji and others who stand by him. I drew the attention of the Muslims to this fact and waged my struggle. I brought about a revolution in the minds of lakhs of Muslims. I have not been able to control my feelings in this matter, and I must tell you that so long as you continue to have a narrow-minded approach to such matters, you cannot achieve your objective. Your objective will, on the other hand, be harmed everyday.

These people read out a list when they referred to this matter. They made mention of the Hindustani Prachar Sabha, Wardha and the Shibli Academy. Should they also not have made mention of the Hindi Sahitya Sammelan which they praised so much and which has been receiving an annual grant of Rs. 40,000 from the Government of India for the last five years.

Shri Tondon : . . . .

Maulana Azad: Only when I reminded of it.

Shri Tandon: ....

Mr. Deputy-Speaker: The hon. Minister is emphasising the other aspect which was not so prominently put by Shri Tandon.

Maulana Azad: What I mean to say is that for years together we have been giving grants to those Hindi institutions in regard to which it has been said that they are not receiving any grant. A mention of this fact should also have been made. He says he did mention it but as far as I remember he mentioned it only after I had invited his attention to the fact. Actually I brought this to his notice twice, once in regard to the Nagari Pracharni Sabha for which the Government sanctioned a sum of rupees one lakh. Then he admitted that this amount had been given. But while adducing facts in support of his argument, he overlooked this thing. Only when I made reference to it he said that these institutions were also receiving the aid.

I would take a little more of your time. Thereafter Seth Govind Dass will make his speech.

Some Hon. Members: Why not pass it over?

Maulana Azad: He started by saying that there were just two hurdles in the path of Hindi. One of these, he said, was English. He also said that he considered those people who had liking for English to be the offsprings of Macaulay.

An Hon. Member: He has not read English.

An Hon. Member: He has not read English.

Maulana Azad: Then he said that Urdu was the second obstacle. I am at loss to understand how Urdu comes in here.

Shri Nand Lal Sharma (Sikar): On a point of order: Is it not unparliamentary to use such language? (*Interruptions*).

Several Hon. Members: No.

Seth Govind Das : . . . .

Maulana Azad: How is Urdu concerned with this? So far as the Education Ministry is concerned it has not created any Section for Urdu, but it has established a Hindi Section. It has chalked out a programme for Hindi and not for Urdu. Urdu in no way comes into the picture.

I do not want to speak any more on that. But I wish to bring it to your notice that he said at the top of his voice, "The Education Ministry has decided to keep the international terms for science. This is absolutely wrong. I went to England and to France and everywhere I found that they had not adopted the international terms". I do not understand what was the source of such information for Sethji. Did he stand at the Charing Cross of London and call "International Terms", "International Terms", but none turned up.

Seth Govind Das: On a point of personal explanation. (*Interruptions*). I am entitled to a personal explanation. I seek the protection of the Chair. (*Interruptions*) I did said this . . . .

Mr. Deputy-Speaker: The hon. Member does not gauge the sense of feeling in the House; therefore he need not come forward with any personal explanation at present. Let him allow the hon. Minister to proceed. If any personal explanation has to be offered, I will give him a chance at the end.

Maulana Azad: I do not know how Sethji has come to the conclusion that there are no international terms in science which we are going to retain. In the first instance, let me tell him how this decision came to be arrived at. It is not correct to say that the Education Ministry made this decision. The Education Ministry has nothing to do with it. The Government set up a University Education Commission. This Commission submitted a report in which it was recommended that for science studies international terms should be adopted in Hindi. This thing was put before the Central Advisory Board of Education. This Board is a body which represents the State Governments, the Universities and the educationists of the country. Naturally the Government attaches value to its recommendations. When the matter was with the Board I received a letter from Dr. Raghuvira in which he said that he was not a member of the Board but he wanted to say something in the matter. I replied that it did not matter if he was not a member of the Board, that I was empowered to extend a special invitation to him and that he should gladly take part in the deliberations. So I invited him. He attended the meeting and spoke for an hour and a half. The members of the Board took it ill. Dr. Mudaliar stood up and said that it was not a school where a teacher could teach things to the students collected there. I interrupted him and pointed out that it was a matter of vital importance and we should invite and consider all points of view. He was therefore given full chance to express himself. Thereafter the Board unanimously accepted the recommendation of the Enquiry Commission, which says that for science international terms should be adopted in Hindi. Thus they endorsed the recommendation of the Enquiry Commission. The Government received this recommendation of the Board and it was considered in a Cabinet meeting. There we arrived at the decision that a body of expert educationists and scientists be formed which should take up the work of preparation of the terms. Consequently the Education Ministry established the Board which is functioning. What I want to suggest is that it is wrong to say that the decision was made by the Education Ministry. As a matter of fact this proposal was made by the University Enquiry Commission. The Board agreed with them and the Government also accepted the proposal. I would ask Sethji that when the question arises as to what should be done in regard to education in science, should the Government consult him or should they consult scientists like Dr. Bhatnagar. Dr. Ghose, Dr. Bhabha, Dr. Saha and Dr. Mudaliar who are already in that line? I am sure that Sethji would never claim that he has ever in his life served in the sphere of science. Let him say whether he has devoted a single minute of his life to science. His mere statement that there should be no international terms has no value. Let him think if such Devanagiri would be of any use. Anyhow, I am not going to draw too much on your time and would like to be brief. It is our duty to abolish English as the official language of the Central Government in a period of 15 years and to make earnest efforts to adopt Hindi. But how are we going to do so? Would it serve to repeat the word Hindi over and over again. Certainly it would not. It is quite a difficult task to replace one language by another in administration which is not an ordinary thing. It involves difficulties. We have to overcome and remove them. The Education Ministry considered this question in the year 1951 and chalked out a programme. The preliminary and fundamental thing was that we adopted a provision in the Constitution that Hindi shall be the official language after fifteen years. If we do not pay full attention to Hindi during these fifteen years and we think that in the sixteenth year Hindi will automatically become the official language and then all work will be done in Hindi, that is simply an illusion. In this way, not to talk of fifteen years, Hindi will not become the official language even in twenty-five or thirty years. Hence we must keep this basic fact in view that at least five years should be allotted for replacing English by Hindi in the Central Secretariat, for completely adopting Hindi in all the Ministries and Departments and for arranging the publication of all circulars, reports and Gazettes in Hindi in Devanagari script. That would enable us to have a trial and to know what shortcomings are there and what difficulties are to be encountered. For purposes of the administration it is necessary to have a specific pattern of language as we have in the case of English. Hindi will have to adopt a pattern on similar lines. This would take us at least five years. The Education Ministry has a programme before it that after ten years *i.e.* in the eleventh year, Hindi should be the official language side by side with English. Our friends from the South will have no cause for complaint because in the eleventh year we will not abolish English. We are going to keep it for full fifteen years, though Hindi will be adopted alongside with it. As for the possible objection that this would involve heavy expenditure on the part of the Government, almost double, I would say that this question of Hindi is of such a great importance that the Government should gladly bear the increased expenditure. But, let me reassure you that the expenditure will not increase to that extent. All States in Northern India have already declared Hindi to be their official language and they are advancing rapidly in their bid to realise that objective. When in the eleventh year the Central Government begins work in Hindi, it will not be necessary for them to send a single paper in English to all such States as U.P., Madhya Bharat, Madhya Pradesh and Rajasthan. If all the need arises to have some duplication in work, even then, as I have already said, this work is of such vital importance that we should gladly bear the extra burden. One might object and say why eleven years, why should it not be adopted in the fifth year. My reply to that is that that would be just as wrong as not to adopt it in the eleventh year. This is a matter in regard to which we cannot move ahead unless we prepare the ground. Anyhow, the Education Ministry have made their programme for Hindi. They have divided these 15 years into three periods of 5 years each. The programme for the first five years is to prepare terms. So far as education is concerned all terms upto the school standard must be finalised. Similarly, terms for administration should also be formulated. In so far as the State Governments are concerned, attempts should be made to make Hindi a compulsory subject at the secondary stage. Now, three years out of the first five have already passed. During these three years, one is glad to find that in the matter of schools, Travancore-Cochin State has given us its full co-operation and, notwithstanding the fact that they are strangers to Hindi, they have made Hindi compulsory at the secondary stage. I was pleased to learn that the Government of Mysore had also made it compulsory. It is also compulsory in Orissa and Assam. In two States only, *viz.*, Madras and Andhra, although Hindi has been introduced at the secondary stage, it is an optional subject and has not yet been made compulsory. From the requests that are received, we, however, find that, in spite of this, considerable number of people there take up Hindi and qualify in it. We hope the time is not far when these States will also make Hindi compulsory at the secondary stage.

Shri Algu Rai Shastri: Will do surely.

Maulana Azad: As for the terms eighteen thousand have already been prepared. I have called another meeting of the Board from the 20th. They have been asked to submit a report on all their activities, so that we might know how to put through our programme in future and what new steps we should take in this direction.

As for the Hindi centres, it is well known that the Dakshin Prachar Sabha has been doing a very useful and valuable job for many years. There were three places, *viz.*, Assam, Orissa and Bengal, where no regular centre has yet been started. There too the Education Ministry has now established three centres. Teachers are being trained and efforts are afoot to organise the propagation of Hindi there in the same manner as is being done in the Southern States.

I shall not take any more of your time. There are just two matters of which I shall make a brief mention. Shri Chatterji has in his speech refered to Manbhum. The Central Government is aware that there is a group in Manbhum whose mother tongue is Bengali and who want their children to be educated through the medium of Bengali. The issue was brought before us in 1949. Similar complaints had also come from one or two other States. Accordingly, I called a conference of State Ministers and placed the matter before them. The Conference resolved unanimously that if in any State there were some people whose mother tongue happened to be different from the official language of the State, they should be given the opportunity to receive education through the medium of their mother tongue. A rule was laid down that if there happened to be 40 students in any school or 10 students in any class who wanted to receive their primary education through the medium of any particular language, arrangements should be made to that end. This recommendation came up before the Government of India who accepted it and incorporated it in their resolution of the 9th August. In the reports received by the Government of India from the Government of Bihar the former have been assured by the latter that they are acting in accordance with this decision.

Some Hon. Members: They are doing it.

Maulana Azad: The complaint now made relates to quite a different matter. I am not yet in a position to form any opinion in this behalf. We must first of all ascertain the views of the Bihar Government without which we cannot form any opinion. If Shri Chatterjee could send me a short note I shall forward it to the Bihar Government and ascertain the real position.

Shri N.C. Chatterjee (Hooghly): I shall send it to the hon. Minister.

Maulana Azad: There was reference to a certain matter in the speech of Shri Chettiar. I was not present on the day when my friend, the Minister of Finance delivered his speech. He was stated to have hinted in the course of his speech that the Ministry of Education had given up as unspent a sum of two crore rupees out of the current year's allocation. I made enquiries from the Ministry and from the facts and figures that I have received from them I have found that the sum involved is not two crores but just 84 lakhs. But even this sum of 84 lakhs includes some big items in regard to which no fault could be found with the Ministry of Education. The very nature of the grant was such that the money could not be spent at all. For instance, rupees ten lakh had been earmarked for the purchase of essential equipment for the Science Institute, Bangalore. This equipment was not received and the money could not, therefore, be spent. Whom should we have paid this money?

Mr. S.S. More....

Maulana Azad: Similarly a sum of several lakhs of rupees had been set apart for the Kharagpur Institute, for the purchase of equipment. That too has not been received yet but may possibly be recieved in May next. Obviously the money could not be spent. We pay a certain sum every year to the Asiatic Society, Bangalore, for the acquisition and publication of Sanskrit manuscripts. This sum is provided for every year. At the very commencement of the year the Society is asked to submit their scheme and the money is paid on the receipt of the same. This time they have not been able to submit a scheme in spite of repeated reminders with the result that the year is over. During this period Shri Beni Prasad happened to call on me and I asked him about the scheme but he replied that he had none yet. Thus the money remained unspent. It would not be correct to say that this was due to any fault on the part of the Ministry of Education. This sum comprises some big items on which the money could simply not be spent.

I shall not take any more time. I would ask you not to imagine even for a minute that the Ministry of Education has grown static. It has an active brain. It has made every possible effort in the past and will continue doing so in the future. It will gladly welcome any suggestion that you might make for any reform or improvement in its methods. But if ever any doubts arise or any whispers are heard I would like you to come to me. I am not a far away. I sit at a distance of just five yards from the Hall. You can meet me and find out what the matter is. I assure you that in so far as it is a question of the development of Hindi the Education Ministry realise its duty and will not be found wanting.

Seth Govind Das: . . .

Mr. Deputy-Speaker: The hon. Member is fully aware that after he has concluded his speech if some reference is made to portions of his speech, all that he can claim to have is that he can get up and remove a misunderstanding to that extent, in as brief and as few words as possible. No further additions should be made.

Maulana Azad: Let me tell you that the Government have no intention of hindering the growth of education; on the other hand, they wish to promote it. This question is under the consideration of the Government and all that I can say for the present is that as far as possible they will not try to put an end to a going concern.

Mr. Deputy-Speaker: Order, order. Hon. Members ought not to get up when I am standing. However big an hon. Member might be he ought not to get up when I am standing. There must be some order and decorum observed in the House.

I will now put all the cut motions relating to the Ministry of Education to the vote of the House.

The cut motions were negatived.

Mr. Deputy-Speaker: Now I will put the Demands to the vote of the House.

The question is:

"That the respective sums not exceeding amounts shown in the third column of the paper in respect of Demands Nos. 17, 18, 19, 20 and 21 be granted to the President, *to complete* the sums necessary to defray the charges that will come in course of payment during the year ending the 31st day or March, 1955, in respect of the corresponding heads of Demands entered in the second column thereof."

The motion was adopted.

[The motions for Demands for Grants which were adopted by the House are reproduced below.–Ed. of P.P.]

DEMAND NO. 17 – MINISTRY OF EDUCATION

"That a sum not exceeding Rs. 37,56,000 be granted to the President to complete the sum necessary to defray the charges which will come in course of payment during the year ending the 31st day of March, 1955, in respect of 'Ministry of Education'."

DEMAND NO. 18 – ARCHAEOLOGY

"That a sum not exceeding Rs. 44,72,000 be granted to the President to complete the sum necessary to defray the charges which will come in course of payment during the year ending the 31st day of March, 1955, in respect of 'Archaeology'."

DEMAND NO. 19 – OTHER SCIENTIFIC DEPARTMENTS

"That a sum not exceeding Rs. 2,00,53,000 be granted to the President to complete the sum necessary to defray the charges which will come in course of payment during the year ending the 31st day of March, 1955, in respect of 'Other Scientific Departments'."

DEMAND NO. 20 – EDUCATION

"That a sum not exceeding Rs. 11,13,30,000 be granted to the President to complete the sum necessary to defray the charges which will come in course of payment during the year ending the 31st day of March, 1955, in respect of 'Education'."

DEMAND NO. 21 – MISCELLANEOUS DEPARTMENTS AND EXPENDITURE UNDER THE MINISTRY OF EDUCATION

"That a sum not exceeding Rs. 30,17,000 be granted to the President to complete the sum necessary to defray the charges which will come in course of payment during the year ending the 31st day of March 1955, in respect of 'Miscellaneous Departments and Expenditure under the Ministry of Education'."

Mr. Deputy-Speaker: The House will now take up the Demands relating to the Ministry of Food and Agriculture. Those Demands are Nos. 43, 44, 45, 46, 47, 122, 123 and 124. They must be treated as having been moved by the hon. the Finance Minister in accordance with the practice which we have been following in the past five years.

Document No. 67

Letter from Maulana Azad to Dr. Karan Singh

New Delhi
1954

My dear Karan Singh,

Although it is difficult for me to leave Delhi at present, I have decided to come to Srinagar for a couple of days to have a brief respite from the extreme heat of Delhi. I shall leave Delhi on the 16th June at 8 A.M. by plane.

I hope you are doing well.

Yours sincerely,
A.K. Azad

Yuvaraj Karan Singh,
Sadar-i-Riyasat,
Jammu and Kashmir,
Srinagar

Document No. 68

Maulana Azad's address dated 5-4-1954 by inaugurating the Lalit Kala Academy

I am happy to welcome you all on the occasion of the inauguration of the National Academy of Art. Some of you will remember that when I addressed the All India Conference on Arts at Calcutta on August 29, 1949, I told you that at the recommendation of the Asiatic Society of Bengal, the Government had decided to set up three academies, *viz*., an Academy of Letters to deal with Indian languages and literatures, an Academy of the Visual Arts and Architecture and an Academy of Dance, Drama and Music. The Academy of Dance, Drama and Music was accordingly set up in 1953 under the name Sangeet Natak Akademi. Similarly the Academy of Letters was set up under the title Sahitya Akademi in March this year. With the inauguration today of the Academy of Art under the title Lalit Kala Akadami, the programme for the establishment of the National Cultural Trust, which I had set before myself, is now complete.

I have always been of the view that apart from the intrinsic value of art for its own sake, it is an essential element in education as it develops the feelings and aesthetic sensibilities of man. I may remind you of what I said at that conference in Calcutta in defence of art in education and life:

> "It is today realised that no education can be complete which does not pay proper attention to the development and refinement of the emotions. This can be done best through the provision of facilities for training the sensibilities by the practice of one of the fine arts. Apart from the general question of developing the finer aspects of personality through artistic education, there is also the immediate utility of such education in developing our manual skill and perceptive sensibility. It is recognised today that education at pre-primary or nursery stage can be best imparted through

training the child in the matching of colour, shapes and sizes. This releases the creative instinct in the child and thus diverts his superfluous energy from merely destructive channels into those of social behaviour and decorum. Thus, whether from the point of view of the training of the emotions or refinement of sentiments or development of manual skill and creative urge, the importance of art as an element of education cannot be overemphasised."

I may tell you briefly what the Ministry has tried to do in furthering the development of art since the holding of the All India Conference. One of the recommendations of that conference was that regional surveys of indigenous art, including folk art, painting, sculpture, bronze-casting, etc., should be undertaken so that authoritative handbooks concerning art designs and techniques and methods and material used in India could be published. The Government of India accepted that recommendation and awarded five scholarships of the value of Rs.3,500 each for the survey of indigenous art in Madras, Bombay, West Bengal, Orissa, Jammu and Kashmir.

The Government also set up a body called the Bharat Kala Samiti to advise the Government in all matters pertaining to art and to promote the cause of art in the country until the establishment of the National Academy of Art. The Samiti has decided to sponsor a critical and comprehensive history of Indian art and has taken in hand the immediate publication of a Moghul album, a contemporary art album and a set of colour picture postcards. It is expected that these three volumes will be published before the end of the year. The Samiti is also considering the publication of a representative volume of Indian paintings, ranging from the earliest Ajanta frescoes to modern times. At the instance of Unesco, we have assisted the New York Graphic Society in bringing out an album of 32 colour reproductions of Ajanta paintings.

In accordance with another resolution of the conference, a fund called the National Art Treasure Fund has been created with contributions from the Central and State Governments and private organisations and individuals.

The Government have also instituted a system of scholarships for young workers in art and other cultural fields. The object of this scheme is to provide effective encouragement to young artists in order to give them suitable facilities for the development of their talents in the right direction. Applications for the first batch of such scholarships have been received and the selection of suitable candidates will be made in the near future.

I must also make a special mention of the establishment in August 1949 of the National Museum in Rashtrapati Bhavan. Here we have collected, under one roof, specimens of Indian art from the earliest times to this day.

Another important event in the world of art was the inauguration of the National Gallery of Modern Art in March this year. Jaipur House was acquired for the purpose and some of the masterpieces of modern Indian painting are displayed there. Efforts are constantly being made to make the collection richer and more representative. On the occasion of the opening of the National Gallery, an All India Exhibition of contemporary sculpture was organised at Jaipur House and prizes awarded to artists who had done distinguished work in this field.

In addition to these activities of the Ministry, voluntary efforts in the field of art have also been supported by suitable grants to various organisations. Special mention may be made of the grants paid to *Shankar's Weekly* for the annual organisation of an International Exhibition of Children's Paintings since 1952. A selection from those paintings has been published in an album entitled *Child Art*. We also arranged for an exchange of paintings between Indian and Japanese children. A grant was made to Rabindra Bhavan, Visva-Bharati, to organise exhibitions of Rabindranath Tagore's paintings in Delhi, Calcutta, Bombay and Madras. Grants have also been made to the Indian Academy of Fine Art, Amritsar, and the All India Fine Arts and Crafts Society, New Delhi.

Of special interest was the exchange of exhibitions of paintings and other forms of visual art with foreign countries. Since 1949 exhibitions from China and the U.S.S.R. have visited India while Indian exhibitions have been sent out to the U.K., Egypt, Turkey, Iraq, China, Japan, Australia, the U.S.A., Canada and the U.S.S.R. A special tribute is due in this connection to Unesco which brought to India an exhibition of the paintings of Leonardo Da Vinci, a travelling exhibition of colour reproductions of paintings from 1860 to date, an exhibition on "Education and Peace," another on "Man against the Jungle" and a scientific exhibition: Our Senses and the Knowledge of the World. We have also participated this year in the international Art Exhibition in Venice and are helping to send an exhibition of Indian Art through the Ages to several middle Eastern, European and South American countries as well as to the U.S.A.

I have, however, always held that in the field of art the role of the Government must be secondary. The Government should, no doubt, take an interest in the development of art but the truth is that art cannot really flourish until there are strong non-official agencies working for it. This is the main reason for the setting up of the Lalit Kala Academy which, though established by the Government, will work as an autonomous body and without any intereference from the Government in its activities. It is true that it is being set up by the Government but this is only because someone had to take the initiative in setting it up. Now that this has been done, the work of the Government is over and from now on it will be your function as members of the Akademi to provide inspiration to artists throughout the country.

I may very briefly describe the constitution of the Lalit Kala Akademi. It is a corporate body and will work through a General Council, an Executive Board, a Finance Committee, and any other committee or committees set up by the General Council or the Executive Board.

The General Council will include, besides officers of the Academy, nominees of the Central and State Governments, representatives of recognised art organisations, eminent artists and the Directors of the National Museum and the National Art Gallery.

The General Council will elect the Vice-Chairman and the members of the Executive Board, and the Finance Committee will approve the budget and appoint auditors.

The Executive Board will be responsible for the supervision and control of the work of the Academy and its office, while the Finance Committee will consider the budget estimates, make recommendations to the Executive Board and prescribe the limit for annual expenditure.

I referred earlier to the assistance received from Unesco in bringing to India an exhibition of European art. Unesco has now taken the initiative in organising a regional Seminar on "Arts and Crafts in General Education and Community Life" in Tokyo this very month. The object of this Seminar is to study ways and means whereby arts and crafts can enrich general education and contribute to the amenities of community life. I am particularly happy that Shri D.P. Roy Chowdhury, our first Chairman of the Lalit Kala Akademi, has been invited by Unesco to serve as the Director of this first Asian Seminar on Art.

It appears to me right and proper that the Unesco Seminar should lay such stress on the place of art in everyday life. Here in India we have always recognised that art is an essential element in the culture of the individual and the community. We have our simple village women who do beautiful *alpana* and decorate their homes. We have our village craftsmen who weave designs and patterns that are the envy of trained artists in the sophisticated countries of Europe and America. If we ask how even the poor in India have developed such pure taste in art, the answer to my mind is that this is due to the splendid architectural and sculptural work we find in our religious buildings. From earliest times, the temple was not only a place of worship but a place of beauty. During the Middle Ages magnificent mosques were built which combined great nobility with great simplicity. The common man who was continually seeing these splendid works of art could not but develop a pure and refined taste. A country which produced Konark or the Brihadeswara Temple or the Taj Mahal had not only a high conception but also inimitable skill in art. The minds which conceived these noble edifices, the hands which shaped them and the patronage which made their construction possible evoke our admiration to this day.

The patronage to art which in former days was extended by kings and nobles will have to be given by the people and the State in contemporary India. I am attracted by a system which, I understand, is in vogue in Sweden. Under this system whenever any public building is constructed, a percentage of the estimated expenditure is earmarked for sculpture, painting and other decoration. I have under consideration a similar proposal so that in future all public buildings, constructed with State funds, may provide opportunities to our artists of today to display their talent.

I need hardly repeat to an audience like the present one, the record of India's glorious heritage of art. In the field of architecture, she has monuments which challenge comparison with the best anywhere in the world. Her sculptures have a plastic quality and vitality that have evoked the admiration of the most carping critics. Her paintings, whether they are the ageless frescoes of Ajanta or the exquisite miniatures of the Middle Ages, are a precious heritage for the whole world. Not only in such traditional works of art, but also in articles of everyday use – made of clay or stone, brass or ivory, silver or gold, or bamboo, cane or wicker – her artists and artisans display wonderful skill.

The Lalit Kala Akademi, which is being set up today, must work to preserve the glorious traditions of the past and enrich them by the work of our modern artists. It must also seek to improve standards and refine public taste. If it serves this purpose, and I have every hope it will, the Academy will have justified itself to India and the world.

I am glad to announce that the Government have decided to give land and to provide funds for the construction of suitable buildings for the three academies. I hope that in a year's time these academies will be lodged in their own buildings.

Document No. 69

Maulana Azad's Address dated 14-8-1954 at the Conference on Sports

I have put you to the inconvenience of coming all the way to Delhi in this weather, but I am sure that in view of the importance of the subject we are going to discuss, you will not consider any apology necessary. I also hope that the results which this conference may achieve will more than make up for the inconvenience caused you.

As you probably know, the Government of India have initiated several schemes for Youth Welfare. Something has already been achieved within a short period but a great deal remains to be done. With regard to games and sports, I have been watching the scene for some time now with increasing concern but I have so far abstained from intervening. I believe that, in such matters, we should rely on voluntary effort and self-help rather than on arrangements, howsoever good, imposed from above. I understood that certain efforts were being made by persons actually concerned with sports organisations to set their house in order, and I therefore thought it best for the Government to await the result of those efforts and, if those efforts bore fruit, to give all possible support to the new arrangements. It appears, however, that conditions are such that they are difficult to reform and that it will in any case be a long process. I do not wish to go into the rights and wrongs of it, I cannot, however, ignore the fact that not only are we far behind even much smaller countries in games and sports but also that our general standards are poor and our interests meagre. Sports and games have a very important role to play in the building up of a healthy nation but one cannot say that they are playing that role in our country at all effectively. Indeed, I am not sure whether the popular interest in games and sports was not greater and standards comparatively higher thirty or forty years ago.

It is against this background that I have invited you today to consider what measures should be adopted to improve the existing state of affairs. I have deliberately not put before you any fixed agenda as I would like you to feel free to raise whatever points you may consider specially important. It will, of course, not be possible for this conference to go into details, and we can perhaps leave that to a smaller body which may be set up to advise the Government from time to time on all matters concerning sports and games. Here we can usefully confine ourselves to a discussion of the main questions.

We must consider the resources, both human and material, at our disposal and examine how they can be utilised to the best advantage. As for the human material, I see no reason to believe that it is in any way inferior to the human material in any other country, but we must devise effective means for its mobilisation and training. It is in my opinion a question of organisation. You, with your rich and intimate experience of sports, can no doubt suggest the most effective concrete steps to take. It appears to me, however, that the greatest need is to have not only effective but clean organisations which will be free from defects that one hears so much about. The sports organisations must command general confidence and respect; they must therefore not merely be good but also appear to be good, so that their leadership is accepted and the largest possible numbers come into the fold of sports. We must draw into sports, leaders and organisers who are genuinely devoted to sports and eliminate those who merely seek personal advantage.

Another point which I would like to emphasise in this connection is that while the Government should undoubtedly do all that lies in their power to encourage and support sports, the main responsibility must remain with those institutions and organisations which are actively engaged in the work, so that sports rest on voluntary, spontaneous and popular effort.

The main problem therefore appears to be to evolve an organisation which will (a) be democratic, resting on the willing and enthusiastic endeavour of the largest number of persons possible, (b) build on the good work already done by the existing organisations and (c) be both efficient and on healthy lines, ensuring fairplay and the spirit of sportsmanship, the participation of the largest number from the lowest levels (school and district) upwards and good competitive standards at all levels.

A very important part of the problem of organisation is the provision of coaching and training facilities. I am aware that certain *ad hoc* coaching schemes were initiated in the past; unfortunately they were not only too few but also inadequate in their approach. It is not enough that some hurried coaching arrangements should be made in preparation for a particular competitive event. Not only does it fail to yield the desired result but it also places the wrong emphasis on competitive events. While we would all be gratified by the success of Indian participants in international contests, what is really important is not success in particular competitive events but the building up of a nation physically fit and imbued with the spirit of sportsmanship. Even from the point of view of competitive events, real success can only be achieved if specialised coaching is based on wide playing facilities and training arrangements from the lowest level upwards, *i.e.* from school onwards.

The two main problems of material resources are those of palygrounds and finances. Here also it is the duty of the Government to give the utmost help possible but I must again emphasise that no constructive endeavour of a self-respecting people can depend entirely on Government help. While therefore the Government and the other public authorities must be urged to make their due contribution, the various sports organisations must continually explore all possible means of strengthening themselves by their own efforts and by enlisting wide popular support. They must, in other words, try to stand on their own legs and look to the Government only to supplement their efforts.

I have put before you briefly some of my own thoughts on the subject and I now invite you to a full and frank exchange of ideas, so that before we disperse we not only have a clear picture of the problems before us but we also have a reasonably definite plan of tackling these problems. As I have said before, I do not think it will serve any useful purpose to find fault with others in a negative way. We should acknowledge that, in spite of severe handicaps and limitations, many organisations and individuals among you and elsewhere have rendered valuable service in the cause of sports, but we should also acknowledge that the total picture at present is far from gratifying. Having done that, we should evolve concrete and constructive steps to improve the present position as speedily as possible. As for myself, I shall listen to you eagerly to find out in what ways the Government can help, and I assure you that your suggestions will receive the fullest and the most earnest consideration of the Government. I am personally determined to do everything possible, with your co-operation, to give our youth a better deal than they have had so far.

Document No. 70

Reply of Maulana Azad to the questions asked in the House of People by Mr. M. Valiulla on August 26, 1954

Scholarships to Foreign Students

Shri M. Valiulla: Will the Minister for **Education** be pleased to state:

(a) the number of scholarships granted to foreign students for study in India during the year (i) 1953-54, and (ii) 1954-55;

(b) the countries to which these scholarships were allotted; and

(c) the terms under which these scholarships were granted?

The Minister for Education and Natural Resources and Scientific Research (Maulana Abul Kalam Azad): (a), (b) and (c) A statement is laid on the Table of the House. (*See* Appendix VIII, Annexure No. 34.)

Document No. 71

Reply of Maulana Azad to the questions asked by Mr. Dwivedy in Rajya Sabha on August 26, 1954 about N.R.S.R.

Shri S.N. Dwivedy: Will the Minister for **Natural Resources and Scientific Research** be pleased to state:

(a) whether it is a fact that a Mineral Advisory Board has been set up recently by Government to report on the establishment of a plant for the benefication of low grade mineral ores;

(b) if so, whether Government have received any report from this Board; and

(c) what are the findings of the Board?

The Minister for Education and Natural Resources and Scientific Research (Maulana Abul Kalam Azad): (a) On the recommendation of the Mineral Advisory Board a Committee was set up on 11th June 1954 to examine and recommend ways and means of persuading private enterprise to set up a ferro-manganese plant and to advise on beneficiation of ores generally.

(b) and (c) The report of the Committee is awaited.

Document No. 72

Answer dated 1-9-1954 given by Maulana Azad in the Council of States (Rajya Sabha) to the questions asked about the Research Fellowship Scheme

Shri M. Valiulla: Will the Minister for **Education** be pleased to state:

(a) whether a Research Fellowship Scheme has been put into operation from June 1954 as indicated by the Ministry in their annual report for 1953-54;

(b) if so, the nûmber of scholarships awarded so far; and

(c) the number of scholars carrying on research under this scheme at present?

The Minister for Education and Natural Resources and Scientific Research (Maulana Abul Kalam Azad): (a), (b) and (c) Six scholarships are to be awarded under the Scheme but as the necessary information from universities was not received in time the selections have not yet been finalised.

Document No. 73

Answers dated 1-9-1954 of Maulana Azad to the questions asked in the Rajya Sabha

INDIAN HISTORICAL RECORDS COMMISSION

Shri M. Valiulla: Will the Minister for **Education** be pleased to state:

(a) the number of important old records and historical materials brought to light in 1953-54 by the Indian Historical Records Commission; and

(b) which are those records and materials?

The Minister for Education and Natural Resources and Scienctific Research (Maulana Abul Kalam Azad): (a) The Indian Historical Records Commission is not concerned with the acquisition and bringing to light of historical records. If, however, the hon. Member desires to know how many papers were read and on which subjects at the last annual meeting of the Commission, a list is attached. [*See* Appendix VIII, annexure No. 62.]

(b) Does not arise.

Document No. 74

Answers dated 1-9-1954 of Maulana Azad to the questions asked in the Rajya Sabha

Training in Archives Science

Shri M. Valiulla: Will the Minister for **Education** be pleased to state:

(a) the year from which the National Archives Department has been conducting post-graduate courses in Archives Science:

(b) the number of trainees admitted each year to the post-graduate course; and

(c) the number of under-graduate trainees receiving training in the year 1953-54?

The Minister for Education and Natural Resources and Scientific Research (Maulana Abul Kalam Azad): (a) There is no post-graduate course in Archives Science; but from 1942 training courses in Archives are being conducted.

(b) The figures are as follows:

Year	One year's Diploma course in Archives Keeping	Three months short course of training in Archives Keeping
1942	1	3
1943	2	4
1944	2	2
1945	2	2
1946	2	4
1947	2	3
1948	3	6
1949	1	3

1950	2	1	
1951	5	3	
1952	7	29	
1953	4	29	
1954	..	15	(upto January-March Session)
	33	104	

Document No. 75

Answers, dated 1-9-1954, of Maulana Aazd to the questions asked in the Rajya Sabha

MAPS COLLECTED BY NATIONAL ARCHIVES

Shri M. Valiulla: Will the Minister for **Education** be pleased to state:

(a) the number of maps and charts collected by the National Archives so far; and

(b) out of them, how many are of historical importance and how many are of geographical interest?

The Minister for Education and Natural Resources and Scientific Research (Maulana Abul Kalam Azad): (a) About 10,000.

(b) All are historical importance.

Document No. 76

Answers, dated 1-9-1954, of Maulana Azad to the questions asked in the Council of States

MOBILE MICROFILM UNIT IN THE NATIONAL ARCHIVES

Shri M. Valiulla: Will the Minister for **Education** be pleased to state:

(a) whether a mobile microfilm unit has been installed in the National Archives to microfilm rare manuscript collections on the spot; and

(b) the number of places at which this mobile microfilm unit has worked so far?

The Minister for Education and Natural Resources and Scientific Research (Maulana Abul Kalam Azad): (a) Not yet.

(b) Does not arise.

Document No. 77

Answers, dated 1-9-1954, of Maulana Azad to questions asked in the Council of States

PHOTO DUPLICATION SERVICES TO FOREIGN SCHOLARS AND INSTITUTIONS

Shri M. Valiulla: Will the Minister for **Education** be pleased to state:

(a) the number of institutions and scholars from outside India for whom photo duplication services were made available during the year 1953-54 and so far in 1954-55;

(b) whether any fee was levied for making these services available; and

(c) if the answer to part (b) above be in the affirmative, what was the amount collected during the above period?

The Minister for Education and Natural Resources and Scientific Research (Maulana Abul Kalam Azad): (a) 10.

(b) Yes.

(c) Rs. 847-12-6.

Document No. 78

Maulana Azad's replies to questions asked in the Rajya Sabha on 1-9-1954

HISTORICAL ENQUIRIES MADE TO THE NATIONAL ARCHIVES

Shri M. Valiulla: Will the Minister for **Education** be pleased to state:

(a) the number of enquiries of a historical nature from scholars outside India received by the National Archives of India during the year 1953-54;

(b) the number of such cases attended to in that year; and

(c) the names of the countries from which such enquiries were received?

The Minister for Education and Natural Resources and Scientific Research (Maulana Abul Kalam Azad): (a) Nil.

(b) and (c) Do not arise.

Document No. 79

Answers dated 9-9-1954, of Maulana Azad in Rajya Sabha to the questions asked about the Committee appointed to undertake a study and appraisal of Promising Ideals etc.

The Minister for Education and Natural Resources and Scientific Research (Maulana Abul Kalam Azad): (a) Yes, Sir. A Committee has been appointed.

(b) (i) The personnel of the Committee is as follows:

1. Dr. K.L. Shrimali.
2. Shri J.C. Mathur.
3. Shri R.K. Patil.
4. Shri L.K. Elmherst (U.K.)
5. Dr. L.H. Foster (U.S.A.)

(ii) The Committee will undertake a study and appraisal of promising ideas, institutions and experiments in the field of higher education in rural areas. The team will visit existing institutions doing experimental work in this field, and make recommendations to Government for the reorientation of rural higher education.

Document No. 80

Maulana Azad's Answers to questions asked in Rajya Sabha on 14-9-1954

RECORDS OF THE EAST INDIA COMPANY

Shri Govinda Reddy: Will the Minister for **Education** be pleased to state:

(a) whether there is a scheme for the publication of all the records of the East India Company; and

(b) if so, what are the particulars of the scheme?

The Minister for Education and Natural Resources and Scientific Research (Maulana Abul Kalam Azad): (a) No.

(b) Does not arise.

Document No. 81

Maulana Azad's Answers dated 14-9-1954 to the questions asked in Rajya Sabha

Preparation of National Calendar

Shri Govinda Reddy: Will the Minister for **Natural Resources and Scientific Research** be pleased to state:

(a) whether a National Calendar is under preparation; and

(b) if so, when it is expected to be ready?

The Minister for Education and Natural Resources and Scientific Research (Maulana Abul Kalam Azad): (a) Yes, Sir.

(b) The work is almost completed. It is expected that it will be finished by the end of 1954.

Document No. 82

Answers of Maulana Azad and his Parliamentary Secretary in Lok Sabha to the questions asked on 20-9-1954 regarding the education of Scheduled Caste students

The Parliamentary Secretary to the Minister of Education (Dr. M.M. Das): (a) Yes – to Madhya Pradesh Government.

(b) A sum of Rs. 45,2000 was paid by the Government of India to the Madhya Pradesh Government in 1953-54 under the Scheme for the Removal of Untouchability, which included the grant of scholarships to Harijan students for Middle School, High School and College education.

Dr. M.M. Das: I think that question may conveniently be put to the State Government of Madhya Pradesh.

The Minister of Education and Natural Resources and Scientific Research (Maulana Azad): Whatever the grant by the Central Government, it is made to the State Government.

Document No. 83

Replies of Maulana Azad and his Parliamentary Secretary to the questions asked in Lok Sabha on 20-9-1954

ARABIC TRANSLATIONS OF RAMAYANA ETC.

Shri R.S. Lal: Will the Minister of **Education** be pleased to state:

(a) whether it is a fact that the copyright of the Arabic Translations of some of the Sanskrit Classics such as the *Mahabharata, Ramayana, Shakuntala*, etc. have recently been purchased by Government;

(b) if so, the number and the names of the books; and

(c) the price paid for them?

The Parliamentary Secretary to the Minister of Education (Dr. M.M. Das): (a) Yes, Sir.

(b) Six. The *Ramayana*, *Mahabharata*, the *Bhagwad Gita*, *Shakuntala*, *Nala Damayanti* and the Divine Chronicles (a summary of Indian Mythology).

(c) Rupees eighty thousand.

Shri M.L. Dwivedi: May I know whether translations in other languages have also been ordered? If so what are those languages.

The Minister of Education and Natural Resources and Scientific Research (Maulana Azad): No. other translation work is, at present being done.

Shri M.L. Dwivedi: May I know whether the Education Ministry will try to have translations in other languages also?

Mr. Speaker: The question is not clear to me.

Shri M.L. Dwivedi: The question is whether translations in other languages will also be purchased in due course?

Maulana Azad: Yes, if any such proposal comes before the Government, the Government will, gladly, think over it.

Shri S.N. Das: May I know whether Government can give an idea of the number of copies likely to be sold in these countries?

Dr. M.M. Das: That has not yet been determined. The mauscripts are still lying with our Embassy in Egypt.

Document No. 84

Replies of Maulana Azad and his Parliamentary Secretary to the questions asked in Lok Sabha on 20-9-1954

EDUCATION OF CHILDREN

Shri Dholakia: Will the Minister of **Education** be pleased to state:

(a) whether Government have formulated any policy regarding the education of children between three and six years of age;

(b) if so, the main aspects of the policy formulated; and

(c) the amount of expenditure proposed to be spent over its implementation?

The Parliamentary Secretary to the Minister of Education (Dr. M.M. Das): (a) No.

(b) and (c) Do not arise.

Shri S.N. Das: May I know whether there is any proposal under the consideration of the Government to send a team of officers or educationists to study the experiments going on in this regard in other countries?

Dr. M.M. Das: So far as pre-primary education is concerned, no such scheme is there, so far as I know.

Shri Dholakia: May I know whether Government intend to appoint a Commission just as they have appointed a Commission regarding secondary education?

Dr. M.M. Das: I must submit to the hon. Member that pre-primary education is the responsibility of the State Governments, and so far as the Central Government is concerned, the highest priority has been given to universal primary education.

Shri S.N. Das: May I know whether in any institute under the control of the Central Government any experiment in this regard is being made?

The Minister of Education and Natural Resources and Scientific Research (Maulana Azad): The experiment is going on in this connection.

Shri S.N. Das: Regarding the education of these children between three and six years of age.

Maulana Azad: There is no institution under direct control of the Central Government.

Document No. 85

Answers of Maulana Azad and Mr. Tyagi in Lok Sabha to the questions asked on 20-9-1954

ENGLISH IN THE ARMED FORCES

Shri Gidwani: Will the Minister of **Defence** be pleased to state what is the policy of Government in regard to the position of English in the Army and of the medium of instruction in the Defence Academy in Poona?

The Minister of Defence Organisation (Shri Tyagi): The policy of the Government is that withing a period of fifteen years from the commencement of the Constitution, English should be replaced by Hindi. Till then English may have to be the medium of instruction at the National Defence Academy which is expected to move to Khadakvasla by the beginning of 1955.

Shri Gidwani: May I know whether the change will be made after fifteen years or whether some start will be made earlier?

The Minister of Education and Natural Resources and Scientific Research (Maulana Azad): In this connection the policy of the Government is to have Hindi as the medium of instruction after ten years, but English will continue to be there till the fifteenth year.

Shri Velayudhan: May I know whether the particular words or terminology in Hindi for those now used in the Army are being discovered by the scholars, so that they may be used for the training of the Military personnel?

Shri Tyagi: Yes, Sir.

Shri T.N. Singh: May I know whether it is proposed to start instruction in the medium of Hindi language only at the end of ten years or any begining will be made right now in certain classes?

Shri Tyagi: There are quite a large number of subjects in the Army in which the medium of instruction is already Hindi. But in highly technical subjects which are scientifically very intricate and require a lot of scientific phraseology, there of course, Hindi could not be taken up.

Shri G.P. Sinha: May I know how many books necessary for Army training have been translated in Hindi?

Shri Tyagi: I have no information about that.

Document No. 86

Answers of Maulana Azad to the questions asked in the Council of States (Rajya Sabha) on 21-9-1954

FELLOWSHIPS TO FRENCH STUDENTS

Shri M. Valiulla: Will the Minister for Education be pleased to state:

(a) the number of Fellowships awarded to French nationals during 1953-54 for–

(i) research work; and

(ii) teaching at Indian universities; and

(b) the number of scholarships awarded by France to Indian students during the same period?

The Minister for Education and Natural Resources and Scientific Research (Maulana Abul Kalam Azad): (a) Six. They do research work as well as teach the French language at Indian Universities.

(b) Twelve fresh awards and 14 renewals.

Document No. 87

Answers of Maulana Azad and his Parliamentary Secretary to the questions asked in Lok Sabha on 23-9-1954

SOCIAL WELFARE INSTITUTIONS

Shri Bhagwat Jha Azad: Will the Minister of **Education** be pleased to state:

(a) the number of social welfare institutions which are expected to receive aid from the Central Social Welfare Board within the Five Year Plan period; and

(b) how much of the amount set apart for the year 1953-54 has been utilised by the Central Social Welfare Board in that year?

The Parliamentary Secretary to the Minister of Education (Dr. M.M. Das): (a) It is not possible to state the number till the period is over.

(b) The Board has sanctioned grants to the extent of Rs. 20,21,000 during 1953-54. Out of this, an amount of about Rs. 10.5 lakhs has been disbursed to the institutions up-to-date.

Shrimati Jayashri *rose* —

Shri Bhagwat Jha Azad: May I know whether the units of the Social Welfare Board have been organised in all the States? If not, in which States have not been organised?

Dr. M.M. Das: In a large number of States – I have not the figures with me,— but it will be about ten States where State Boards have not yet been organised.

Mr. Speaker: Shrimati Raijee may put her question.

Shrimati Jayashri: I wanted to ask the same question.

Shri Bhagwat Jha Azad: May I know whether any condition is imposed before giving such grant to the institution, and is it a fact that in some cases the institution consists of only one person to whom the grant is given?

The Minister of Education and Natural Resources and Scientific Research (Maulana Azad): No! any such case has not come to our notice.

Shri Bhagwat Jha Azad: I asked in my first question and the Government said that they had no figures up till now of the number of institutions to whom the grant has been given. May I know what action has been taken where the branch of this Board has not been organised?

Dr. M.M. Das: I have not said that there is no record of the different institutions to which grants have been given. I only said that at present I do not know what are the States of India in which the State Boards have not been constituted. I can name the States where grants have been given. I have got with me the amounts of grants and the different institutions to which the grants have been given.

Document No. 88

Answers of Maulana Azad and his Parliamentary Secretary to the questions asked in Lok Sabha on 23-9-1954

TRAINING IN DISCIPLINE

Shri Bhagwat Jha Azad: Will the Minister of **Education** be pleased to state:

(a) whether it is a fact that a three weeks training course was conducted in Kasturba Niketan, Delhi, for inculcating a sense of discipline among children; and

(b) if so, whether Government now propose to conduct similar courses in other places also?

The Parliamentary Secretary to the Minister of Education (Dr. M.M. Das): (a) Yes, Sir.

(b) The Delhi State Government has been advised to consider the desirability of trying this scheme in other Schools also.

Shri Bhagwat Jha Azad: May I know whether the Government has ascertained whether, in such a training which is only for three weeks there is any extra cost involved and whether it is a fact that this training can be introduced without any cost?

Dr. M.M. Das: Nothing can be produced without any cost. For this training also we have to appoint, according to the scheme, *ex*-service men as instructors in the schools.

Shri Bhagwat Jha Azad: May I know if it is in the knowledge of the hon. Parliamentary Secretary that such a training was imparted to the Kasturba Niketan girls and boys at no cost, without incurring any extra expenditure?

Dr. M.M. Das: In that case – I speak subject to correction, – the Deputy Minister of Rehabilitation took the charge of instructor on himself; but even so, approximately Rs. 5,000 or so were spent on the scheme.

Shri Raghuramaiah: May I know whether the Government is considering to take up this with the other State Governments also besides the Delhi Government?

The Minister of Education and Natural Resources and Scientific Research (Maulana Azad): Yes, this is under consideration.

Document No. 89

Maulana Azad's address at the 9th annual session of A.I.T.E., held in New Delhi on 30.10.1954

I have great pleasure in welcoming you to the 9th annual meeting of the All India Council for Technical Education.

Since our last meeting, the constitution of the Council has been further revised to ensure better co-ordination in the work of the Committees and the Boards of the Council. I am happy that we have, with us here today, the Chairmen of the Regional Committees and the Chairmen of the Boards of Studies of the Council.

In view of the importance of improving the quality of higher education, the Central Government decided last year to set up a University Grants Commission. This body has been entrusted not only with the task of assessing the financial needs of the universities but also with taking other appropriate steps for the maintenance and improvement of standards. I am glad to note that freindly relations have already been established between the University Grants Commission and the Council in the field of technical education. The University Grants Commission has accepted the suggestion of the Co-ordinating Committee to utilise the machinery of the Council for the assessment of the needs of the Technological Departments of the universities. I welcome on the Council, the Chairman of the University Grants Commission as an *ex-officio* member.

We are meeting today after a lapse of more than a year and a half. During this period, our Co-ordinating Committee has been active in carrying out the policy and programme laid down by us at the last meeting. The successful implementation of the Five Year Plan on the general lines indicated by the Council is, in no small measure, due to the untiring efforts of the Regional Committees and other Special Committees.

It is heartening to see that as a result of the work of these Committees of the Council, before the close of the first Five Year Plan period, we shall have in the country a fair number of post-graduate courses in engineering and technology as also arrangements for advanced work and research. We shall also have a network of facilities in management studies, a subject which has assumed great importance in recent times. An Administrative Staff College and a National Institute of Management will also have been set up largely through the efforts of industry and commerce. At least three, if not more, of the regional schools of printing technology will also have been functioning. The provision for architectural studies will have been expanded considerably and a Central School of Town and Regional Planning will have been established on firm foundations. As you all know, in the past we have had to send a large number of our students abroad for study in these subjects.

Last, but by no means least, the needs of all existing institutions, preparing students for the first degree and diploma courses, will not only have been assessed but the majority of them will have largely completed their programme of development. All this is, by no means, small achievement when one considers that the work was started only after February 1953 when the Council gave general directives on new developmental projects.

The increasing interest, which the State Governments are taking in the work of the Council, is evident from the reports of the work done by the Regional Committees as also the items put forward for consideration of the Council by some of the State Governments. I am glad that the State Governments are working hard to improve the provision for technical education within their States. I am sure that your deliberations on the points raised by them will help us to formulate policies and ensure co-ordinated development.

The Indian Institute of Technology, Kharagpur, has, as you will remember, been established in terms of the recommendations of the Council. Its progress has been remarkable. It has on its rolls today 1090 students receiving instruction for the first degree and post-graduate courses in various branches of engineering and technology. Some are also doing advanced work and research. Its Board of Governors has decided to introduce a number of courses at the post-graduate level commencing with the July 1955 session. Having regard to all the developments that have taken place in the country, the Board has drawn up a plan under which the Institute will ultimately have 1800 students in all – 1200 for the first degree and 600 for post-graduate courses and advanced work. I have every hope that, in course of time, this Institute will develop into an institution of which India may well be proud.

One of the important items on the agenda is the preparation of the Second Five Year Plan. I realise that it has come soon after the framing of detailed schemes to implement the First Five Year Plan. The work done by the Council during the brief space of a year and ten months has, however, brought to the forefront the various problems of technical education. We are therefore in a position to indicate the general lines of development for the five-year period, 1956-61. Although final decisions have not yet been taken, the general expectation is that the Second Five Year Plan will be an "Industrial Plan." It is important therefore that we should plan ahead and be ready to meet its demands. Since it takes three to four years to train technical personnel, it is necessary to decide immediately what steps to take to speed up our machinery of training to cope with the possible requirements for the next five years.

Tentative suggestions in regard to what might be included in the Second Five Year Plan have been made in the notes circulated to you. I think the time has come when we should seriously consider the setting up of more higher technological institutions. The site for the Western Institute has already been acquired and the Government of Bombay has expressed its eagerness to go ahead with the project. The Central Government therefore propose to start the preliminary work so that the second Institute may come into being with the commencement of the Second Five Year Plan.

I also feel that greater activity, both in intensity and scope, is necessary in the field of co-operative projects with the industry. Apprenticeship training schemes at all levels have not yet received the attention they deserve. In this, the active interest and co-operation of the industry are the forerunners of any successful schemes. The Government has already accepted the recommendations of the Secondary Education Commission to provide diversified courses at the secondary level. Such courses can be useful only if opportunities are available to children leaving school to go into industry as learner-workers or apprentices having at the same time facilities for part-time instruction in technical schools. Such schools could be set up by industry. Provision should also be made for such part-time instruction in the existing engineering colleges, which are at present doing mostly full-time work.

I am glad to note that in so far as graduate apprenticeship training is concerned, it has been possible to secure fairly good response from the industry. All the same, what has been done is not enough. Much more will have to be done at all levels. I take this opportunity of making a special appeal to the representatives of the industry and commerce on the Council and the industrialists outside to participate fully in the apprenticeship schemes, which must be worked out and put into effect.

Of late, I have seen tendencies, particularly amongst the Government Departments, to set up separate institutions for their staff members. Their plea is that the establishment of such training centres will lead to greater efficiency than can be obtained if training were arranged in the existing institutions. I think this matter requires further consideration, and I would request the Council to devise the necessary measures to see that the special needs of the various organisations are adequately fulfilled by the existing institutions. If this requires the provision of special courses, expert staff or additional equipment, we should be prepared to sponsor them. I am sure that such arrangements would prove beneficial both to the organisations and the institutions concerned. They should help to tone up the standards at the institutions and make them alive to the needs of the industry, commerce and other technical departments. A further advantage would be that the job could be done more economically in this way. This is by no means an unimportant consideration in our training programmes. Short-term refresher courses would go a long way in meeting such needs and I have no doubt that the Council will direct its attention to this problem.

Document No. 90

Remark, dated 24-11-1954, of Maulana Azad on the University Grants Commission Bill in the House of People

The Minister of Education and Natural Resources and Scientific Research (Maulana Azad): Yes, this is a different thing. Such a question did not arise in this connection. If the hon. Member wants that the Constitution be changed in this respect, they can bring forth an amendment to this effect; but this question does not arise in connection with the University Grants Commission.[1]

---

1. See next Volume VIII for full text of the Bill.

APPENDICES

APPENDIX 1

Document No. 91

Maulana Abul Kalam Aazd's remaks on Muslim Wakfs Bill Moved by Mr. Kazmi[1] in Rajya Sabha on 13-3-1953

The Minister of Education and Natural Resources and Scientific Research (Maulana Azad): I want the position to be clarified. Therefore I would like to say a few words with your permission. My friend, the Law Minister has explained the attitude of Government in this regard. If the majority of Muslim Members of the House want to pursue this Bill, Government would not come in their way. Regarding the point, which he has expressed in the form of his personal opinion *i.e.* Government should frame a new Bill, we should bear in mind that no such decision has been made by the Government as yet and it is too early to say whether it will be able to make such a decision. If in future a Bill seeking to preserve and administer all the Wakfs belonging to Hindus, Muslims, Jainis and Sikhs comes before Parliament, the present Bill, it is clear, would not prove an obstruction. By passing this Bill, Government would repeal this Act.

There is no doubt that this Bill contains many things which require further consideration, but if it is referred to the Select Committee, it is hoped these will be fully considered and then Parliament will have ample opportunity to pass its verdict.

Further remark to the question raised by Mr. Radhey Lal regarding the formulation of the Bill.

Maulana Azad: It does not apply to all, but it has been so formulated that it may be extended to any community which likes to have it.

---

1. See Enclosure.

Enclosure

Muslim Wakfs Bill

Shri Kazmi (Sultanpur Distt.–North-*cum*-Faizabad Distt.–South-West): I beg to move:

> "That the Bill to provide for the better governance and administration of Muslim Wakfs and the supervision of Mutawallis' management of them in India, be referred to a Select Committee consisting of Dr. Syed Mahmud, Shri M. Hafizur Rahman, Shri Ahmad Mohiuddin, Shri Gurmukh Singh Musafir, Pandit Krishna Chandra Sharma, Shri Hira Vallabh Tripathi, Maulana Mohammad Saeed Masuodi, Col. B.H. Zaidi, Shri Mohanlal Saksena, Chaudhri Hyder Husein, Shri Amjad Ali, Shri Syed Ahmed, Dr. N.M. Jaisoorya, Shrimati Subhadra Joshi, Shri C.C. Biswas, Shri S.V.L. Narasimham, Shri Atma Singh Namdhari, Shri Piare Lall Kureel Talib, and the Mover, with instructions to report by the last day of the second week of the next session."

Mr. Chairman: I do not find in the copy of his motion before me any mention of the second week of the next session.

Shri Kazmi: Instead of 8th May I am moving "the last day of the second week of the next session".

Mr. Chairman: Very well.

Shri Kazmi: This Bill was with the permission of the House circulated for eliciting opinion. At the time I moved for eliciting opinion I had given a short summary of the Bill. I may just say that this Bill as a matter of fact is the result of a study of all the Wakf Acts which are in force in various States. But there is a large number of States which have got no Wakf Act at all. And it was for the purpose of co-ordinating the various States in the matter of supervision of Mutawallis in the administration of Wakfs that it was considered proper to have a Central Bill which can be applied to any of the States in which there is no Wakf Act at the present time. As a matter of fact for that very reason Delhi, U.P. and Bihar were exempted from the operation of the provisions of this measure in so far as they had Wakf Boards already constituted in those places.

Now, a very large number of opinions has been received. Some of them have already been circulated to hon. Members of this House. And hon. Members will find that the majority of them, with the exception of those that oppose it on sentimental ground, are in favour of the Bill and in favour of the principle of the Bill.

The only comments adverse to the Bill are in connection with the constitution of the Central Board, that it may prove to be an expensive one. But as a matter of fact, if you, Sir, will look to the scheme of the Bill, probably the Central Board will be the least expensive and will do probably very useful work.

In addition to the opinions that have already been circulated to the hon. Members there is a very large amount of opinion that has been received by the Government, which has not been published but which has been placed in the Library of the House. And from that it appears that a very overwhelming majority of people is in favour of the constitution of Boards of Management to look to and supervise the activities of Mutawallis in various States of India. For this reason I do not think it is necessary for me at this stage to deal with the various points that have been raised, because it is for the Select Committee to consider them.

Mr. Chairman: Motion moved:

> "That the Bill to provide for the better governance and administation of Muslim Wakfs and the supervision of Mutawallis' management of them in India, be referred to a Select Committee consisting of Dr. Syed Mahmud, Shri M. Hafizur Rahman, Shri Ahmed Mohiuddin, Shri Gurmukh Singh Musafir, Pandit Krishna Chandra Sharma, Shri Hira Vallabh Tripathi, Maulana Mohammad Saeed Masuodi, Col. B.H. Zaidi, Shri Mohanlal Saksena, Chaudhuri Hyder Husein, Shri Amjad Ali, Shri Syed Ahmed, Dr. N.M. Jaisoorya, Shrimati Subhadra Joshi, Shri C.C. Biswas, Shri S.V.L. Narasimham, Shri Atma Singh Namdhari, Shri Piare Lall Kureel Talib, and the Mover, with instructions to report by the last day of the second week of the next session."

APPENDIX 2

Document No. 92

Maulana Azad and Indian Income-Tax (Amendment) Bill April 23, 1953

LAW MINISTER'S SPEECH RE. SPEAKER'S CERTIFICATE ON INDIAN INCOME-TAX (AMENDMENT) BILL

Pandit Thakur Das Bhargava (Gurgaon): Sir, under the Constitution, a Money Bill has been defined under clause.....

The Minister of Law and Minority Affairs (Shri Biswas): Before my friend goes on, may I make my position clear? I believe, Sir, you have received a communication from the Chairman of the Council of States, and he must have conveyed not only his own statement but also a copy of a Resolution which was unanimously adopted in the other House. By that Resolution, I am directed not to attend here either in my capacity as Leader of the Council in order to answer a charge which my friend Mr. Bhargava might choose to bring against me in respect of certain remarks reported to have been made by me in the other House the other day in connection with the Income-tax (Amendment) Bill. Therefore, if that is the matter which is going to be discussed, and if there is to be any charge brought against me, I cannot be here.

Shri Feroze Gandhi (Pratapgarh Dist.–West-*cum*-Rae Bareli Distt.–East): The Resolution passed in the Upper House may be read out.

Shri Syed Ahmed (Hoshangabad): Has the Resolution of the other House been received by you?

The Minister of Education and Natural Resources and Scientific Research (Maulana Azad): The real question before us is to hear the statement of the Law Minister in this regard.

Shri Biswas: I may at once state here that in the statement which came from the Chairman of the Council of States you will find....

Mr. Depty-Speaker: I have not got the Resolution.

Shri Biswas: I do not know. The Resolution must have been sent. Possibly, it will follow.

Mr. Deputy-Speaker: I shall read out the message I have received.

Shri Biswas: If you read out that message, that will make my position clear, because it was read out to me by the Chairman before he read it out to the Council, and I accepted that statement as quite correct.

Mr. Deputy-Speaker: I understand this is a copy that was given to the Secretary. Formally I have not received a copy, but anyhow, in view of the statement, I think this is correct. I shall, for the information of the House, read it out.

Shri Feroze Gandhi: On a point of order, Sir. When this communication has not been received by you, shall we take it as having been received by this House?

Several Hon. Members: No, no.

Mr. Deputy-Speaker: I understand that it was personally given by the Chairman to the Secretary.

Shri P.N. Rajabhoj: That is all right.

Mr. Deputy-Speaker: This is what I understand was read out in the other House by the Chairman. Now, when once a statement is made in the other House and a copy has come here, that is sufficient property so far as this House also is concerned. Let us see what exactly it says:

> "A mere complaint is not precluded and does not involve any breach of privilege of a member or of the Council. I am afraid that I cannot give my consent to this motion for privilege.
>
> There seems to be some misapprehension in regard to what happened in the Council on the 29th instant. Some members expressed a doubt whether the Bill in question was a Money Bill according to the requirements of article 110(1). A few felt that doubts could be raised even after the certificate was issued by the Speaker. At this stage the Leader of the Council referred to these doubts and suggested that it would reassure the House if it was told categorically that the Speaker had applied his mind to this question and issued the certificate after a full and fair consideration of all aspects of the matter. When that statement, which reiterated the obvious, came to us yesterday from the House of the People, the matter was concluded. It was nobody's intention, least of all, of the Leader

of the Council to cast aspersions on the integrity and impartiality of the Speaker. It is our anxiety in this Council to do our best to uphold the dignity of the Speaker and the privileges of the other House as we expect the other House to protect our interest and privileges."

I believe the hon. Minister associates himself with everything that has been said here.

Shri Biswas: Yes.

Mr. Deputy-Speaker: In view of this, I think any further discussion on this matter is not necessary or called for.

Shri Gadgil (Poona Central): The point is whether it is a fact that the other House has passed a Resolution directing the Law Minister not to appear in this House in any capacity. If that is passed, may I know whether it is not a matter of which proper notice can be taken by this House?

Mr. Deputy-Speaker: So far as this matter is concerned, we have the hon. Law Minister in flesh and blood before us. Now, the hon. Law Minister has been kind enough to come and explain to us and reiterated what was already said in the other House. This matter is closed.

As regards the other matter, let me wait and see what exactly the Resolution is. I have not got a copy of the Resolution. Hon. Members have not got it either. Let it be taken up later on in due course as soon as a copy is available. I will try to send for the proceedings, and we will take it up in a proper manner. This matter is closed.

Pandit Balkrishna Sharma (Kanpur Distt.– South-*cum*-Etawah Distt.–East): May I draw your attention only to this matter, that the Law Minister himself has said in this House that if his speech or statement in the Upper House regarding Money Bill is to be considered here, then he is bound by the Resolution of that House and it will not be possible for him to be present here to answer these charges? In view of this, is it not proper that we should take notice of this statement of the hon. Minister – let alone that Resolution?

Maulana Azad: Sir, the proceedings in the other House have been related to you by my hon. colleague. The other remaining question has been dealt with in the statement of the Chairman of the Council. And this settles the matter.

Pandit Thakur Das Bhargava: Not the statement of the hon. Minister.

Maulana Azad: The hon. Minister has agreed with him and has supported his statement.

Shri Gadgil *rose* –

Mr. Deputy-Speaker: Order, order. If there is anything to be heard, I will certainly call upon him to elucidate any point. The position, as it is, is this. The hon. the Law Minister was kind enough to tell us that it is true that the other House has passed a Resolution. But later on, when this was read out, he said he entirely agreed and stood by that. Now, therefore, he is here and he also says that he never intended anything against the Chair. Therefore, so far as this matter is concerned, it may be treated as closed.

Regarding the other one that the other House has given a direction to the Law Minister not to appear here, I have to say that we are both of us limbs of the Parliament, and particularly a Minister is a Minister in both the Houses. Unlike other Members, the Minister belongs to both the Houses, and I will consider as to the appropriateness of any particular Resolution in due course. I would like to request hon. Members, as far as possible, to avoid any kind of criticism. We do not know exactly under what circumstances and for what purpose the other august House has passed a resolution of that kind. We shall try to find out from the proceedings in a calm atmosphere; so that constanly we must develop a kind of family relationship between the two Houses. Under the Constitution, both the Houses form a single Parliament. (*Interruptions*). Order, order. That ought to be the spirit in which we understand the proceedings of the other House. As the hon. Chairman of the other House has observed. "It is our anxiety in this Council to do our best to uphold the dignity of the Speaker and the privileges of the other House as we expect the other House to protect our interests and privileges", I am sure we will also do the same.

Shri Syed Ahmed *rose* –

Mr. Deputy-Speaker: Order, order. Permit me to speak also.

Now, it is open to us to look into the proceedings of the other House and if really there is anything objectionable, as it is said, certainly there are methods of seeing that such things do not occur.

But so far as this matter is concerned, it will be treated as closed. It is unfortunate that we had to interrupt the present proceedings regarding the PEPSU Budget.

Dr. S.P. Mookerjee (Calcutta South-East): May I place one matter before you, Sir?

Shri Gadgil *rose* –

Dr. S.P. Mookerjee: If I may say so Sir. I agree with you entirely that this matter should be treated as closed. The hon. the Law Minister has assoicated himself with the statement of the Chairman of the other House, and the matter should be closed. But one quesiton of fundamental importance arising out of this, apart from what has been raised by my friend, Pandit Balkrishna Sharma, is this: supposing in the other House a statement is made, whether by a Minister or by a Member of the other House, which may amount to reflection on the Speaker of this House, has this House any authority to consider that matter? That is a question of supreme importance which cannot be decided now. But along with the other question which you have raised, the propriety of the Council of States passing that Resolution, I would earnestly request you to consider this matter also, because, in my opinion, if the Speaker's authority is challenged or any reflection is cast on him, the authority of this House is long enough, wide enough, and big enough to bring that man before this House, whoever he may be. That is the position of this House – it is the sovereign Parliament of this country. This question has to be gone into quite apart from the other. This matter may be treated as closed, but the main question is, if any reflection is cast on the Speaker, has this House the authority to bring that person before this House and call for an explanation?

Shri Gadgil *rose* –

Pandit Thakur Das Bhargava: As the Deputy-Speaker has been pleased to close this episode, I request the hon. Minister also to treat it as closed for ever. But at the same time, I beg to bring to the notice of the House and the Deputy-Speaker one matter of very great import – the prestige and dignity of the Chair of this House. Now in regard to this matter also – I will not go into the merits – I never raised any charge against anybody. I simply requested you to give me an opportunity...

Maulana Azad: Sir, when my hon. friend has agreed that this matter is closed, it is not at all proper for him to dilate upon it.

Pandit Thakur Das Bhargava *rose* —

Shri Biswas: I have to withdraw from the House, Sir, when a discussion on his motion is going on. May I have your permission to withdraw. (*Interruptions*).

Some Hon. Members: Withdraw permanently.

Mr. Deputy-Speaker: I am afraid....(*Interruptions*)

Shri Gadgil: May I ask for one minute. (*Interruptions*).

Mr. Deputy-Speaker: Order, order

Pandit Balkrishna Sharma: The cat is out of the bag.

Statement by the Leader of the Council is as follows:

> "Sir, you will of course give your ruling on the motion moved but I want to submit only this with reference to the two points which were raised by my hon. friends. First of all, I may assure my hon. friend and all others concerned that I never cast any slur upon the Speaker in what I said nor was it ever my intention to do so. I would be unworthy of the position I hold if I had said something which would sully the integrity of the Speaker or of the Chairman of the other House of Parliament. I have sufficient responsibility to be conscious of the honour which is due to their position. Secondly, as regards the other point whether I should be permitted to go to the other House at the invitation of the Deputy-Speaker, I do not propose to raise the constitutional question. I shall go there. I was present in that House and I did not hear the Deputy-Speaker making a request to me but he said to me afterwards that he had made that request. If that request was made, I owe it to him as a matter of courtesy – not as a matter of constitutional obligation – that I should be there to show as an example of good behaviour."

Dr. N.B. Khare: On a point of clarification. It is said here that the Resolution has been passed unanimously. May I know through you whether the hon. the Law Minister also agrees with it?

Maulana Azad: There is no doubt about it that the proceedings in the Council of States have given rise to some important questions, the significance of which I do not deny. These should certainly be considered, but you will agree with me that it would not at all be proper to prolong this discussion. The proceedings of the House have been interrupted; they should be resumed. You will be able to consider at leisure as to what further action is required in this matter.

Shri B.S. Murthy (Eluru): We would like to know what the Deputy Leader said.

Mr. Deputy-Speaker: I have already said that I will read the message from the other House and leave it at that stage and consider calmly what ought to be done. I assure the House that nothing shall be wanting on my part to uphold the prestige of this House and to see that nothing is done to impair it from whichever quarter it may be.

I am equally interested in seeing that both the Houses of Parliament carry on amicable terms maintaining the prestige of each other.

There is no harm in putting it off till some other day. I will take it up as early as possible and consider this matter with the leaders of the various groups and decide what action is to be taken in consultation with the Leader and Deputy Leader of the House.

APPENDIX 3

Document No. 93

Letter from Maulana to Bhimsen Sachar

New Delhi,
9th June, 1953

My dear Bhimsen Sachar,

In reply to your wireless message regarding Mahendra Singh Bedi I have sent you one yesterday saying that in this matter I leave it to you to do what is proper. There is, however, one aspect of this matter which has been brought to my notice and which I would like you to consider. While it is true that service of the Punjab Government Officers is not generally lent to the Delhi State for more than five years and should not be so lent, this practice does not affect the loan of such officers to the Central Government. There are in fact many officers in the Central Government who were lent by the States and have been here for more than five years. Since it is the Central Ministry of Food & Agriculture that has asked for Bedi's services and not the Delhi State, the case stands on a different footing than if the Delhi State had asked for an extension of his services. Moreover, the Ministry of Food & Agriculture are not likely to choose another officer from the Punjab Government in place of Bedi, if the latter's services are not lent. I do not wish to press you in this matter but if you think that there is any force in these arguments, you might reconsider your previous objection and let Bedi's services be lent to the Food & Agriculture Ministry.

Yours sincerely,
A.K. Azad

Shri Bhimsen Sachar,
Chief Minister, Punjab

APPENDIX 4

Document No. 94

Joint replies dated 10-12-1953 by Mr. K.D. Malaviya and Maulana Abul Kalam Azad in Rajya Sabha

ESTABLISHMENT OF A UNIVERSITY FOR MADHYA BHARAT

Shri V.S. Sarwate: Will the Minister for **Education** be pleased to state:

(a) whether Government have, after the receipt of the Report of the Experts Committee appointed to consider the establishment of new universities, given any advice to the Madhya Bharat Government regarding the establishment of a university for Madhya Bharat; if so, what advice has been given; and

(b) what action has been taken by the Government of Madhya Bharat on receipt of such advice?

The Deputy Minister for Natural Resources and Scientific Research (Shri K.D. Malaviya): (a) A copy of the Report submitted by the Expert Committee which was appointed to consider the establishment of new universities generally and of the Madhya Bharat University in particular has been forwarded to the Government of Madhya Bharat with the suggestion that the recommendations made by the Committee may be considered fully before it is decided to set up a university in Madhya Bharat.

(b) The Government of India have not received any communication from the State Government regarding the action taken by them in the matter.

Shri V.S. Sarwate: What does the Government of India propose to do if the Madhya Bharat Government is silent on this subject?

Shri K.D. Malaviya: Nothing, Sir.

Shri V.K. Dhage: What has been the recommendation of this Expert Committee, Sir, with regard to this University?

Maulana Abul Kalam Azad: A copy thereof is available in the Parliament Library.

Shri V.S. Sarwate: My question was, "What does the Government of India propose to do?"

Shri K.D. Malaviya: We appointed a committee. The committee made certain recommendations and these have been forwarded to the Madhya Bharat Government. It is open to them to take any decision. It is not for us.

Shri H.C. Mathur: Is not the Madhya Bharat Government free and independent to take any action as it desires?

Shri K.D. Malaviya: Yes.

Maulana Abul Kalam Azad: Under the Constitution, education is the responsibility of the Centre. Since the Madhya Bharat Government brought up a Bill for the establishment of a new university, the Government of India appointed this Committee so that it might, after deliberation, make its recommendations in the matter. The Committee considered this matter. It is of the opinion that under the existing circumstances there is scope for a new university in Madhya Bharat, but it requires at least Rs. 50 lakhs on account of non-recurring expenditure and Rs. 10 lakhs on account of recurring expenditure. The Government of India have passed this recommendation on to the State Government and have advised them to consider the matter and act accordingly.

Shri H.C. Mathur Besides money, is there no other question which the Government of India might like to refer to them?

Maulana Abul Kalam Azad: It is not merely a question of money.

Dr. Kalidas Nag: May I ask the hon. Minister if in view of the historical and cultural importance of Madhya Bharat which started the Vikrama University and such institutions at all stages of higher education – as has been noticed in the recent University Commission and other Reports – that the Government of India also will do something to expedite the foundation of this University in Madhya Bharat, the land of Kalidasa and Varahamihira?

Maulana Abul Kalam Azad: This depends on the financial position.

APPENDIX 5

Document No. 95

Joint replies, dated, 10-12-1953, of Maulana Azad and Mr. K.D. Malaviya to the questions asked in Rajya Sabha

CO-ORDINATION AND DETERMINATION OF STANDARDS OF EDUCATION IN UNIVERSITIES

Maulana M. Faruqi: Will the Minister for **Education** be pleased to state:

(a) whether Government propose to introduce comprehensive legislation to co-ordinate and determine the standards of education in Universities.

(b) whether a draft Bill prepared in this connection was considered by the State Education Ministers and Vice-Chancellors; if so, what are their main recommendations; and

(c) when Government will introduce the Bill in Parliament?

The Deputy Minister for Natural Resources and Scientific Research (Shri K.D. Malaviya): (a), (b) and (c) The Conference of State Education Ministers and Vice-Chancellors convened in April 1953 considered a Bill to set up a Central Council of University Education. It recommended the creation of a statutory University Grants Commission with the co-ordination and determination of standards in Universities as one of its functions. Government is taking steps to introduce necessary legislation for the purpose as soon as possible.

Prof. N. G. Ranga: Is it not a fact, Sir, that the Vice-Chancellors who had assembled here were not in favour of the proposals made by the Education Ministry?

Shri K.D. Malaviya: Sir, the original proposal of the Government of India was to constitute separate bodies, one, the Central Council of University Education and the other, the University Grants Commission. This proposal was not accepted by this Conference of University Vice-Chancellors and Ministers.

Prof. N. G. Ranga: Do Government propose to go ahead with their own proposals in spite of that?

Maulana Abul Kalam Azad: Let me make it clear. Government had first thought that there should be two agencies, one to look after university education and co-ordination, and the other the University Grants Commission. The Conference which had becn called proposed that instead of two agencies there should be only one agency, *viz.*, the University Grants Commission, and it should also be given the powers which it was proposed to give to the other agency. Government have accepted this proposal and have drafted the Bill in accordance with it. In order that these few remaining months of the year may not be wasted, Government have appointed a Commission of five members, which is starting work in a few days. During the next session when this Bill comes up, the number of members on this Commission will be increased and it will then become a statutory body.

Shri Govinda Reddy: Did the Conference agree, Sir, that common standards should be prescribed by a Central authority?

Mr. Chairman: No, this question of co-ordination is also assigned to the new Commission.

Shri Govinda Reddy: I wanted to know whether on that there was any difference in the conference.

Maulana Abul Kalam Azad: The Conference did not go into these details.

Shri H.N. Kunzru: When are the Government introducing this Bill?

Maulana Abul Kalam Azad: The Bill is ready and will be introduced during the next session.

Shri H.N. Kunzru: Is it not possible to introduce this Bill in this session itself? This would enable hon. Members to look into it for it is very important and urgent matter.

Maulana Abul Kalam Azad: The hon. Member knows that only a few days are left for this session to end and it has to end on the 24th. Nevertheless, Government will try.

APPENDIX 6

Document No. 96

Joint replies, dated 10-12-1953, of Maulana Aazd and Mr. K.D. Malaviya to the questions asked in Rajya Sabha

MAYO COLLEGE, AJMER

Shri H.C. Mathur: Will the Minister for **Education** be pleased to state:

(a) whether there is any representative of the Central Government on the management of the Mayo College, Ajmer; and

(b) whether this institution is receiving any aid from the Central Government?

The Deputy Minister for Natural Resources and Scientific Research (Shri K.D. Malaviya): (a) Yes, Sir.

(b) No, Sir. But an *ad hoc* grant of Rs. 50,000 was paid to the College during 1952-53 on account of its financial difficulties.

Shri H.C. Mathur: This is a fine institution and there is scope for great development, but, situated as it is in an impoverished Part C state, it is faced with financial difficulties. In view of this are Government considering the necessity of a recurring grant to this College, particularly in view of their responsibilities to a Part C State?

Shri K.D. Malaviya: No, Sir, just now there is no consideration for a recurring grant, but we know that it is a useful institution.

Shri H.C. Mathur: Is the Government aware that in changing this from a princely college to a public school it is faced with great financial difficulties and because the Government has a special responsibility to Part C States does not this institution deserve their consideration?

Maulana Abul Kalam Azad: That is why an *ad hoc* grant of Rs. 50,000 was made. This and other similar Chiefs' colleges used to have various kinds of income which are no longer there. So the Government of India thought that they should be given some aid. A sum of Rs. 3 lakhs was set apart for three years. Various institutions are being aided one after the other.

Shri H.C. Mathur: Is anything being done in regard to making a recurring grant?

Maulana Abul Kalam Azad: There is no proposal for a recurring grant. I may inform the hon. Member that the condition of the Mayo College is now improving, and it is hoped that in a short time it will stand on its own legs and will no longer be in need of aid.

Shri D. Narayan: May I know how mnay boys are there in this school?

Maulana Abul Kalam Azad: One hundred and forty.

APPENDIX 7

Document No. 97

Joint replies dated 10-12-1953, of Maulana Azad and Mr. K.D. Malaviya to the questions raised in Rajya Sabha

AGREEMENT WITH THE FORD FOUNDATION FOR STUDYING EDUCATIONAL PROBLEMS

Shri S. Mahanty: Will the Minister for **Edcuation** be pleased to state whether Government have entered into any agreement with the Ford Foundation of America for studying the problems of secondary education in India?

The Deputy Minister for Natural Resources and Scientific Research (Shri K.D. Malaviya): No.

Shri S. Mahanty: May I ask him if the services of Mr. H.C. Dent and Dr. Zilliacus, the two experts who visited India, were requisitioned by the Government of India and if so under what authority?

Shri K.D. Malaviya: Four experts who are members of the Ford Foundation are associated with the survey of Secondary Teacher Preparation. They came here – the Government had not to incur any expenditure on their behalf – and they toured the country along with four other Indian experts. They have gone out now to Denmark; they will go to the U.S.A., and the U.K. and they will come back and submit their report to us. This has nothing to do with Secondary Education Commission Report work.

Shri S. Mahanty: That is not the question. I asked if these two gentlemen visited India in connection with secondary education.

Maulana Abul Kalam Azad: No.

Shri K.D. Malaviya: They visited this country in connection with the survey work of preparing teachers of secondary school stage.

Mr. Chairman: The question raised was "were they invited by the Government of India for studying the problems of secondary education in India?" And the answer is 'No'.

Shri S. Mahanty: Problems of secondary education may mean anything and everything. What I ask is....

Mr. Chairman: No, no.

Shri S. Mahanty: Take the preparation of syllabus for secondary education. Does it not come under secondary education, Sir?

Maulana Abul Kalam Azad: No assistance of any kind has been taken from the Ford Foundation in respect of secondary education.

Shri S. Mahanty: May I know for which purpose Mr. Dent and Dr. Zilliacus visited India?

Maulana Abul Kalam Azad: The object of this proposal was to give the Indian teachers the opportunity of acquainting themselves with the new developments in other countries of the world. It had nothing to do with the system of education.

Shri S. Mahanty: May I draw the attention of the hon. Minister to the statement which is circulated in connection with Question No. 257 and from which he will find that these two gentlemen visited India very much for purposes of secondary education.

Mr. Chairman: Now, we go on to that question.

APPENDIX 8

Document No. 98

Joint replies, dated 10-12-1953, of Maulana Azad and Mr. K.D. Malaviya to the questions asked in Rajya Sabha

VISIT OF FOREIGN EDUCATIONAL EXPERTS TO INDIA

Shri B. Rath: Will the Minister for **Education** be pleased to state:

(a) the number of foreign educational experts who visited India during the period from 1st October, 1952 to 1st November, 1953;

(b) the name, nationality, qualifications and purposes of visit of each of these experts and the amount spent on each of them; and

(c) whether any report has been submitted to Government by any of those experts?

The Deputy Minister for Natural Resources and Scientific Research (Shri K.D. Malaviya): (a) and (b) A statement giving the required information is laid on the Table of the House. [*See* Appendix VI, annexure No. 76.]

(c) Yes.

Shri M.S. Ranawat: What is the total number of experts who visited the country?

Shri B. Rath: I will tell you; it is about 41. How many experts have been engaged in the survey of Secondary Teacher Preparation?

Shri K.D. Malaviya: The hon. Member can get the information from the Table there.

Shri B. Rath: I want the hon. Minister to hear and understand the question. I am not concerned with the Ford Foundation business only. How many persons have been engaged? Is it only these four American experts obtained through the Ford Foundation who have been engaged for this survey work? Is there any Indian expert also?

Shri K.D. Malaviya: Four Indian experts are also associated with the examination of all these questions.

Shri B. Rath: I want to know how many experts in all have been engaged.

Shri K.D. Malaviya: Four *plus* four is eight. But they have nothing to do, as I said in my answer to the previous question, with the Secondary Education Commission.

Shri B. Rath: What is the scheme of survey?

Maulana Abul Kalam Azad: I shall draw your attention, Sir, to the question which was: How many foreign experts visited India during 1952-53? What has this got to do with the scheme of survey?

Shri B. Rath: The experts have come in connection with a survey work. I want to know the scheme of the survey that is being undertaken.

Mr. Chairman: The Question Hour is over.

APPENDIX 9

Document No. 99

Maulana Azad's Answers dated 10-12-1953 in Rajya Sabha to question asked by Mr. B.V. Kakkilaya

SURVEY OF THE SOUTH EASTERN COAST OF INDIA

Shri B.V. Kakkilaya: Will the Minister for **Natural Resources and Scientific Research** be pleased to state:

(a) whether any survey has been made in regard to the availability of lime from the coral reefs off the South Eastern Coast of India; and

(b) if so, what are the results of the survey?

The Minister for Education and Natural Resources and Scientific Research (Maulana Abul Kalam Azad): (a) and (b) A statement giving the information required is laid on the Table of the Council.

Statement

During February and March 1952, a detailed survey of the Coral islands in the Gulf of Manaar, between Tuticorin and Pamban, Madras, was taken up by the Geological Survey of India. The results of the survey are as follows:

Coral reefs ranging from a few feet to 400 yards in width were found fringing the numerous small islets in the Gulf of Manaar, between Tuticorin in the south and Pamban in the north. The reefs are porous, soft and of light material containing over 96 per cent. of $CaCo_3$ (Calcium Carbonate) and very little of impurities. They can be used for small scale manufacture of bleaching powder, caustic soda and materials requiring high lime content. They can also be powdered and used as 'whiting' in distempers and paints. The estimated reserves of coral material in the Gulf of Manaar is about 2.25 million tons spread over a distance of about 80 miles:

(i) Pamban area — 9,24,000 tons.

(ii) Killakarai area — 1,056,000 tons.

(iii) Tuticorin area — 286,000 tons.

But as the lime in the reefs is deposited by living corals and other organizms, the reefs can grow again even if they are removed. It is possible for the coral masses to be replenished in a few years under suitable conditions. About 200,000 tons of coral reefs may be available annually from all sources without reserves being depleted.

An upraised reef near Rameswaram may yield 80,000 tons of good quality limestone.

APPENDIX 10

Document No. 100

Letter from Maulana Azad to Mr. Punjabrao Deshmukh

1953

My dear Punjabrao Deshmukh,

I am very glad to see the copy of the *Statesman* printed on the new kind of newsprint which you have sent me. My best wishes for the means of this experiment.

Yours sincerely,
A.K. Azad

APPENDIX 11

Document No. 101

Letter from Maulana Azad to Pandit Jawaharlal Nehru

1953

My dear Jawaharlal,

At the last meeting of the Working Committee we passed a Resolution drawing the Government's attention to the desirability of extending the benefit of Life Insurance to the rural population. Since then I have been thinking over this matter and feel that it is of great importance and should be implemented as soon as possible. The right way of doing so would be to nationalise. The business of Life Insurance covering salaries of Rs. 5,000 and below and of entrusting it to some official agency. I am sending you a draft resolution on these lines for discussion by the Working Committee the day after tomorrow.

Yours sincerely
A.K. Azad

APPENDIX 12

Document No. 102

Maulana Azad and the Children Bill 1953

(Moved in Rajya Sabha on 19-12-1953)

THE MINISTER FOR EDUCATION AND NATURAL RESOURCES AND SCIENTIFIC RESEARCH (MAULANA ABUL KALAM AZAD):

مولانا ابوالکلام آزاد : جناب ! میں تحریک کرتا ہوں کہ جو بل
لاوارث اور آوارہ بچوں کی دیکھ بھال کیلئے پیش کیا گیا ہے وہ ہاؤس
کی ایک سلیکٹ کمیٹی کے سپرد کیا جائے - اس بل کا مقصد اتنا
کھلا اور صاف ہے کہ میں نہیں سمجھتا ہوں کہ اس بارے میں زیادہ
بحث اور تفصیل کی ضرورت ہے -

Shri V.K. Dhage (Hyderabad): Sir, may I raise a point of order?

Mr. Deputy Chairman: No. That stage is gone. You may speak for the rejection of the Bill.

Shri C.G.K. Reddy (Mysore): Sir, he thinks that there is a point of order. The Bill has been introduced. Its further consideration can be objected to.

Shri V.K. Dhage: Sir, this is a very important point.

Mr. Deputy Chairman: What is that?

Shri V.K. Dhage: Sir, the Bill has been moved for consideration. I wanted to say something with regard to the question whether it can be taken into consideration or not. Sir, in the Statement of Objects and Reasons it has been stated that an Expert Committee that was appointed has gone into this question and that Expert Committee has made certain recommendations in its report. Now, Sir, we haven't got that report at our disposal. That report forms the basis of this Bill and that basis of the Bill has not been given to us for consideration. I, therefore, feel, Sir, that unless that report, which is the basis of this Bill, is placed before us, it will be difficult for us to proceed with the Bill.

Mr. Deputy Chairman: It is not a point of order, Mr. Dhage. You can move for the rejection of the Bill. That is a different thing.

Shri H.N. Kunzru (Uttar Pradesh): Sir, I do not know whether what has been stated by Mr. Dhage is factually correct or not, but if it is, I think we can certainly object to any further proceedings being taken in connection with the Bill.

Mr. Deputy Chairman: The Bill has been before the House for a long time. The hon. Members could have got the information from the Ministry of Education.

Shri H.N. Kunzru: That is not our responsibility. It is the responsibility of the Government to send the thing. That responsibility cannot be cast on us. The Government cannot say "You could have got this information from us whenever you wanted". It is their business to see that the information is sent to the House.

Mr. Deputy Chairman: Anyway, that cannot be a point of order.

Shri Rajendra Pratap Sinha (Bihar): I want to say for your information, Sir, that I made enquiries from the Ministry and I was told that we could not have that report because that was a confidential and private report.

Mr. Deputy Chairman: I have already given my ruling that that is not a point of order. Let the hon. Minister proceed.

MAULANA ABUL KALAM AZAD:

مولانا ابوالکلام آزاد : میں نہیں سمجھ سکتا کہ ہمارے ان دوستوں نے اس وقت یہ سوال کیوں اٹھایا ہے ؟ ایکسپرٹ کمیٹی اس لئے بٹھائی گئی تھی کہ وہ اس معاملہ پر غور کرے اور اسکے بعد ایک رپورٹ تیار کرے - چنانچہ اس نے اپنی رپورٹ تین برس پہلے پیش کی تھی - اسکے بعد ایجوکیشن منسٹری نے اس پر غور کیا اور لا منسٹری سے مشورہ کیا گیا - اور پھر ایک بل تیار کیا گیا جو اسوقت ہاؤس کے سامنے ہے - اگر سلیکٹ کمیٹی کے ممبر چاہینگے کہ جو رپورٹ آج سے تین برس پہلے ایکسپرٹ کمیٹی نے پیش کی تھی وہ رپورٹ بھی ان کے سامنے رکھی جائے تو منسٹری اسے خوشی سے رکھ دیگی - لیکن میں یہ بات تسلیم نہیں کرتا کہ چونکہ وہ رپورٹ ہر آنریبل ممبر کی گود میں نہیں رکھ دی گئی ہے اسلئے یہ بل......

SHRI V. K. DHAGE:

श्री वी० के० डागे : हमारे गोद में रखने की जरूरत नहीं है। टेबल पर रखिए।

MAULANA ABUL KALAM AZAD:

مولانا ابوالکلام آزاد : آپکو ضرورت نہیں ہے مگر اور آنریبل ممبروں کو ضرورت ہے - اگر سلیکٹ کمیٹی میں سوال اٹھایا گیا تو وہ رپورٹ منسٹری خوشی سے سب کے سامنے رکھ دیگی - اکثر بل اسی طریقہ سے تیار کئے جاتے ہیں - پہلے مشورہ کیا جاتا ہے، پھر کمیٹی بنتی ہے، اور وہ کمیٹی اپنی رپورٹ پیش کرتی ہے، اور اس رپورٹ کی روشنی میں بل تیار کیا جاتا ہے - یہ ضروری نہیں ہوتا کہ اس رپورٹ کو بھی بل کے ساتھ پیش کیا جائے -

SHRI V. K. DHAGE:

श्री वी० के० डागे : मसला यह है कि यह जो बिल आपने पेश किया है वह उस रिपोर्ट पर मुनहसिर है।

Sir, may I say a word?

Mr. Deputy Chairman: Please don't disturb him.

Shri V.K. Dhage: He has yielded.

Mr. Deputy Chairman: Let there be no interruption in the middle of the speech.

Shri V.K. Dhage: I have got the right to know as to what that report is and as to whether that report will be placed on the Table of the House. Why has that report not been placed on the Table of the House when that report had been submitted three years ago?

Mr. Deputy Chairman: You can raise your objection in your speech.

Shri Rajagopal Naidu (Madras): Sir, it is not a question of objection. It is a question of our effectively taking part in this debate. The Chair should help this House in seeing that the document is available. Otherwise how can we take part in the debate without knowing what it is?

Shri C.G.K. Reddy: How can we discuss the Bill, Sir? If it was a secret document, he should not have mentioned it in the Statement of Objects and Reasons. How do we know that the Bill has been drafted entirely according to the recommendations of that Committee unless we have that report?

Shri Rama Rao (Andhra): The Bill that has been brought before this House is sufficiently self-explanatory. In fact there is no sense in saying that the report is not here.

Shri V.K. Dhage: Would you remove the words "Expert Committee" from the Statement of Objects and Reasons on the basis of what you have said now?

Mr. Deputy Chairman: Mr. Dhage, order, order. The hon. Minister may proceed.

Shri H.N. Kunzru: Sir, it is well understood; Maulana Saheb may be perfectly correct. I am not against the Bill. But you will allow us to raise this point again and it will be raised, Sir, if you do not allow us to raise it now, we shall raise it on Monday. It is an important point, and I am sorry to say that you are attaching no importance to it. It concerns the rights and privileges of the Members of this House. I do not want to prevent Maulana Saheb from moving the Bill, but I take strong exception to the Maulana Saheb's remark that the Government is not bound to place the report on the Table. After having referred to it in the Statement of Objects and Reasons, they are bound and in duty bound to supply the information before asking us to consider this Bill.

Shri Akhtar Husain (Uttar Pradesh): May I know under which rule of the Rules of Procedure of the Council of States my hon. friend is claiming this as of right?

Shri H.N. Kunzru: My hon. friend has been here long enough to understand what is meant by the words 'rights and privileges of this House'.

(Shri Akhtar Husain Rose)

Mr. Deputy Chairman: Order, order. Dr. Kunzru has not resumed his seat. Two hon. Members cannot speak at the same time.

Shri H.N. Kunzru: Sir, it is not merely a question of rule. And perhaps there is rule 211. But it is a question of the rights and privileges of the Members which are not defined in any rule. My hon. friend must have read the Constitution of India, and he must have known, before he rose to make his objection, that it provides that the rights and privileges of the members of the Indian Parliament will be same as those of the British Parliament.

Mr. Deputy Chairman: I am afraid rule 211 does not apply.

Shri H.N. Kunzru: Rule 211 may or may not apply. But there is the Constitution of India and there is the unwritten law relating to the duty of the Government.

Mr. Deputy Chairman: What is the provision of the Constitution under which we can compel the Minister incharge to place the report on the Table of the House?

Shri H.N. Kunzru: We have every moral right to see that report.

Mr. Deputy Chairman: I fully concede that point. But what is the provision of the Constitution?

Shri H.N. Kunzru: If I may say so, instead of casting your moral weight on the side of the Government, if you were to cast it on our side, I am sure that Maulana Saheb would then yield and the report would be placed immediately on the Table of the House.

Mr. Deputy Chairman: Under what provision? May I know from the hon. Minister whether he can place the report on the Table of the House?

MAULANA ABUL KALAM AZAD:

<u>مولانا ابوالکلام آزاد</u> : ضرور رکھی جائیگی - لیکن جو سوال یہاں اُٹھایا گیا ھے کہ یہ بل پیش نہیں کیا جا سکتا - جب تک ایکسپرٹ کمیٹی کی رپورٹ ممبروں کے سامنے نہیں رکھی جاتی -

Shri C.G.K. Reddy: I would explain that point if the hon. Minister would listen to me for a few minutes without getting impatient. Sir, you have asked: under what provision of the Constitution this can be done? Sir, so far as the Council is concerned, the general procedure is to follow the House of Commons procedure where our rules are silent. Now, Sir, can the hon. Minister quote even one instance where in the Statement of Objects and Reasons it has been mentioned that the Bill has been drafted on the basis of a Committee's report and they have not placed that report before the House? Such a thing cannot happen. No Minister could survive in the House of Commons if he did so. Sir, we are following the procedure of the House of Commons. Where our rules are silent,we must go to the conventions of the House of Commons. Is there a single instance where a Bill has been introduced or placed for consideration on the basis of a report which has not been placed before the House?

Shri V.K. Dhage: I may also say. Sir, that a similar question arose in the other House with regard, I think, to the Banking Companies Bill that was before the House, and the Speaker held that unless and until that Expert Committee Report or even the letters which the hon. Deputy Minister exchanged with the Chief Justice of Hyderabad were placed before the House, the Bill could not be proceeded with. An objection was taken and the Bill was not proceeded with till those papers were given to the Members.

Mr. Deputy Chairman: Let us not talk under supposition. You show me a ruling.

श्री किशन चन्द (हैदराबाद) : मेरा यह कहना था कि जिस तर्ज और लहजे में मौलाना साहब ने यह कहा "गोद में रख दिया जायेगा मेम्बरों के" यह अनपार्लियामेंटरी (unparliamentary) है।

SHRI H. P. SAKSENA (Uttar Pra-desh):

श्री एच० पी० सक्सेना (उत्तर प्रदेश) : आगोश में कहिये।

MAULANA ABUL KALAM AZAD:

مولانا ابوالکلام آزاد : مقصد کا یہی لہجہ ہے -

MR. DEPUTY CHAIRMAN: Please speak in English. I cannot follow.

SHRI C. G. K. REDDY: He said that it would be put in the lap of the Members

SHRI KISHEN CHAND: The hon.

Minister said: "The report will be placed in your lap "*God men rakhi jaigee*' (गोद में रखी जायेगी). That, in my opinion, is unparliamentary.

MAULANA ABUL KALAM AZAD:

مولانا ابوالکلام آزاد : یہ سمجھ لیا جانا چاہیئے کہ ایجوکیشن منسٹری نے اس معاملہ پر غور کرنے کے لئے ایک کانفرنس بلائی ہی - کانفرنس نے ایک ایکسپرٹ کمیٹی بنائی جس سے یہ درخواست کی گئی کہ وہ معاملہ پر ور کرنے کے بعد اپنی رپورٹ پیش کرے جسکی روشنی میں ہم آگے بڑھ سکیں - چنانچہ کمیٹی نے رپورٹ پیش کی اور اس کی رپورٹ کے مطابق یہ بل تیار کیا گیا ہے - پہلی مرتبہ جو بل تیار کیا گیا تھا وہ بہت کچھ رجڈ (rigid) اور ٹھوس تھا - اس لئے کوشش کی گئی کہ اسکو زیادہ سمپل (simple) کیا جائے - چنانچہ منسٹری نے اس میں بہت کچھ کاٹ

چھانٹ کی- اگر ہاؤس یہ چاہتا کہ تین برس پہلے ایکسپرٹ کمیٹی نے جو رپورٹ تیار کی تھی ، وہ سلیکٹ کمیٹی کے سامنے رکھدی جائے تو وہ خوشی سے رکھہ دی جائیگی - لیکن جس طریقہ سے یہ سوال اٹھایا گیا ہے اس کا مطلب یہ ہے کہ بل یہاں پیش نہیں کیا جا سکتا جب تک کمیٹی کی رپورٹ ہاؤس کے سامنے نہ آئے ، میں اسے ایک لمحہ کے لئے بھی ماننے کیلئے تیار نہیں ہوں - جب بل تیار ہوتے ہیں تو انہیں مختلف اسٹیجز سے گزرنا پڑتا ہے - پہلے صلاح اور مشورہ ہوتا ہے ، کانفرنس ہوتی ہیں ، پھر کمیٹی بٹھائی جاتی ہے ، وہ اپنی رپورٹ پیش کرتی ہے - اس طرح بہت سی کڑیوں سے گزرنے کے بعد ایک بل تیار ہوتا ہے اور یہ ضروری نہیں ہوتا کہ یہ تمام کڑیاں ہاؤس کے سامنے رکھی جائیں -

SHRI C. G. K. REDDY:

श्री सी० जी० के० रेड्डी : कभी नहीं !

MAULANA ABUL KALAM AZAD:

مولانا ابوالکلام آزاد : اگر ہاؤس کمیٹی کی یہ خواہش ہے کہ ایکسپرٹ کی رپورٹ سلیکٹ کمیٹی کے سامنے رکھی جائے تو وہ نہایت خوشی سے رکھدی جائیگی - اس سے مجھے اختلاف نہیں ہے - جس چیز سے میں نے اختلاف کیا وہ صرف یہ تھا کہ یہ پوزیشن میں تسلیم نہیں کرتا کہ چونکہ ایکسپرٹ کمیٹی کی رپورٹ ہاؤس کے ٹیبل پر نہیں رکھی ہے اس لئے یہ بل پیش نہیں کیا جا سکتا -

SHRI H. N. KUNZRU:

श्री एच० एन० कुंजरू : मैं मौलाना साहब के गौर करने के लिये दो बातें पेश करना चाहता हूं । एक तो यह कि जो कान्फ्रेंस एजूकेशन मिनिस्ट्री की हुई थी उसकी सिफारिश यह थी कि गवर्नमेंट श्राफ इंडिया एक चिल्ड्रेन्स ऐक्ट ऐसा बनाये कि जो श्रौर स्टेट्स के लिये भी मुफीद हो, यानी जो कि बतौर नमूने के उनके सामने पेश की जा सके श्रौर जिसको अगर वे चाहें तो जरूरत के मुताबिक तरमीम कर लें। यह बिल सिर्फ श्रापके "सी" स्टेट्स के लिये नहीं है, बल्कि जैसा कि मैं स्टेट्मेंट श्राफ श्राब्जेक्ट्स एण्ड रीजन्स

(Statement of Objects and Reasons) की इबारत से हूं, यह बिल सिर्फ पार्ट "सी" स्टेट्स के लिये नहीं बनाया गया है बल्कि इस गरज से भी बनाया गया है कि और भी जो स्टेट्स हैं वे भी इस मसले पर गौर करें और इस बिल के मुताबिक कुछ तरमीम करके......

MAULANA ABUL KALAM AZAD:

مولانا ابوالکلام آزاد : اپنا بل بنائے

SHRI H. N. KUNZRU:

श्री एच० एन० कुंजरू : अपने बिल्स बनायें। दूसरी बात यह है कि स्टेटमेंट आफ आब्जेक्ट्स एंड रीजन्स में लिखा हुआ है कि

"The present Bill is based gen- erally on the recommendations of the Expert Committee."

अगर यह बिल एक्सपर्ट कमेटी की सिफारिशों के ऊपर बना है और इसकी गरज यह है कि और स्टेट्स भी ऐसा ही बिल पेश करें तो यह नहीं कहा जा सकता कि जो एक्सपर्ट्स (experts) मुकर्रर हुये थे या कोई डिपार्टमेंटल कमेटी बनी थी उनका गवर्नमेंट ने अपने स्टेट्मेन्ट आफ आब्जेक्ट्स एंड रीजन्स में बेकार जिक्र कर दिया।
यह कमेटी अगर बनाई जाय तो इसकी अहमियत को देखते हुये गवर्नमेन्ट के लिये यह लाज़िम है कि इसकी रिपोर्ट को पेश करे। गवर्नमेन्ट ने कुछ मुद्दत हुये, कम्पनीज ला (Companies Law) में तरमीम के लिये एक कमेटी मुकर्रर की थी, उसकी रिपोर्ट छप गई और उस पर लोगों की राय लेने के बाद एक नया बिल लाने की कोशिश की गई। क्या चेयर से मैं यह दर्याफ्त कर सकता हूं कि अगर इस कम्पनीज ला कमेटी की रिपोर्ट पेश न की जाती तो कोई हाउस नये बिल के ऊपर गौर करने के लिये एक लमहे के लिये भी तैयार होता?

SYED MAZHAR IMAM (Bihar):

سید مظہر امام (بہار) : میں یہ

کہنا چاہتا ہوں کہ اس طرح کا کلونشن اگر ہاؤس کرد ے......

Shri V. K. DHAGE:

श्री वी० के० ढागे : अंगरेजी में बोलिये।

SYED MAZHAR IMAM:

سید مظہر امام... : تو اسکا نتوجہ

یہ ہوگا کہ آیندہ تمام چیزوں کی رپورٹ گورنمنٹ کو ہاؤس کے سامنے
پیش کرنی ہوگی - اسلئے اگر ایسا کلیریفکیشن ہو جائیگا ......

MAULANA ABUL KALAM AZAD:

مولانا ابوالکلام آزاد : ممبر نے کہا
کہ کمیٹی کی رپورٹ ایک پوشیدہ چیز تھی - مجھے معلوم نہیں کہ
یہ بات انہوں نے کس طرح معلوم کی -

SHRI S. N. MAZUMDAR:

श्री एस० एन० मजूमदार : आपके दफ्तर से आया है।

(Interruptions.)

Mr. Deputy Chairman: It is not a Parliamentary Committee or a Committee of the House. The Government may print it for distribution and sale. I think there is no rule by which I can compel the Government to place it before the House.

Shri H.N. Kunzru: You may not be able to compel the Government to do so, but....

Mr. Deputy Chairman: The hon. Minister has promised that it will be supplied to Members.

Shri H.N. Kunzru: May I respectfully submit that you can tell the Government that in future, such documents should be supplied to the House before any question relating to them is discussed? That is the real point at issue.

Mr. Deputy Chariman: It will be helpful to Members, I agree, but it cannot be a point of order. I cannot compel the Government. I can only say that it will be helpful to Members.

Shri H.N. Kunzru: Before now discussions have been stopped on this very ground. It is for you to decide.

Mr. Deputy Chairman: So far as I know, there have been no precedents.

Shri V.K. Dhage: I quoted a precedent only a week old in the House of the People.

Mr. Deputy Chairman: You give me the ruling in any House of Parliament.

Shri S. Banerjee (West Bengal): You create a precedent.

Mr. Deputy Chairman: I do not want to.

Shri Rama Rao: If there is to be any ruling, it must be in favour of the Bill being considered.

Shri S.N. Mazumdar (West Bengal): We are not expressing ourselves against the Bill.

Mr. Deputy Chairman: So far as the point of order is concerned, I have held that there is no point of order, the hon. Minister may continue.

Shri B.M. Gupte: May I point out....

Mr. Deputy Chairman: It is not necessary, Mr. Gupte.

श्री एच० एन० कुंजरू : यह तो खुद आपने ही फरमाया कि हम रिपोर्ट को पेश नहीं करेंगे। आपने यह नहीं कहा, लेकिन जब आपके डिपार्टमेन्ट से पूछा गया तो उन्होंने कहा कि रिपोर्ट कंफीडेंशल है। अब आप कहते हैं कि अगर सेलेक्ट कमेटी चाहेगी तो वह रिपोर्ट पेश की जायगी। आपके ऐसा कहने से जरूर ही इस खयाल की ताईद हुई कि वह रिपोर्ट पोशीदा है। अगर आप समझते हैं कि रिपोर्ट पोशीदा नहीं है तो यह सवाल कभी पैदा ही नहीं होता।

MAULANA ABUL KALAM AZAD:

مولانا ابوالکلام آزاد : آنریبل ممبر کے کہنے کا مقصد یہ ھے — یہ کہنے سے کہ کمیٹی کی رپورٹ سیلیکٹ کمیٹی کے سامنے رکھ دی جائیگی یہ ثابت ھو گیا کہ کمیٹی کی رپورٹ ایک پوشیدہ چیز تھی - اگر یہی انکی لاجک (logic) ھے تو میں تسلیم کرتا ھوں کہ میں اس بارے میں کچھ نہیں کہہ سکتا -

श्री एच० एन० कुंजरू : सवाल यह है कि आप हाउस को इस वक्त रिपोर्ट नहीं देना चाहते थे।

MAULANA ABUL KALAM AZAD:

مولانا ابوالکلام آزاد : میں یہ بات صاف طور پر واضح کر دینا چاهتا ھوں کہ گورنمنٹ یہ بات کسی حال میں بھی تسلیم نہیں کر سکتی کہ ایک بل کے تیار کرنے کے لئے اسے جن کارروائیوں کے انجام دینے کی ضرورت پیش آتی ھے

وہ سب اسے ہاؤس کے سامنے رکھنی چاہئیں - اگر وہ ہاؤس کے سامنے
نہیں رکھی گئیں تو وہ بل بھی پیش نہیں کر سکتی - گورنمنٹ
کو پورا اختیار ہے کہ جس کاغذ کو چاہے ہاؤس کے سامنے رکھے اور
جسکے رکھنے کی ضرورت نہ ہو نہ رکھے - یہ بات گورنمنٹ کے وہم و
گمان میں بھی نہیں آئی تھی کہ اس کمیٹی کی رپورٹ کو ہاؤس
کے آنریبل ممبر دیکھنا ضروری سمجھیں گے - یہ کمیٹی ہاؤس نے مقرر
نہیں کی تھی - گورنمنٹ نے مقرر کی تھی - لیکن بہرحال چونکہ
اس رپورٹ میں کوئی بات ایسی نہیں ہے جسے گورنمنٹ پوشیدہ
رکھنا چاہے اسلئے گورنمنٹ تیار ہے کہ اگر سلیکٹ کمیٹی نے اسکے
دیکھنے کی خواہش کی تو اسکے سامنے رکھ دی جائے گی -

SHRI C. G. K. REDDY:

श्री सी० जी० के० रेड्डी: दफ्तर से तो कहा गया है।

MAULANA ABUL KALAM AZAD:

مولانا ابوالکلام آزاد: بہرحال، میں یہ
سمجھتا ہوں کہ جہانتک بل کے مقصد کا تعلق ہے - وہ اتنا صاف ہے
کہ اس بارے میں کسی لمبی چوڑی بحث کی ضرورت نہیں ہے -
آج کل دنیا کے تمام مہذب ملکوں کی گورنمنٹوں (Governments)
نے یہ بات تسلیم کر لی ہے کہ سوسائٹی (society) میں جو لاوارث
بچے ہوں یا ایسے بچے ہوں جن کا خاندان انکی دیکھ بھال کی فکر
نہیں کرتا ہو - گورنمنٹ کو ان کی تعلیم و تربیت کا انتظام کرنا
چاہئے اور گورنمنٹ اس کے لئے ذمہ وار ہے - ساتھ ہی یہ بات بھی
عام طور پر تسلیم کر لی گئی ہے کہ اگر بچوں سے کوئی جرم سرزد
ہو جائے تو ان کے ساتھ اس ڈھنگ سے سلوک نہیں ہونا چاہئے جیسا
کہ عام عدالتوں کا ڈھنگ ہے کیونکہ جونہی ایک بچے کو قانون کی
عام سزاؤں میں سے کوئی سزا دی جاتی ہے ہمیشہ کے لئے اسکی اخلاقی
زندگی برباد ہو جاتی ہے - انکے لئے تنبیہ اور نگرانی کا دوسرا طریقہ
اختیار کرنا چاہئے - چنانچہ تمام مہذب ملکوں میں اس کا خاص
انتظام کیا گیا ہے - لیکن افسوس ہے کہ اس بارے میں ہمارا ملک
ابھی بہت پیچھے ہے -

سنہ ۱۹۴۷ء میں جب میں نے ایجوکیشن منسٹری (Education Ministry) کا چارج (charge) لیا تو اسوقت جو چند اہم کام میرے سامنے خاص طور پر آئے تھے ان میں ایک کام یہ بھی تھا - میں نے پہلے یہ معلوم کرنا چاہا تھا کہ جہانتک اس معاملہ کا تعلق ہے مختلف صوبوں کا کیا حال ہے - معلوم ہوا ہے کہ چند صوبوں میں اگر کوئی قدم اٹھایا گیا ہے تو صرف ایک بات کے لئے اٹھایا گیا ہے یعنی اسکی کوشش کی گئی ہے کہ کم عمر کے مجرموں کے لئے الگ قیدخانے بنائے جائیں اور وہاں تعلیم کا بھی انتظام کیا جائے -

مگر یہ انتظام بھی تمام صوبوں میں نہیں ہے - چند گنے ہوئے صوبوں میں ہے - ان میں بمبئی کے صوبہ نے سب سے زیادہ اس کام میں دلچسپی لی ہے لیکن وہاں بھی یہ کام ایک خاص حد سے آگے نہیں بڑھا ہے - جب یہ معلومات ایجوکیشن منسٹری کے سامنے آگئیں تو خیال کیا گیا کہ بہتر یہ ہوگا کہ تمام صوبوں کے ایجوکیشن منسٹروں کی ایک کانفرنس (conference) بلائی جائے اور وہ پوری طرح غور و فکر کرکے ایک فیصلہ کرے اور اسکے مطابق قدم اٹھایا جائے - چنانچہ اگست سنہ ۱۹۴۹ء میں یہ کانفرنس بلائی گئی - کانفرنس نے بالاتفاق یہ فیصلہ کیا کہ سنٹرل گورنمنٹ (Central Government) کو اس بارے میں قدم اٹھانا چاہیئے اور ایک ایسا بل تیار کرنا چاہیئے جو تمام صوبوں کی گورنمنٹوں کے لئے (کیونکہ اسوقت ملک صوبوں میں بٹا ہوا تھا، اسٹیٹ (State) نام کی گورنمنٹیں نہیں تھیں) نمونے کا کام دے اور اپنے اپنے صوبوں کے لئے اس قسم کا بل وہ اپنی اسمبلیوں (Assemblies) میں منظور کرائیں - کانفرنس نے ایجوکیشن منسٹر (Education Minister) سے درخواست کی کہ وہ ایک ایکسپرٹس کمیٹی (Experts Committee) اس غرض سے مقرر کر دیں کہ وہ اس معاملہ کے تمام پہلوؤں پر غور و فکر کر کے ایک بل کا مسودہ تیار کر دے - ایجوکیشن منسٹری اس مسودہ پر غور کریگی اور پھر پارلیمنٹ (Parliament) میں پیش کرنے کے لئے ایک موزوں اور مناسب بل تیار ہو جائے گا - چنانچہ ایکسپرٹ کمیٹی مقرر کر

دی گئی اور اس نے فوراً کام شروع کر دیا - کمیٹی کا پہلا کام یہ تھا
کہ دوسرے ملکوں میں اس سلسلہ میں جو کچھ ہوا ہے اسے پوری
طرح معلوم کرے اور پھر ملک کی حالت سامنے رکھتے ہوئے اپنی
تجویزوں کا نقشہ تیار کرے - کمیٹی نے اپنا کام پورا کرنے کے بعد اپنی
رپورٹ مرتب کر کے پیش کی اور اس طرح ایک بل کا مسودہ تیار
ہوا - یہ بل بہت لمبا چوڑا تھا - اس میں کوشش کی گئی تھی
کہ ہر طرح کی تفصیلی باتوں کو طے کر دیا جائے - جو انسٹی
ٹیوشن (institution) قائم کئے جائینگے انکے ضابطے اور
قاعدے کیا ہونگے - وہ کس طرح کام کرینگے - ان سب باتوں کو بل
میں بیان کیا گیا تھا - لیکن جب گورنمنٹ نے اس پر غور کیا
تو یہ رائے قائم کی کہ اس بل میں اس طرح کی تفصیلات تک جانا
ضروری نہیں ہے - بل کا مقصود یہ ہے کہ اسٹیٹ گورنمنٹوں
(State Governments) کے لئے نمونے کا کام دے - اس لئے اس
میں صرف موٹی موٹی اور بنیاد کی باتوں کو لینا چاہیئے -
نیچے کی تفصیلات کو چھوڑ دینا چاہیئے کہ اسٹیٹ کی

گورنمنٹیں اپنی اپنی حالت کے مطابق جس طرح چاہیں انہیں
طے کریں - مثلاً اگر ہم ضروری سمجھتے ہیں کہ بچوں کے لئے ایک
لا کورٹ (Law Court) ہو تو ہمیں لا کورٹ کا ذکر کر دینا چاہیئے
اور جو اس کی موٹی موٹی باتیں ہیں انہیں بل میں واضح کر دینا
چاہیئے - اب رہی یہ بات کہ وہ لا کورٹ جو بنے گا اس کے قاعدے
کیا ہونگے اور اس میں کام کس طرح ہوگا - تو ان باتوں میں ہمیں
جانے کی ضرورت نہیں - اسے چھوڑ دینا چاہیئے کہ ہر اسٹیٹ اپنی
حالت اور ضرورت کے مطابق اسکے رولس اور قاعدے بنالے -
چنانچہ اس چیز کو سامنے رکھ کر کوشش کی گئی کہ یہ بل جتنا
سیدھا سادھا اور سمپل (simple) کیا جا سکتا ہے کیا جائے - چنانچہ
اب جو بل آپکے سامنے ہے اس میں آپ دیکھ رہے ہیں کہ صرف ٦
چیپٹرس (chapters) ہیں اور ٥٢ کلازیز (clauses) ہیں - ٦

چیپٹرس میں سے پہلا چیپٹر ٹائٹل وغیرہ کے بارے میں ہے -
گویا ۵ چیپٹرس اصلی بل کے ہیں - بنیادی طور پر ۵ انسٹی ٹیوشنس
ہیں جن پر زور دیا گیا ہے - پہلا انسٹی ٹیوشن وہ ہے جس کی
نسبت کہا گیا ہے "After-care-organisation" یعنی کوئی
جگہ ایسی ہونی چاہئے جہاں وہ لڑکا جسکو پولیس (police) نے
دیکھا ہو کہ آوارہ پھر رہا ہے اسے پکڑنے کے بعد رکھا جاسکے اور اسکے بعد
اسکے حالات کی انکوائری (enquiry) کی جائے - جبتک انکوائری
جاری رہے گی وہ وہیں رکھا جائیگا - چنانچہ پہلی بات یہ ہے -

اس کے بعد دوسرا انسٹی ٹیوشن ہمارے سامنے آتا ہے - بچوں
کا ایک گھر ہونا چاہئے جہاں ان بچوں کو رکھا جاسکے جو لاوارث
مان لئے جائیں ساتھ ہی ان کے لئے ایک خاص قسم کا اسکول (school)
بھی ہونا چاہئے - ظاہر ہے کہ جو عام اسکول موجود ہیں ان کے لئے
موزوں نہیں ہونگے - ان کے لئے ایک خاص اسکول ہونا چاہئے -

تیسرا انسٹی ٹیوشن وہ ہے جسے آبزرویشن ہوم (Observation
Home) کا نام دیا گیا ہے - یعنی دیکھ بھال کا گھر - یہ ان
لوگوں کے لئے ہوگا جن کے لئے عدالت کوئی فیصلہ کر دیگی -
گویا انہیں سزا دی گئی ہے - لیکن یہ قید کی سزا نہیں ہوگی صرف
نگرانی ہوگی اور نگرانی کا مقصود ان کی اصلاح ہوگا -

چوتھا انسٹی ٹیوشن چلڈرنز کورٹس (Children's Courts) ہے -
ان کے لئے ایک خاص قسم کی عدالت ہوگی کیونکہ جو عام عدالتیں
موجود ہیں وہ انکے لئے موزوں نہیں ہو سکتیں - انکی خاص
حالت ہے، ان کی خاص ذہنیت ہے اور خاص سائیکالوجی
(psychology) ہے - انکے لئے خاص عدالتیں ہونی چاہئیں اور
خاص مجسٹریٹ - یورپ اور امریکہ میں یہ مجسٹریٹ عموماً
عورتیں ہوتی ہیں کیونکہ وہی بچوں کی حالت کو، ان کے دماغ کو،
طور طریقے کو بہتر طریقہ پر سمجھ سکتی ہیں - یہ بنیادی
چیزیں ہیں جن پر کہ بل میں زور دیا گیا ہے ان آرگنائزیشنس
(organizations) کو کیسے قائم کیا جائے - ان کے رولس (rules)

اور قاعدے کیا کیا ہوں - یہ ہر اسٹیٹ کو اپنی حالت اور ضرورت کے مطابق بنانے ہونگے - اس بل نے انہیں چھوڑ دیا ہے - اگر ہم ان باتوں میں جاتے تو یہ بل ایک ایسا ٹھوس اور رجڈ (rigid) ہو جاتا کہ اسٹیٹوں کے لئے کوئی راستہ اسکے سوا نہیں رہ جاتا کہ یا تو وہ اسے پوری طرح لے لیں یا پورا کا پورا چھوڑ دیں - ہم چاہتے ہیں کہ ایسا نہ ہو - دوسری اہم بات جو سامنے رکھی گئی ہے وہ یہ ہے کہ اس معاملہ کا اہم پہلو خرچ کا ہے - اسٹیٹ گورنمنٹوں کو یہ بات دیکھنی ہوگی کہ وہ روپیہ کہاں تک نکال سکتے ہیں اور کسطرح نکال سکتے ہیں - اسلئے بل اس طرح کا ہونا چاہئے کہ اگر خرچ کی مشکلات کی وجہ سے پورے اسٹیٹ میں یہ قانون نافذ نہ کیا جا سکے تو اسکے ایک حصہ میں نافذ کیا جاسکے اور یہ کام شروع کرنے کے لئے کم سے کم خرچ کی ضرورت ہو - مطلب یہ ہے کہ اگر کوئی اسٹیٹ ایک ہی مرتبہ میں پورا قانون نافذ نہیں کر سکتا تو بتدریج نافذ کرے - چنانچہ بل میں اس بات کی پوری گنجائش رکھی گئی ہے - آپ نے یہ بل منظور کیا تو فوراً اس کا نفاذ پارٹ سی اسٹیٹس (Part C States) میں ہو جائیگا پارٹ اے اور بی اسٹیٹس (Part A and B States) میں یہ نمونہ کا کام دیگا - جو اسٹیٹ چاہے گا اس طرح کا بل اپنے یہاں منظور کرا کے عمل میں لائیگا -

جو انسٹی ٹیوشن اس بل میں قرار دئے گئے ہیں اگر وہ ابتدا میں پورے اسٹیٹ کے لئے نہ بنائے جائیں صرف ایک ضلع اور ایک خاص حصے کے لئے بنائے جائیں تو ایسا کیا جا سکتا ہے - اور اسکی پوری گنجائش اس بل میں رکھی گئی ہے مثلاً اگر ایک اسٹیٹ ابتدا میں صرف کسی ایک حلقہ میں یہ کام شروع کرنا چاہے تو اسکے لئے ضروری ہوگا کہ یہ پانچوں انسٹی ٹیوشن اس حلقہ میں قائم کردے اور پھر بتدریج دوسرے حلقوں میں کام پھیلائے - ان پانچ انسٹی ٹیوشنوں کے خرچ کا اندازہ ۶۲ هزار روپیه

سالانہ کیا گیا ہے - گویا ایک اسٹیٹ اگر سردست زیادہ روپیہ نہیں نکال سکتا تو صرف ۶۲ ہزار سالانہ کی قلیل رقم خرچ کرکے یہ کام شروع کر سکتا ہے -

ایک اہم سوال یہ ہے کہ بچوں کی تعریف کیا ہو یعنی انکی عمر کی قید کیا معین ہونا چاہئیے - دوسرے ملکوں میں جو کچھ کیا گیا ہے اسکو سامنے رکھ کر یہ فیصلہ کیا گیا ہے کہ ۱۶ برس کی عمر رکھی جائے - چنانچہ اس بل کا جہاں تک تعلق ہے بچوں کا اطلاق ایسے لڑکوں پر ہوگا جو ۱۶ برس کی عمر کے اندر ہوں - ۱۶ برس کی عمر کے بعد کے لڑکے اس بل کی تعریف کے اندر نہیں آئینگے - بہرحال میں یہ تحریک آپ کے سامنے پیش کرتا ہوں کہ یہ بل ہاؤس کی ایک سلیکٹ کمیٹی کے سپرد کر دیا جائے - سلیکٹ کمیٹی اپنی رپورٹ ہاؤس کے سامنے رکھے گی - چنانچہ سلیکٹ کمیٹی کے ممبروں کے نام یہ ہیں :

Shrimati Rukmini Arundale,

Shrimati Violet Alva,

Dr. Shrimati Seeta Parmanand,

Kunwarani Vijaya Raje,

Shri J.N. Kaushal,

Shri Onkar Nath,

Shri Lavji Lakhamshi,

Shri T.R. Deogirikar,

Shri Rahmath-Ullah,
Maulana M. Faruqi,
Shri Indra Vidyavachaspati,
Shri S.D. Misra,
Dr. K.L. Shrimali,
Shri Kishori Ram,
Shri H.C. Mathur,
Shri Kishen Chand,
Shri S.N. Mazumdar,
Shri Abdul Razak,
Shri Amolakh Chand,
Shri K.D. Malaviya, and
The Mover.

یہ بل جونہی منظور ہوگا اسکا نفاذ تمام سی کلاس اسٹیٹوں میں ہو جائیگا - لیکن اے اور بی کلاس کی ریاستوں کے لئے یہ نمونہ کا کام دے گا -

میں یہ بات نوٹ کر لیتا ہوں کہ ایکسپرٹ کمیٹی کی رپورٹ سلیکٹ کمیٹی کے سامنے رکھدی جائیگی -

SHRI H. P. SAKSENA:

श्री एच० पी० सक्सेना : मै आनरेबल मिनिस्टर साहब से यह जानना चाहता हूं कि इसमें क्या राज़ मख्फी है कि इस कानून को सरेदस्त पार्ट "सी" स्टेट में ही चालू किया गया है ?

MAULANA ABUL KALAM AZAD:

مولانا ابوالکلام آزاد : پارٹ اے اور بی اسٹیٹوں میں کانسٹی ٹیوشن (Constitution) اسکی اجازت نہیں دیتا۔ اس میں کوئی راز کا سوال ہی نہیں ہے

Mr. Deputy Chairman: Let me put the motion first.

Shri H.P. Saksena: Sir, just a point of clarification.....

Mr. Deputy Chairman: Yes, but let me put the motion to the House first.

Motion moved:

> "That the Bill to provide for the care, protection, maintenance, welfare, training, education and rehabilitation of neglected children and juvenile delinquents in Part C States be referred to a Select Committee consisting of the following members:

Shrimati Rukmini Arundale,

Dr. Shrimati Seeta Parmanand,

Shrimati Violet Alva,

Kunwarani Vijaya Raje,

Shri Onkar Nath,

Shri Lavji Lakhamshi,

Shri J.N. Kaushal,

Shri T.R. Deogirikar,

Shri Rahmath-Ullah,

Maulana M. Faruqi,

Shri Indra Vidyavachaspati,

Shri S.D. Misra,

Dr. K.L. Shrimali,

Shri Kishori Ram,

Shri H.C. Mathur,

Shri Kishen Chand,

Shri S.N. Mazumdar,

Shri Abdul Razak,

Shri Amolakh Chand,

Shri K.D. Malaviya, and

The Mover."

Shri V.K. Dhage: Sir, in view of the discussion that has taken place here on the point that I had raised, it is felt that without the report of the Committee being placed before us and without it being in our hands, it will not be possible for us to effectively participate in the debate upon this Bill. Therefore, on our side, we shall not be able to take part in the discussion at all without the report being placed in our hands.

Shri C.G.K. Reddy: Sir, I should like to associate myself with Mr. Dhage's remarks and say that it should not be mistaken that so far as we are concerned, we are opposed to this Bill. In fact, we wish that it could have been possible for us to enact it in all the States together. We should not, therefore, be mistaken and our non-participation does not mean that we have nothing to say about it; certainly we have not anything to say against it. Therefore, I endorse fully all the remarks of my hon. friend Shri Dhage. I very much deprecate the attitude that has been taken up by the Government, because I can recall no instance where the report has been first denied to us. From the Ministry it was stated that it is confidential. We are not aware whether suddenly the confidential aspect of it has been lifted since the point was raised. With the best of efforts we tried to get the report. It was refused to us. And I do not know how the hon. Minister can think that he can introduce a motion for reference to a Select Committee without our being able to know what the recommendations of the previous Committee were on which the Bill is based. For aught we know, the recommendations of that Committee may have gone beyond or may have fallen far short of the measure that he is now adopting through this Bill. Therefore, we have to register this protest and we hope that in future at least, the Government will not think of bringing forward a Bill which, according to their own Statement of Objects and Reasons, is based on the report of a Committee which was appointed by them, without that report being circulated for the benefit of the Members.

Shri S.N. Mazumdar: While associating myself with the remarks made just now by Shri Dhage and Shri Reddy, I would also like to make it clear that my non-participation in the discussions at this stage does not mean that we are opposed to this Bill. On the other hand, I do feel that the Bill is a very important one and the subject of the treatment of children that is involved here is a very important one and demands serious consideration. But for that it is absolutely necessary that the report of the Expert Committee should be with us and only after going through the report of that Committee shall we be able to make some contribution to this debate.

That is why, Sir, as a mark of protest against this attitude of Government I am not participating in the discussions at this stage.

Syed Mazhar Imam: Sir, I think this is a protest against the decision of the Chairman.

Mr. Deputy Chairman: They are free to do as they like. I cannot compel them.

MAULANA ABUL KALAM AZAD:

مولانا ابوالکلام آزاد: ہاؤس کے ہو ایک ممبر کو اختیار ہے کہ وہ اپنے خیالات پیش کر سکتا ہے -

Mr. Deputy Chairman: I cannot compel them to participate in the debate.

Shri Rajagopal Naidu: Mr. Deputy Chairman, Sir, I also join along with other Members of the House in lodging a protest against the Government not taking into confidence all the Members of the House and not supplying the documents. I am not here questioning the ruling of the hon. Deputy Chairman but what rule 211 says is this: "If a Minister quotes in the Council a despatch or other State Paper which has not been presented to the Council he shall lay the relevant paper on the Table."

Mr. Deputy Chairman: What is the rule?

Shri Rajagopal Naidu: Rule 211. So, Sir, as this has been quoted in the Statement of Objects and Reasons....

Mr. Deputy Chairman: He has not quoted it. Mr. Naidu, that is the difficulty.

Shri Rajagopal Naidu: He has quoted, Sir.

Shri C.G.K. Reddy: He has quoted in the speech.

Mr. Deputy Chairman: He has not quoted it. If he had, then I would certainly compel him to lay it on the Table.

Shri Rajagopal Naidu: May I read it once again, Sir?

Mr. Deputy Chairman: If he has quoted it or anything else, I would certainly compel him to place it on the Table. He said that 'an Expert Committee went into this question and made a report and on their recommendations we have brought forward this Bill'.

Shri Rajagopal Naidu: Now, Sir, that itself is a quotation.

Mr. Deputy Chairman: Government appoint so many expert committees who go into these cases. In fact, there is a ruling which I will read for you: "A Select Committee of this House cannot have greater powers than what the House itself enjoys under the Constitution. Under the existing Constitution this House has not got the right to compel either the Government or any other person to produce documents and papers or to compel persons to appear as witnesses." It follows, therefore, that the Government have the right to place before the Select Committee only such papers, records, as they are prepared to place. I have no power to compel them. It will certainly help the Members and the House if the Report is supplied. The hon. Minister has said in his speech that it will be placed before the Select Committee and that it will also be supplied to the Members of the House. It is really unfortunate if the Members now choose not to participate in the debate. I cannot compel them to participate.

Shri C.G.K. Reddy: May I respectfully ask you, Sir, how the Chair expects the Members to take part in a debate on the motion for reference to Select Committee?

Mr. Deputy Chairman: This is the ruling.

Shri C.G.K. Reddy: Quite right; I agree that you cannot compel them and even if you ask them the hon. Minister can say that he refuses to place it because it is against public interest.

Mr. Deputy Chairman: He has said that he will supply it.

Shri C.G.K. Reddy: But, Sir, our protest is why they did not do it before.

Mr. Deputy Chairman: I cannot compel you if you choose not to take part.

Shri Rajagopal Naidu: I had not concluded my speech, Sir.

I have no other option in these circumstances but to lodge my protest against the way in which this Bill is being moved. Probably it is the intention of the hon. Mover that there should not be an effective participation of the Members in this debate and so, in these circumstances, I would also wish to join the other Members from the Opposition in not participating in the debate.

Maulana Abul Kalam Azad: Thank you.

Shrimati Mona Hensman (Madras): Mr. Deputy Chairman, I rise to congratulate the Government on introducing this Bill which has been, in part, already passed in my State. In Madras, the juvenile courts started in 1932, and I would have you know, Sir, that many of us women have been serving on those courts since that date. In speaking on this Bill I may say that there are many points that have been raised in it which provide for neglected children and those children who have not had a fair chance are going to be given special treatment by the State, special education in a congenial environment, to be given the right of citizenship in our Republic. We have, Sir, in our Constitution provided the rights of citizenship for all but, Sir, when we, have allowed begging and crime and neglected members among the youth of our nation, there cannot be effective participation in this citizenship. Therefore, Sir, I welcome this Bill but I would like to point out a few things that would, from my experience, make it a little difficult to implement this Bill in this form. Sir, I am well aware that at the first reading, we do not usually refer to clauses, nor should we speak on the clauses but, with your permission, Sir, I would point to a few particular facts that I wish to palce before the House with reference to certain clauses but I will not speak on them. I think you will agree, Sir, that it would make matters much more plain if I point out to the Members of the House exactly where our observations will occur.

Sir, in the first part regarding the children's courts, I cannot understand why only one Magistrate may be appointed. I feel that there should be an insistence or a Government order providing for the fact, when this Bill is being implemented, that there should be a Board. I feel that as a human family is composed of a father and a mother, there should be a Board consisting of at least one man and at least one woman because otherwise the defective points to be brought out from the parents, to be brought out from the children, to be brought out from the juvenile court will not be properly or effectively complemented and supplemented. If there is only one person, whether a man or a woman, a great deal of proper material can be overlooked. So, I would plead, Sir, that in the implementing of this Bill, there should definitely be a provision for the constitution of a Board where a woman and a man shall sit together – whoever has the senior powers does not matter – and there should be both points of view put forward in each case. There is a clause which says that there should be special knowledge of dealing with juvenile delinquency in the Magistrates selected. So far, in the Part C States, there have not been efficient, sufficient or perhaps any juvenile courts. So, how would there be men and women who have already had experience in this branch of law in those parts of the country? I would point out to the hon. Minister for Education that he should see that definite instruction, to those lacking sufficient experience, are given to those who are presiding in the courts for the first time. Otherwise many things would slip past them and the child might suffer. I feel, Sir, that when there is a District Magistrate presiding in a court, special care should be taken to see that the very principles of a children's court are observed; that is for instance, that the police should not be in uniform, that the forms that are used should not hold a child guilty, that the child should not be called an accused but a juvenile offender. All these points, Sir, will, I am sure, be implemented. When it is a District Magistrate's court, the District Magistrate must make himself into two parts, as it were one the District Magistrate judging and one the non-official trying the case of a child. I am quite sure that in several parts of the country they will not be able to have any one else to appoint and, therefore, the District Magistrate would be the safest person for this duty.

Then, Sir, I have no knowledge about these Observation Homes, except it be that Government means thereby the Remand Homes, where temporary reception is given to a child before and during the time the trial is going on. Then the custody of the child matters a great deal when brought to the Court from its own place, whether outsdie the quarters where the court is held or within the precincts of that city or town. These children, Sir, should never be kept in a police thana or in any police official's house for even an hour or two, let alone for a day or a night, or anywhere but in a Remand Home. Although, in my State, this has been made very clear, it sometimes occurs that, for the sake of convenience they seem to think it is for the welfare of the child to be kept in a safe place where the law obtaines rather than in a safer place where human values are preserved as well as the law. Especially in the case of girl juveniles, we should guard against any outside influence whether from the police or from others. There should be Remand Homes within a reasonable distance of the juvenile courts wherein these girls and boys could be kept safely under the charge of people specially appointed by the law to look after these cases. For them there should be a special procedure. It is a matter of observation that these enquiries and the contacts of children and their guardians should be made solely through the Probation Officers. The police may enquire as to the address of a child or as to the occupation of a parent but the Probation Officer should investigate the conditions of the home of the child. The court will certainly enquire personally and otherwise as to the position of the child in his home, and as to the security, neglect, etc., of the child in general.

But the complete investigation for the purpose of report should be in the hands of the Probation Officers who are independent of the court, but who are definitely Government servants appointed and trained for this confidential business.

Now as regards the class called uncontrollable children. Owing to their economic conditions many parents would like their children to be brought up, to be cared for, to be educated by the State, but it is not possible for the State to look after every child and to give them a proper education. Although our schools are somewhat on a compulsory basis, yet there is not enough room for every child and if the compulsion were made really compulsory, many parents, to my knowledge and experience, would immediately come forward to declare that their children are beyond their control, and they would do so because of the feeling that their children would then get good food, healthy surroundings, good influences and an education which otherwise, they as parents could not give them. It is the Probation Officer, Sir, who can recommend and who can investigate such cases, but I feel that the word 'uncontrollable' has got to be very carefully used in regard to children, because, otherwise it will be abused by those who wish to saddle their family responsibility on the State and the State of course will not be able to obtain enough funds to carry this burden.

About the payment of a fine by the child, Sir, even when a child is earning, say, 8 annas or 11 annas or even one rupee a day, these earnings do not accrue to the child. It is always the guardian or the parent who takes most of the money and the child is given only say, two annas a week, the balance going for the maintenance of the family used by the guardian or by the parent. No child can look upon its earnings as its own. In such circumstances, if a child is made to pay a fine it would be made ridiculously low. Now it has got to be made a deterrent fine made upon a parent, not so much on the child for the parent gains by the child's delinquency. In the case of 'Prohibition' such as we have in Madras and wherever rationing of rice obtains, very often children are employed to carry illicit liquor or to carry illicit rations to and fro, and Sir, there is a regular agency about this. The agent comes to the juvenile court and he pays the fine, Sir, whether it is Rs. 10, Rs. 15, or Rs. 20. These agents are running a little racket whereby the children, the boys, and girls are given 8 annasa or one rupee each time and the agents get all the profits from the illicit distillation of liquor or illegal carriage of rations. Therefore, Sir, when it comes to be a case of a fine for the child I would plead that Government should give instructions that this provision be used as little as possible and a further clause provided whereby the fine is realisable from the parent whether the child is earning or not, and it should be a deterrent fine in the case of those parents who can bear it, or in case of the repetition of the offence.

The next point I would raise is about the very striking order at the bottom of page 7 where it says: "No juvenile delinquent shall be sentenced in default of payment of fine" and in the proviso it goes on to say that in a very serious case the juvenile may be imprisoned because he may not be fit company for the others in the certified school or in the State school. Well, Sir, I would plead: Let there be senior certified schools such as we have in our State in Chingleput where children between the ages of 14 and 16 years can be put. There is a little more restriction there. There is more physical and stricker kind of training. There is some correctional treatment on the lines of the Borstal School but there is no imprisonment. The same facilities will not be available if the child is imprisoned, and the child of 14-16 is very susceptible to bad influences of evil men in a prison.

Then, Sir, Clause 23 is a very fine clause which provides "No child shall be charged with, or tried for, any offence together with an adult". The two cases are separable. We have not got this provision in our State. I would congratulate the Government on making such a provision in this Bill which deals with Part 'C' States. The hon. Minister can easily urge our own State to adopt this because very often there are cases where the man and the child have committed the same offence. The case of the adult gets adjourned and adjourned, his case sometimes drags on for months through difficulties that he cannot foresee and sometimes through various wilful acts such as non-appearance, etc. and the child naturally has to be kept for these two or three months together in a certified school or in an Observation Home. I am specially grateful for this clause whereby the two cases are separable in the interests of the child as the Bill certainly puts before us the interests of the child whereby unnecessary detention is considered undesirable.

Then the next point I would speak about is on page 10 where it says: "No order of a competent court shall be invalidated merely by any subsequent proof" etc. Now we have to think of those cases where, especially, in the case of girls who have been brought forward, and have been declared as juveniles under sixteen years of age by our doctors who appear before the juvenile courts, and the competent court orders that the girl should not be restored to the guardian or agent – not the parents usually, I do not think just now of those cases where the girls are restored to their parents because in such cases it is usually the alleged guardian or agent who is brought to justice – because the Probation Officer has said that the girl has been used for evil purposes while the girl had been in the custody of the alleged guardian or agent. Then, Sir, the matter has been taken up to the High Court from the lower court by this guardian or agent – where another doctor over-rules the previous order and says that the girl who was said to be 14 or 15 years by another doctor is now 16, though it is very difficult to say exactly that a girl is 16. It may be six months or one year this way or that way and a girl may be 15 according to one doctor and she may be 16 according to another doctor. This sort of appeal on the ground of age is preferred to the High Court and the High Court, according to the evidence it has before it, happens to declare a girl as 16 and thus the decision of the lower court is affected and reversed. But it must be remembered this sort of appeal is usually made by the alleged guardian or agent who has been using the girl and will use the girl for immoral purposes. I would plead that if the juvenile court declares a boy or a girl as a juvenile according to the medical evidence produced before it, this should be taken as final, and no appeal should be allowed on the ground of age. On any other ground, of course, an appeal should be permissible because nobody can deny the right of appeal to any free citizen of our country who has the right of appeal from one trial court to another. But even some parents do not know the exact date of birth of their children. So I feel there is real danger especially for the girls who may be used for immoral purposes if the decision of the juvenile court that she was a juvenile when brought there was reversed on an appeal on the ground of age only.

Finally I would point out a slight printing error in clause 30 where the word 'persuasion' has been printed as 'pursuation'. According to the dictionary we know the word as 'persuasion' and I point this out so that it might be corrected, for it is not seemly that wrong spellings should be passed in a Bill put before this House.

Finally I commend this Bill to the House. I feel that it has behind the real backing of the country for the noble purposes for which it has been drawn up.

[THE VICE-CHAIRMAN (SHRIMATI VIOLET ALVA)
IN THE CHAIR.]

श्रीमती सावित्री निगम (उत्तर प्रदेश) : उपाध्यक्ष महोदया, मैं इस बिल का हार्दिक समर्थन करने के लिये खड़ी हुई हूं । ऐसा प्रतीत होता है कि देश के लाखों भूखे शिशुओं का करुण क्रंदन और वात्सल्यमयी नारियों के हृदय की पुकार सुन कर माननीय शिक्षा मंत्री ने यह बिल लाकर सरकारी रक्षा के द्वार प्रथम बार अरक्षित बच्चों के लिये खोले हैं ।

शायद देश के सभी नरनारी और राज- नीतिक दल इस बिल का हार्दिक समर्थन करेंगे, क्योंकि इस बिल के द्वारा एक ऐसी कमी पूरी होने जा रही है जिसके कारण देश के लाखों बच्चे तरह तरह के कष्टों, तकलीफों, मुसीबतों और शोषण को बरदाश्त करते हुये देश के ऐसे असामाजिक तत्व, ऐसे व्यक्ति, बनते थे जो कि स्वयं अपने हा अपना जीवन नष्ट कर देते थे और दूसरों के लिये कष्टकारी

और दुःखद बन जाते थे। महोदया, बच्चा के रक्षण का प्रश्न देश के सुख और सौभाग्य का प्रश्न है। यद्यपि यह विधेयक इस देश में कोई इतना अधिक महत्त्व नहीं रखता जैसा कि इस प्रश्न को सुलझाने के लिये उसे रखना चाहिये, किन्तु फिर भी यह विधेयक उन सब तमाम सरकारी प्रयत्नों का श्रीगणेश है जो कि आगे चल कर इस बिल के पास हो जाने के बाद सरकार के द्वारा हमारी संतान के संरक्षण के लिये किये जायेंगे।

महोदया, अरक्षित बच्चों में केवल वही अभागे और अनाथ बच्चे नहीं होते, जिनको दुर्भाग्य ने उनकी मां-बाप की छत्रछाया से वंचित कर दिया है, बल्कि अनेक संख्या में वह बच्चे भी आते हैं जो आर्थिक परिस्थितियों- वश माता-पिता तथा परिवार वालों की दुश्चरित्रता के शिकार होकर घर से बाहर निकल जाते हैं और उन्हें घर से न किसी प्रकार का सहारा और न संरक्षण ही प्राप्त होता है और न उनकी निगरानी होती है। आगे चल कर यही बच्चे जेबकट, डाकू और लुटेरों के गिरोहों में शामिल हो जाते हैं और देश के लिये ही नहीं, मानवता के लिये भी अभिशाप प्रमाणित होते हैं। महोदया, यह बच्चे बड़े होने पर जिस प्रकार देश के लिये अहित करने वाले साबित होते हैं उसका तो सब को भली भांति पता है, किन्तु बचपन में भी ऐसे बच्चे मोहल्ले के तमाम बच्चों को चोरी, जुवा, गाली और सिगरेट पीने आदि गंदी आदतों के सिखाने में सहायक होते हैं। वास्तविकता यह है कि बच्चे कभी बिगड़ते नहीं, वे बिगाड़े जाते हैं। स्वभावतः बच्चों के दिल बहुत ही कोमल और पवित्र होते हैं और उनके हृदय में सदैव सब कुछ सीखने और सब कुछ ग्रहण करने की और समझने की इच्छा प्रकृति द्वारा उन्हें मिली है। किन्तु अपने आसपास कें

वातावरण से मां-बाप तथा परिवार वालों की लापरवाही से यह बच्चे गंदी आदतों का अनुकरण भी करते रहते हैं और साथ ही जब घर से उनकी ठीक से निगरानी नहीं होने पाती और उन्हें बाहर जाना पड़ता है तो

बाहर के आवारा बच्चे भी उन्हें अपने गिरोह में शामिल कर लेते हैं और इस प्रकार धीरे धीरे ये उनकी ओर झुकते जाते हैं। एक बार गलती करने के बाद जब उनकी कोई रोकथाम नहीं होती, तो फिर उनकी आंखों की शर्म मर जाती है और दिन प्रति दिन उनका झुकाव पतन की ओर होता जाता है। किंतु जब ऐसे बच्चे मां-बाप, परिवार वालों के लिये एक बड़ी विकट समस्या बन जाते हैं और वे उनको किसी प्रकार काबू में नहीं ला पाते तो फिर उनका ध्यान उन तमाम संस्थाओं की ओर जाता है, जो कि बच्चों के नाम पर चलाये जाते हैं और उन बेकाबू बच्चों को वहां भेजने के लिये सभी लोग सुझाव देने लगते हैं। किन्तु, महोदया, बच्चों की संस्थायें, जो आज दया-धर्म के नाम पर जगह जगह चल रही हैं, हर शहर में बड़े बड़े लम्बे-चौड़े साइनबोर्ड और पोस्टर इन संस्थाओं द्वारा लगाये गये हैं और बांटे जाते हैं—नाम भी उनके इतने आकर्षक होते हैं, और रिपोर्टें भी इनकी इतनी हृदयग्राही होती हैं—कि लोग उन पर विश्वास कर लेते हैं और इनसे आकर्षित होकर अनाथ और बेकाबू बच्चों को, परिवार और रिश्ते- दारों के होते हुये भी, संरक्षण के लिये वहां भेज देते हैं। परन्तु जिन्हें असली नक्शा मालूम है, वे जानते हैं कि ये संस्थायें संगठित रूप से शोषण करने वाली संस्थायें हैं और बच्चों पर जिस प्रकार के जुल्म, ज्यादतियां और अत्याचार वहां होते हैं, उनका कहीं ठिकाना नहीं है। इन बच्चों से गाकर भीख मंगवाने और बैंड बजवाने और तरह तरह के चन्दे मांगने का काम निकाल कर पैसा कमाया जाता है। जो लम्बी लम्बी रकमें चन्दों में मिलती हैं उसे संस्थाओं के संयोजक अपने उपयोग में लाते हैं और बच्चों को केवल सूखी रोटी, आधा पेट भोजन और कुछ चीथड़ों में ही गुजर करनी पड़ती है। जो लोग चार्ल्स डिकेन्स के नोवल (novel) में इस तरह के "फौन्डलिंग होम्स" (fondling homes) का जिक्र पढ़ चुके हैं, उसी का सजीव चित्र इन शिशु-रक्षा गृहों में बड़ी आसानी से देखने को मिल सकता है।

महोदया, इन अनाथाश्रमों में जो स्कूल होते हैं उनमें भी बिलकुल यही हालत रहती है। न वहां कोई शिक्षा-दीक्षा दी जाती है, न कोई उद्योग-धंधे ही सिखाये जाते हैं। शिक्षक के नाम पर वहां एक अयोग्य व्यक्ति बैठा कर सौ-पचास बच्चों को लेकर उन्हें पीटने और उठक-बैठक कराने के अतिरक्त और कोई प्रोग्राम नहीं चलाया जाता। इसका नतीजा यह होता है कि ये

बच्चे जब बड़े होकर बाहर निकलते हैं तो वे इतने अयोग्य, स्वास्थ्यहीन और बुरी आदतों के हो जाते हैं कि उन्हें सिवाय फरी लगाने, जेबकटी करने या भीख मांगने के अतिरिक्त और कोई उपाय नजर नहीं आता। इसलिये सरकार ने जहां इस ओर ध्यान दिया है कि इस प्रकार के शिक्षा-गृह, बल्कि रक्षा-गृह, खोलने जा रही है वहां ऐसे शिशु-गृहों और बाल-रक्षा-गृहों को भी, जो पहले से चल रहे हैं, उसे अपने हाथ में लेने की आवश्यकता है, क्योंकि जो सरकारी रक्षालय खोले जा रहे हैं, उनमें बड़ी संख्या में ऐसे बच्चे रख जायेंगे, जिन्हें अपराधियों की कोटि में रखा जाता है या जिन्हें बेकाबू बच्चों की कोटि में रखा जाता है। हमें उन अनाथ बच्चों के लिये, जो कि लाखों की संख्या में हिन्दुस्तान में मौजूद हैं, व्यवस्था अवश्य करनी चाहिये और नियम बना कर सरकारी निगरानी के अन्दर उन अनाथाश्रमों को भी रखना चाहिये जो गैर सरकारी रूप से चल रहे हैं। उनका भी संयोजन, संचालन और निरीक्षण करने का प्रबन्ध अवश्य होना चाहिये।

जिस दिशा में सरकार प्रयत्न कर रही है और बच्चों के लिये आब्जर वेशन होम्स (observation homes), चिल्ड्रेन होम्स (children's homes) आदि खोल कर उन सभी बच्चों को, जिन्हें कि परिस्थितियों ने और हमारे वर्तमान आर्थिक संकटों ने इतना गिरा दिया है, संरक्षण दे रही है, उससे लाखों भावी नागरिकों का जीवन तो सुधर ही जायगा, साथ ही अन्य बच्चों और अन्य व्यक्तियों के चरित्र और स्वभाव पर और जीवन पर इसका बड़ा ही अच्छा असर पड़ने वाला है। सरकार को इस बात के लिये सतर्कता से प्रयत्न करना चाहिये कि वह उन तमाम बुराइयों को जो वर्तमान संस्थाओं में छाई हुई हैं और जिनके कारण ये संस्थायें बिलकुल अनुपयोगी, बल्कि समाज के लिये घातक और हानिकारक सिद्ध होती हैं, दूर कर सके और उनसे इन सरकारी रक्षा-घरों को बराबर बचा सके।

महोदया, यह जो चिल्ड्रेन्स कोर्ट (children's court) बन रहे हैं उनमें दो तीन बातें बहुत ही ध्यान रखने योग्य हैं। पहली बात तो यह है कि बच्चों को, जैसा कि मेरी पूर्व- वक्ता बहन ने कहा, कभी अपराधी की भांति न लिया जाय। साथ ही पुलिस के जो हथकण्डे अपराधियों द्वारा कन्फेस (confess) कराने के लिये होते हैं उनसे तो बच्चों को बिलकुल बचाये रखना चाहिये, क्योंकि जिस प्रकार सभी अमानवीय ढंग से पुलिस अपराधों को कन्फेस कराती है, वह बच्चों को अपराधी बनाने में बड़ा हाथ रखता है। जिस क्रूरता का व्यवहार उनके साथ किया जाता है वह उनके समस्त जीवन को नष्ट करने वाला होता है और

उनके कोमल हृदय पर ऐसा धक्का पहुंचाता है कि फिर उनका सुधार होना ही असम्भव हो जाता है। तीसरी बात ध्यान रखने की यह है कि उन बच्चों को कभी अपराधियों के सम्पर्क में न लाया जाय हालांकि अभी मौजूदा हालत में वे सब बच्चे बड़े अप- राधियों के साथ ही रह सकते हैं।

एक तीसरी बात बहुत ध्यान देने योग्य यह है कि जहां तक हो सके इन बच्चों के मामलों का निर्णय करने के लिये महिला मैजिस्ट्रेट ही रखी जायें और इन बच्चों के मुकद्दमों की पैरवी के लिये महिला एडवोकेट्स (advocates) हों, क्योंकि वही सहानुभूति- पूर्ण ढंग से इन बच्चों की त्रुटियों को समझ सकेंगी और इन बच्चों के अपराध करने के कारणों का पता लगा सकेंगी। आज ऐसे व्यक्तियों की बहुत कमी है जो कि मनोवैज्ञा- निक ढंग से बच्चों के साथ व्यवहार कर सकें और उनके मनोविज्ञान को समझ सकें। इसलिये इस बात की बड़ी आवश्यकता है कि शिक्षा-मंत्रालय की ओर से कोई ट्रेनिंग सेंटर (training centre) ऐसा खोला जाय जिसमें कि ऐसे लोगों को ट्रेनिंग दी जा सके जो कि चिल्ड्रेंस होम में काम करेंगे या चिल्ड्रेंस कोर्ट्स में काम करेंगे या आब्जर्वेशन होम्स में रह कर बच्चों का आब्जरवेशन करेंगे। निरीक्षण गृहों का काम बड़ी जिम्मेदारी का और महत्वपूर्ण है इसलिये निरीक्षण गृहों की व्यवस्था इस प्रकार होनी चाहिये कि उसमें बच्चों को यह कभी महसूस न होने पावे कि उनको किसी अपराध के कारण समाज से बाहर वहां लाया गया है। वहां का वाता- वरण बिलकुल आश्रम के रूप में होना चाहिये। वहां का आपसी सम्पर्क ऐसा हो कि वहां के बच्चों को यह अनुभव हो कि वे अपने घर में ही रह रहे हैं। उनके सुख-दुःख का पूरा ख्याल रखा जाय और इसके साथ ही साथ उनकी शिक्षा-दीक्षा और उनके रहन-सहन का तथा उनकी कोमल भावनाओं की रक्षा का हर प्रकार से प्रबन्ध होना चाहिये। इसके साथ ही वहां का वातावरण ऐसा होना चाहिये कि बच्चे स्वयं अपने अपराधों को और अपनी गलतियों को मान लें और फिर अपने में सुधार भी ला सकें।

महोदया, शिशु-गृहों की योजनायें बहुत सुन्दर बनाई जाती हैं परन्तु अक्सर ऐसा होता है कि देश की वर्तमान परिस्थितियों और आर्थिक कठिनाइयों के कारण वह केवल कोरे कागज़ों में ही रह जाती हैं। जब तक कि शिशु-गृह में एक मनोवैज्ञानिक विश्लेषण-शाला नहीं होगी, तब तक वह कभी भी सफल सिद्ध नहीं हो सकती क्योंकि बच्चे ऐसी बुरी परिस्थितियों का सामना

कर चुके होते हैं, ऐसे बुरे दिन देख चुके होते हैं कि उनके दृष्टिकोणों, उनके मनोभावों को बदलने के लिये उनका मनोवैज्ञानिक विश्लेषण करना भी अत्यन्त आवश्यक है। इसलिये शिशु- गृहों में एक मनोवैज्ञानिक विश्लेषणशाला अवश्य ही होनी चाहिये। अक्सर देखा गया है कि वे बच्चे जो कि कुशिक्षा और कुसंगति के प्रभावों के कारण बिगड़ चुके होते हैं उनको यदि ललितकलाओं, नृत्य, गायन तथा पेंटिंग आदि में लगाया जाय और उनकी दिल- चस्पी बढ़ाई जाय, तो उनमें आश्चर्यजनक परिवर्तन और सुधार आ जाता है। इसलिये जो भी शिशु-गृहों में स्कूल खोले जायं उनमें इन चीजों को प्राथमिकता दी जाय, बच्चों को छोटे-छोटे घरेलू उद्योगधंधों की शिक्षा देने के अतिरिक्त ललितकलाओं और अन्य कलाओं का उचित रूप से ज्ञान कराया जाय। अक्सर ऐसा भी होता है कि उत्साह और जल्दबाजी के कारण बड़े बड़े शिशु-गृहों की स्कीमें चालू कर दी जाती हैं लेकिन उनकी पूरी व्यवस्था पहले से नहीं की जाती, और न उसमें मकानों तथा मनोरंजन का, खेल-कूद आदि का ही कोई प्रबन्ध किया जाता है।

इसलिये जो भी शिशु-गृह सरकार की ओर से बनाये जायं उनमें बच्चों के खेलने के लिये पार्क आदि की पूरी व्यवस्था होनी चाहिये तथा तमाम बच्चों के मनोरंजन का पूरा प्रबन्ध होना चाहिये ताकि बच्चे ऊब कर भागने की चेष्टा न करें। इसके अतिरिक्त इन शिशु-गृहों में अधिकतर ऐसी समाजसेवी बहनों का और ऐसी शिक्षिकाओं का सहयोग लिया जाना बहुत जरूरी है जो कि सचमुच एक सच्ची मां का रूप धारण कर सकें तथा बच्चों के चारित्रिक उत्थान में और उनका उचित मानसिक विकास कराने में पूरा सहयोग दे सकें।

इस विधेयक में जो आफ्टर केयर इंस्टीट्यूशन (after care institution) की बात कही गई है और जिस धारा के द्वारा ऐस इंस्टीट्यूशन खोलने का ज़िक्र किया गया है वह अत्यन्त प्रशंसनीय है क्योंकि अक्सर ऐसा होता है कि इन शिशु-गृहों में रह कर जो बच्चे अच्छी आदता वाले हो जाते हैं तथा सुयोग्य बच्चे प्रमाणित हो जाते हैं और जो कि उचित रूप से विकास-पथ पर चलने लगते हैं तथा जिनकी रिपोर्ट भी अच्छी हो जाती है, वे जब फिर पुराने संस्कारों में लाये जाते हैं तो पुरानी परिस्थितियां ऐसा उन्हें मजबूर कर देती हैं कि वे पतन की ओर उन्मुख होने लगते हैं और पुरानी आदतें बढ़ने लगती हैं। इसलिये अगर आफ्टर केयर इंस्टीट्यूशन खोला गया और इसमें सच्ची समाज-

सेविकाओं और निरीक्षिकाओं को उचित रूप से लिया गया, तो बच्चों के लिये समुचित वातावरण की सृष्टि हम उन घरों में ही कर सकेंगे और उनको तमाम दिक्कतों और परेशानियों से बचा सकेंगे, जिनका सामना उन्हें अक्सर घर जाने पर करना पड़ता है। अक्सर ऐसा होता है कि बच शिशु-गृह में रहने के कारण बदनाम हो जाते हैं और लोग उनके साथ संदेह का व्यवहार करते हैं और उनके साथ इतनी उपेक्षा और अवहेलना प्रदर्शित करते हैं कि बच्चे अपने को ऊपर उठाने का कोई मौका ही नहीं पाते। यदि समाज-सेविकायें और निरीक्षिकायें ऐसे इंस्टीट्यूशन से सम्बन्धित होंगी तो वे उचित रूप से उन बच्चों की सहायता कर सकेंगी और उनको मारल सपोर्ट (moral support) दे सकेंगी और इसमें संदेह नहीं है कि उन बच्चों का जीवन सुधारने में बड़ी आसानी हो जायेगी।

महोदया, सरकार को इस दिशा में भी बहुत शीघ्र ही प्रयत्न करना चाहिये कि जिन स्टेट्स में यह बिल लागू नहीं हो रहा है वहां की सरकारों को इस के लिये प्रेरित किया जाय या एक गाइडेंस (guidance) भेज कर मजबूर किया जाय कि वे भी अपने यहां इसी प्रकार का कोई न कोई कानून लाकर इस तरह के बच्चों के लिये ला कोर्ट्स, आब्जरवेशन होम्स, चिल्ड्रेंस होम्स आदि खोलें।

THE VICE-CHAIRMAN (SHRIMATI VIOLET ALVA): How much more time will you take, Mrs. Nigam?

SHRIMATI SAVITRY NIGAM: Only one minute.

श्रीमती सावित्री निगम : यदि सर- कार ने इस बिल उचित रूप से काम किया तो वह न केवल इन नई संस्थाओं को वर्तमान संस्थाओं की खसखी से बचाते हुये इस दिशा में सफल होकर देश में तेजी से शिशु-गृह खोल सकेगी तथा लाखों बच्चों को शोषण से बचा लेगी वरन् देश के भावी नागरिकों के द्वारा एक नये समाज की रचना में सफल भी हो सकेगी।

महोदया, इन शब्दों के साथ म एक बार फिर शिक्षा मंत्री जी को हार्दिक धन्यवाद देते हुये इस बिल का समर्थन करती हूं।

سید مظہر امام (بہار) : محترمہ! میں حکومت کو اس بات کیلئے مبارکباد دینا چاہتا ہوں کہ وہ ایک ایسا بل (Bill) ہاؤس (House) کے سامنے لائی ہے - میں ہاؤس کو یاد دلانا چاہتا ہوں کہ دو دفعہ بجٹ سیشن (Budget Session) کے موقع پر میں نے حکومت کی توجہ اسطرف دلائی تھی کہ وہ ایسے بچوں کا خیال کرے جن کا دیکھنے والا ملک میں کوئی نہیں ہے اور ان کے لئے ایک ایسا ہوم (home) بنائے - مجھے اس بات کی بیحد خوشی ہے کہ حکومت نے اس بات پر دھیان دیا اور ایک اسکیم (scheme) بنا کر بل کی شکل میں ہمارے سامنے لائی ہے -

آج میں مناسب نہیں سمجھتا کہ اس کے متعلق تفصیل میں کوئی بحث کروں کیونکہ یہ بل سلیکٹ کمیٹی (Select Committee) میں جا رہا ہے اور جو اس میں ہمارے دوست ممبر (Member) منتخب ہوئے ہیں ان کا یہ فرض ہوگا کہ اس بل کو غور سے دیکھیں اور بتائیں کہ ان میں کن کن چیزوں کی کمی رہ گئی ہے - لیکن مجھے اس موقع پر افسوس کے ساتھ کہنا پڑتا ہے کہ ایسے بل کے وقت پر اپوزیشن (Opposition) کے ممبرس اس ہاؤس سے ہٹ گئے اور انہوں نے ہٹ جانا مناسب سمجھا -

میں کہہ سکتا ہوں کہ آزادی کے بعد یہی ایک بل ہے جو کہ حکومت صحیح معنوں میں لائی ہے - حالانکہ یہ چھوٹا سا ہی بل ہے لیکن بہت ہی اہم ہے - دوسرے ملکوں میں بچوں کی سکیورٹی (security) حکومت پر ہے - میں نے اکثر حکومت کے سامنے اس ہاؤس میں عرض کیا ہے کہ بوڑھی عورتوں، بیواؤں اور ایسے بچے جو کہ لاوارث ہیں ان کی سکیورٹی کی ذمہ داری گورنمنٹ (Government) کو لینی چاہیئے اور کم سے کم ان کی دیکھ بھال کیلئے کوئی انتظام ضرور کرنا چاہیئے - جبتک کہ ہمارے یہاں کوئی ایسا پراویژن (provision) نہیں ہو جاتا کہ تمام بیکاروں کی ہم دیکھ بھال کرسکیں تب تک کم سے کم ان لوگوں کی دیکھ بھال تو کرنی ہی چاہیئے -

حکومت نے یہ کام بچوں سے شروع کیا - حقیقت میں یہ ایک بڑا قدم ہے اور گورنمنٹ اس کے لئے بہت ہی قابل مبارکباد ہے - مجھے اس کا نہایت ہی افسوس ہے کہ ایسے اہم بل کو پاس کرنے کے وقت ایک معمولی سی چیز پر ہمارے اپوزیشن پارٹی (Opposition Party) کے ممبرس اس بل سے الگ ہیں اور انہوں نے اپنا کوئی مشورہ اس بارے میں دیڈا قبول نہیں کیا ہے - مجھے نہایت افسوس ہے کہ ہمارے اپوزیشن کے دوست نے اس طرح کے اہم بل پر حصہ نہ لینے کا فیصلہ کیا ہے -

مگر ان کا نام سلیکٹ کمیٹی میں ہے - اگر انہوں نے اسے بھی نامنظور کر دیا تو ہاؤس میں جو بحث ہوگی اور آگے جو بحث ہوگی تو اسطرح سلیکٹ کمیٹی کیسے کام کریگی - ہمارے آنریبل منسٹر (Hon. Minister) تو نہیں ہیں مگر پارلیمنٹری سیکریٹری صاحب (Parliamentary Secretary) جو موجود ہیں اس بات پر غور کریں - میں پھر اپنے اپوزیشن کے دوستوں سے عرض کروں کہ وہ اس اہم بل پر ضرور حصہ لیں - اس میں کسی طرح کی پارٹی (party) کا سوال نہیں ہے -

جیسا کہ میں نے پہلے عرض کیا کہ یہ ایک ایسا بل ہے کہ جس کے ماتحت گورنمنٹ ایک طبقہ کی سکیوریٹی کا بھار اپنے اوپر لے رہی ہے چاہے وہ بچوں ہی کا کیوں نہ ہو - حقیقت یہ ہے کہ یہ ایک بہت ہی اہم کام ہے جو ہماری حکومت نے پہلے پہل اپنے ہاتھ میں لیا ہے اور اسکے لئے حکومت قابل مبارکباد ہے - ہمیں امید ہے کہ اس کے بعد عورتیں اور مرد اور دوسری طرح کے لوگ جو ہمارے ملک میں بیکار مجبور پڑے ہیں ان کی بھی سکیورٹی کا بھار ہماری گورنمنٹ اپنے اوپر لیگی -

جہانتک بل کا تعلق ہے اس میں کوئی شک نہیں ہے کہ اسکو پوری حمایت سب طرف سے ملنی چاہیئے -

مگر میں تو اس خیال کا آدمی ہوں کہ اس کو سلیکٹ کمیٹی میں بھی بھیجنے کی ضرورت نہیں تھی - جو کچھ بھی ضروری ملتمست (amendments) اس میں کئے جانے ضروری تھے ان کو یہیں پر کر لیا جاتا۔ اگر حکومت یہ چاہتی ہے کہ اسکو سلیکٹ کمیٹی ہی میں بھیجا جائے تو پھر کوئی چارہ ہی نہیں ہے -

دیش کا ہر شخص، ہر بچہ اس بل کا خیرمقدم کریگا - بچوں کی ذمہ داری سرکار اپنے اوپر لے رہی ہے - یہ ایک مبارک قدم ہے - جیسا کہ آنریبل محترم صدر نے عرض کیا تھا کہ اگر دیش کے بچوں کی دیکھ بھال نہیں کی گئی تو وہ ہمارے ملک اور سوسائیٹی (society) کے لئے ایک کرس (curse) ہو جائیں گے - آج ہمارے ملک میں بہت سے ایسے بچے ہیں جنکو کھانے کو نہیں ملتا، پہننے کو کپڑا نہیں ملتا - اور ان بچوں کی دیکھ بھال سرکار اپنے اوپر لیتی ہے تو اس سے مبارک قدم اور کیا ہو سکتا ہے - مجھے یہ دیکھ کر شرم آتی ہے کہ ہمارے اپوزیشن والے ان معصوم بچوں کا بھی خیال نہیں کر رہے ہیں جو اس ملک کی گلیوں میں مارے مارے پھرتے ہیں اور جنکی بہتری کے لئے یہ بل لایا جا رہا ہے - کم سے کم اپوزیشن والوں کو ایک چھوٹی سی بات پر اپنے کو علیحدہ نہیں رکھنا چاہیئے - وہ اس بل پر اپنی رائے نہیں دے رہے ہیں اسکا مجھے نہایت افسوس ہے -

مجھے افسوس اس بات کا بھی ہے کہ یہ بل پہلے نہیں لایا گیا اور اس کو اب بھی جلدی سے جلدی پاس نہیں کیا جا رہا ہے - آنریبل منسٹر صاحب نے بتلایا کہ یہ قانون صرف پارٹ سی اسٹیٹس (Part C States) ہی میں لاگو ہوگا پارٹ اے اور بی اسٹیٹس (Part A and B States) میں نہیں لاگو ہوگا - اسکا سبب یہ ہے کہ وہ اس قانون کو قانونی مجبوری کی وجہ سے لاگو نہیں کر سکتی ہے - مگر میں آنریبل منسٹر صاحب سے عرض کروں گا کہ وہ اس بل کو ساری اسٹیٹوں (States) میں لاگو کرنے کے لئے اپنا

اور اپنی پارٹی کے اثر سے کام لیں اور اس بات کی کوشش کریں کہ اس طرح کا قانون سارے پراونسوں (provinces) میں جلد سے جلد پاس ہو جائے اور وہ قانون کی شکل لے لے - یہ تو کسی ایک سٹیٹ کے بچوں کا سوال نہیں ہے بلکہ یہ سارے ملک کے بچوں کا سوال ہے - میں سمجھتا ہوں کہ جناب صدر اسٹیٹوں کو خود اس طرح کا قانون بنانا پڑیگا - یہ قانون ہمارے ملک کے لئے ایک اہم قانون ہے - اس لئے میں پھر آنریبل پارلیمنٹری سیکریٹری صاحب سے عرض کرنا چاہتا ہوں کہ وہ حکومت کے سامنے یہ بات رکھیں گے کہ بچوں کی پرورش کے ساتھ ہی ساتھ سرکار کو اس ملک میں جو بیوہ

اور وڈوز (widows) ہیں ان کا بھی خیال کرنا چاہئے اور ان کے لئے بھی اسی طرح کا قانون بنایا جانا چاہئے - ہمارے ملک میں بہت سی بیوائیں آج کھانے کپڑے کے بغیر گلیوں میں ادھر ادھر ماری ماری پھرتی ہیں - اور انکو سماج سے طرح طرح کی مشکلات کا سامنا کرنا پڑتا ہے - وہ بھی ہماری سوسائیٹی کے لئے ایک بھار ہے جسکو ہمیں دور کرنا چاہئے - مجھے پوری امید ہے کہ سرکار میری اس تجویز پر ضرور غور فرمائے گی -

حقیقت یہ ہے کہ ایک شخص جو اپنی دیکھ بھال کو لئے مجبور ہے چاہے وہ بچہ ہو، مرد ہو، یا عورت ہو کوئی بھی ہو اگر ہم اسکے لئے قانون نہیں بناتے ہیں تو ہمارے لئے یہ ایک شرمناک بات ہے - اور انسانیت کی توہین ہے - اسکی حقیقت یہ ہے کہ آج ہماری حکومت جو بل لا رہی ہے وہ اس ملک کی آزادی کے بعد پہلا ایسا قدم ہے جسکے لئے وہ قابل مبارکباد ہے -

یہ ایک ایسا اہم بل ہے جسکے لئے دیش کا ہر شخص گورنمنٹ کی پوری پوری مدد کریگا - جیسا کہ آنریبل منسٹر صاحب نے اپنی تقریر میں فرمایا ہے کہ فنڈ (fund) کی کمی کی وجہ سے یہ کام جلدی نہیں ہو پا رہا ہے - مگر میں امید کرتا ہوں کہ اس ملک کے

لوگ اس کام کے لئے سرکار کی ہر طرح سے امداد کریں گے، اور
جہانتک ہو سکے گا وہ کچھ نہ کچھ سبسکرپشن (subscription)
دینگے۔ چاہے وہ مرد کے لئے ہو چاہے عورت کیلئے ہو یا بچے
کے لئے ہو۔ یہ تو ملک کے ہر آدمی کا اولین فرض ہے کہ وہ اپنے سے
گرے ہوئے آدمی کو آگے بڑھائے اور ہر مصیبت زدہ کی امداد کرے۔
اگر ہمارے ملک کے لوگوں نے اپنا یہ فرض سمجھا اور ہر طرح کی
امداد کی تو ان بدقسمت لوگوں کی پرورش اور تعلیم و دوسری
ضروری چیزوں کا بندوبست ہو سکے گا۔

ایک سجیشن (suggestion) میں آپکے سامنے اور رکھنا
چاہتا ہوں اور وہ یہ ہے کہ جتنے بھی بچے سرکار اپنے اختیار میں
لیگی انکے لئے ملٹری (military) کی تعلیم کمپلسری
(compulsory) کر دینی چاہیئے۔ ایسے بچے جنکا دنیا میں کوئی
بھی نہیں ہے، جنکو گھر سے کسی طرح کا سروکار نہیں ہے وہ ملک کے
اچھے سولجر (soldiers) ہو سکتے ہیں۔ اگر اس طرح کے بچے ہیں
جو ملٹری کی تعلیم پانے کے قابل نہیں ہیں تو انکو دوسرے کاموں میں
لگایا جا سکتا ہے۔ اس لئے میرا سجیشن آپ سے یہ ہے کہ ان
بچوں کی پڑھائی کی جو بھی آپ اسکیم (scheme) بنائیں اس
میں ملٹری تعلیم ضرور رکھیں۔ اگر آپ نے میرا یہ سجیشن مان
لیا تو آپکو دیش کیلئے ایک اچھے اور بہترین نوجوانوں کی فورس
مل جائیگی۔ اگر کوئی لڑکا فزیکلی فٹ (physically fit)
نہیں ہے تو اسکو دوسرے کام میں لگایا جا سکتا ہے۔ مجھے پوری
امید ہے کہ سرکار میری اسی تجویز پر غور کریگی اور اسکو
عملی صورت بھی دیگی۔

ان الفاظ کے ساتھ میں اس بل کو لانے کیلئے پھر حکومت کو
مبارکباد دیتا ہوں اور تہ دل سے اس بل کی تائید کرتا ہوں۔

[MR. DEPUTY CHAIRMAN in the Chair.]

SHRIMATI SHARDA BHARGAVA (Rajasthan):

श्रीमती शारदा भार्गव (राजस्थान): उपाध्यक्ष महोदय, यह जो विधेयक हमारे सामने आया है, उसके लिये मैं सरकार को और शिक्षा विभाग को बधाई देना चाहती हूं। मगर साथ ही यह भी कहना चाहती हूं कि यह बिल जो कि बहुत ही उपयोगी है, बहुत देर से प्रस्तुत किया गया है। उसकी उपयोगिता को दृष्टि में रखते हुए इसे बहुत पहिले प्रस्तुत किया जाना चाहिये था और जितनी जल्दी यह पास हो जाता उतना ही अच्छा होता। मेरा तो सुझाव यह था कि अगर इसको सलैक्ट कमेटी को न सौंपा जाता तो अच्छा होता। जो कुछ भी इसमें संशोधन की आवश्यकता थी उसको यहां पर ही कर दिया जाता।

इस प्रस्ताव का हमारे विरोधी पक्ष के भाइयों ने जो विरोध किया, उसके लिय मुझे बड़ा दुःख हुआ। किन कारणों से उन्होंने इसका विरोध किया है, यह बात मेरी समझ में नहीं आई। उनका कहना है कि उन्होंने शिक्षा विभाग से कुछ बातें पूछी थीं, उनके जवाब में उनसे यह कहा गया कि चूंकि ये बातें सीक्रेट (secret) हैं, गोपनीय हैं, उनको नही बतलाया जा सकता है। मगर हमारे विरोधी भाइयों ने यह बात नहीं बतलाई कि उन्होंने किसको इस विषय में पत्र भेजा था और किससे उनको उत्तर प्राप्त हुआ और क्या प्राप्त हुआ। अगर वे शिक्षा मंत्री जी के सामने इन बातों को रखते तो उनका विरोध करने का मतलब भी समझ में आ सकता था। मगर जब शिक्षा मंत्री जी बारंबार यह कह रहे हैं कि यह चीज गोपनीय नहीं है, तो विरोधी पक्ष के भाइयों का विरोध करना उचित नहीं मालूम पड़ता है। यह कितना उपयोगी बिल है इसको तो वे मानते हैं, मगर वे यह विचार नहीं करते कि एक थोड़ी सी बात के लिये इस तरह के उपयोगी बिल का विरोध करना क्या इस सदन के सदस्यों को शोभा देता है। वे यहां पर विरोधी बैंचों पर चुप होकर बैठे हुये हैं जो कि उनके लिये शोभनीय नहीं है।

इस बिल के चेप्टर २ में क्लाज़ ४ के सब सैक्शन २ में जहां पर मैजिस्ट्रेटों के सम्बन्ध में कहा गया है कि एक मैजिस्ट्रेट भी हो सकता है और मैजिस्ट्रेट्स की बेंच भी हो सकती है और बेंच के अन्दर एक महिला

होनी चाहियें । इस विषय में मेरा सुझाव यह है कि इसके बदले में यह हो जाय कि "चाहे एक मैजिस्ट्रेट हो या बेंच हो, उसमें एक महिला होना आवश्यक है"। इसका कारण मैं यह बतलाना चाहती हूं कि जितना बच्चों के मनोविज्ञान के बारे में एक स्त्री समझ सकती है उतना पुरुष नहीं जान सकता है। महिला ही बच्चे के लालन और पालन के बारे में अच्छी तरह से जानती है। उसने यह बुरा काम किया है तो उसको क्या सजा मिलनी चाहिये, उसको क्या शिक्षा मिलनी चाहिये, किस तरह की शिक्षा से उसका भविष्य उज्ज्वल हो सकता है, ये सब बातें महिला ही अधिक अच्छी तरह से जानती है। इसलिये मेरा कहना है कि चाहे एक मैजिस्ट्रेट हो, चाहे बेंच हो, उसमें एक महिला तो अवश्य ही होनी चाहिये। इसके अतिरिक्त अगर बेंच में दो मैजिस्ट्रेट होते हैं तो उसमें एक पुरुष को भी लिया जा सकता है। शायद यह भी प्रश्न आ सकता है कि महिलायें किसी किसी स्टेट में मैजिस्ट्रेट होने योग्य न मिले। प्रथम तो मेरा यह मानना है कि आजकल महिलायें काफी शिक्षित हो गई हैं और यह समझने लगी हैं कि मैजिस्ट्रेट किस तरह काम करते हैं और उन्हें क्या क्या करना होता है। और अगर किसी स्टेट में योग्य महिलायें न भी मिलें तो पास-पड़ोस की स्टेट्स से उन्हें लाया जा सकता है, क्योंकि मनोविज्ञान एक ही है और सभी महिलायें उसे समझती हैं। इसलिये मेरा संशोधन है कि बच्चों के कोर्ट (court) में एक महिला मैजिस्ट्रेट जरूर होनी चाहिये ताकि अगर कोई पुरुष बच्चों के मनोविज्ञान को न समझ सके तो वह उसे समझने का प्रयत्न करे।

इसमें एक जगह यह दिया गया है कि बच्चों के मां-बाप अगर यह समझते हैं कि बच्चा कोई कसूर करने का आदी है और उनसे सुधर नहीं सकता तो उनके खबर करने पर उसे बच्चों का जो गृह बनाया जायेगा उसमें लिया जा सकता है। मगर यथार्थ में बच्चों के मां-बाप, चाहे उनके बच्चे कितना भी ऊधम करें या कसूर करें, कभी जाकर शिकायत नहीं करेंगे और न यह चाहेंगे कि उनको अपने बच्चों से अलग होना पड़े क्योंकि मां-बाप का मनोविज्ञान ही कुछ इस प्रकार का है कि वे बच्चों को अपने से दूर नहीं कर सकते, भले ही वह उन्हें धमकी देंगे, मारेंगे पीटेंगे। इसलिये इस जगह भी कोई इस तरह के संशोधन की आवश्यकता है कि अगर बच्चों की ऐसी आदत पड़ गई है कि वे मां-बाप से

नहीं सुधर सकते हैं, और पास-पड़ोस का वातावरण भी अशुद्ध करते हैं तो उनके पड़ोसियों को भी यह अधिकार होना चाहिये कि वे भी यह खबर करदें कि यह बच्चा अगर वहां सुधारा जा सकता है, तो उसको वहां लिया जाना चाहिये। यदि हम जो चिल्ड्रेन होम बना रहे हैं वह सचमुच में बच्चों को सुधारने के लायक होंगे तो उसमें अगर हम मां-बाप की इच्छा न होते हुये भी यह समझें कि उनके बच्चे सुधर सकते हैं, तो मैं नहीं मान सकती कि कोई पड़ोसी जाकर शिकायत न करेगा कि वह बच्चा कोई गलती या अपराध करता है जिसके लिये उसे हमें चिल्ड्रेन होम में ले लेना चाहिये। यहां पर यह संशोधन हो जाना चाहिये।

फिर जो कि स्कूल खोले जाने की बात है वह बहुत आवश्यक है। सब लोग यह कहते हैं कि आज की जो शिक्षा है वह अपूर्ण है और आज के वातावरण के लिये ठीक नहीं है। शिक्षा को यहां समझाया नहीं गया है कि किस प्रकार की शिक्षा दी जायेगी। इसमें जरूरी था कि आप यहां कहते कि उनको तीन प्रकार की शिक्षा मिलनी बहुत आवश्यक है। पहली तो मौरल (moral) शिक्षा, क्योंकि यह निश्चित है कि बच्चों का वातावरण या उनके घर की जो सीख है वह गंदी है या ठीक नहीं है जिसकी वजह से बच्चे खराब काम करते हैं। इसलिये उनको मनोविज्ञान को समझ करके उनके साथ वैसा ही व्यवहार करना पड़ेगा जिससे वह ठीक हो सकें। इसलिये उन्हें मौरल शिक्षा देने की बहुत आवश्यकता है।

दूसरी चीज़ है उनमें अक्षर ज्ञान का होना। पढ़ना-लिखना आ जाना भी बहुत जरूरी है। मगर उस प्रकार नहीं जिस प्रकार कि आज हमारा रवैया है कि पांचवें, छठवें, सातवें या हाई स्कूल पढ़कर किसी नौकरी के पीछे दौड़ते हैं।

अब तक जो एजूकेशन (education) का ढंग चल रहा है उसको तो हम जानते हैं कि उसको ठीक मार्ग पर लाने के लिये कुछ समय लगेगा। जहा हम नये स्कूल खोलते हैं, नई विचारधारायें लाते हैं, वहां हम कोई नई स्कीम को ही क्यों न रखें जिससे वह सब चीजें हट जायें जो कि अनइम्पलायमेंट (unemployment) को बढ़ाने वाली हैं। इसलिये वहां पर बेसिक एजूकेशन (basic education) रखना भी आवश्यक है और वह भी बच्चों के मनोविज्ञान को देखकर उसके अनुसार उसको दी जाय, ताकि उनका मन उसमें पूर्णतः लग जाय और उन्हें बुरे कामों के लिये समय ही न मिले। इस तरह की शिक्षा से बच्चे अपने आप ही बुरी प्रवृत्ति को छोड़ेंगे और चिल्ड्रेन होम में रहने का

लाभ उठाकर भविष्य में अच्छे नागरिक बन सकेंगे। इस- लिये आवश्यक है कि वहां के एजूकेशन को हम नये ढांचे में लाने का प्रयत्न करें, यह नहीं कि चाहे जिस अध्यापक को रख दें। ऐसे मामूली दरजे के अध्यापक जो छठे, सातवें, आठवें या दसवें तक पढ़े होंगे, योग्य अध्या- पक सिद्ध नहीं हो सकते। मैं यह सुझाव देना चाहती हूं कि बच्चों के मनोविज्ञान को समझने वाले अध्यापक को रखना चाहिये जो उनकी आदतों को समझ सकते हैं और उन्हें अच्छे ढांचे में ढालने का प्रयत्न कर सकते हैं। इसलिये इस बात का अधिक से अधिक प्रयत्न किया जाये कि बड़ी उम्र की महिलायें जो बच्चों के मनोविज्ञान को समझती हों उनको अध्यापिकायें नियुक्त किया जाये।

तीसरी बात यह है कि इस कानून के मातहत यह रखा गया है कि हम ऐसे बच्चों को कसूरवार मानेंगे और पकड़कर चिल ड्रन होम में ला सकते हैं, जो गाकर या किसी और प्रकार से भीख मांगते हैं। इसमें मुझे एक बात की कमी मालूम पड़ती है। आप लोगों ने अक्सर देखा होगा कि बहुत से अंधे आदमी भीख मांगते हुये घूमते हैं, जो गाते हुए चलते हैं, हाथ में उनके कटोरा या बर्तन होता है, साथ में उनके छोटे छोटे बच्चे होते हैं जो सिर्फ उनके हाथ पकड़े हुये रहते हैं। क्या इस कानून के अन्दर ऐसे बच्चों को भी शामिल किया जायगा यह मेरी समझ में नहीं आया। अगर ऐसे बच्चों को छोड़ दिया जायगा तो वे आगे चलकर मंगते ही बनेंगे।

एक चीज़ और बड़ी हानिकारक है। मैं एक लेख पढ़ रही थी जिसमें यह लिखा हुआ था कि बहुत से मंगते जो रोग दिखाते फिरते हैं, वास्तव में उस रोग से पीड़ित नहीं होते, बल्कि बहुत से रोग बनावटी बना देते हैं। वे इस प्रकार के रंगों का इस्तेमाल करते हैं जिससे कि मालूम पड़ता है, उनके घाव हो रहा है, कोढ़ या और कोई घृणित बीमारी हो रही हो। बहुत से भले चंगे लोग गूंगे और बहरे बनकर अपने को अपाहिज दिखाते हैं। ऐसे लोग बच्चों को

साथ लेकर भीख मांगने के लिये घूमते हैं। अगर इन बच्चों को इस कानून की मातहत नहीं लाया जाता है तो इन पर क्या असर पड़ेगा? वे झूठ बोलेंगे और आगे चलकर इसी तरह से झूठ तथा फरेब करके भीख मांगेंगे। यहां ऐसे बच्चों का इस कानून में जिक्र नहीं आता है और इसलिये उसको बिल में लाना बहुत जरूरी है। इस प्रकार ये मेरे चार पांच सुझाव हैं जिन पर मैं चाहती हूं कि सेलेक्ट कमेटी विचार करे और इन सब चीजों को कानून में बढ़ा दे। मैं फिर एक बार एजूकेशन मिनिस्ट्री (Education Ministry) को धन्यवाद देना चाहती हूं कि वह एक बहुत उपयोगी बिल हमारे सामने लाई है। इन शब्दों के साथ में इस बिल का समर्थन करती हूं।

श्रीमती चन्द्रावती लखनपाल (उत्तर प्रदेश): उपाध्यक्ष महोदय, लावारिस, अनाथ, उपेक्षित, हैन्डिकैप्ड (handicapped) बच्चों की समस्या जितने भयंकर रूप से आज हमारे सामने उपस्थित है वैसी पहले कभी नहीं हुई। देश के अन्दर बढ़ती हुई जनसंख्या और उससे भी तेजी की रफ़्तार से बढ़ती हुई बेकारी ने इस समस्या को बहुत ही भीषण रूप दे दिया है। देश के विभाजन के बाद तो सचमुच ही यह समस्या हमारे सामने नग्न रूप में उपस्थित हो गई है। हम चाहे जहां भी जायें, बड़े बड़े नगरों के अन्दर विशेष रूप से—कहीं भी चले जायें, गली में, मोहल्लों में, बाजारों में, बस स्टैंड पर, मेले-तमाशे पर—हमें फटे चीथड़े कपड़े पहने हुये भीख मांगते हुये ये अनाथ बच्चे दिखलाई देंगे और यह दुर्दशा कोई एक या दो नगरों में नहीं है, सभापति महोदय, सभी बड़े और छोटे नगरों में अपने देश में यह दृश्य देखने को मिलेंगे। यह छोटे छोटे बच्चे भीख मांगते हैं, लेकिन केवल भीख मांगने तक ही इनकी गतिविधि, इनके कार्य समाप्त नहीं होते। जेब कतरने, चोरी करने और भी तरह तरह के अनाचारपूर्ण काम करना उनका एक स्वभाव सा होता है। यह बच्चे जब बड़े हो जाते हैं तो अपने समाज विरोधी कार्यों द्वारा समाज की सुरक्षा को ही एक प्रकार से खतरे में डाल देते हैं और अपने अनाचार- पूर्ण कृत्यों के द्वारा समाज के नैतिक वातावरण को दूषित करते हैं। वास्तव में इन बच्चों की उपेक्षा करना समाज के सर्वोत्तम हितों की उपेक्षा करना है। कोई भी सरकार अनाथ और लावारिस बच्चों की समस्या को उपेक्षा की दृष्टि से अधिक देर तक नहीं देख सकती परन्तु हमारे देश में इस प्रश्न की ओर कोई ध्यान नहीं दिया गया है। आज शिक्षा मंत्री जी जो इस सम्बन्ध में एक बिल लाये हैं वह वास्तव में हमारे लिये बड़े सौभाग्य की बात है और मैं सब बन्धुओं और बहनों के साथ में

जिन्होंने आज शिक्षा मंत्री जी को इस विषय पर बधाई दी है, अपना भी स्वर मिलाती हूं और उनको इसके लिये हार्दिक धन्यवाद देती हूं ।

जैसा कि शिक्षा मंत्री जी ने कहा है, यह बिल बहुत ही सोच और विचार के बाद और विशेषज्ञों के अध्ययन के बाद यहां पर लाया गया है। इसमें संदेह नहीं कि यह बड़ा सुन्दर, व्यापक और कम्प्रेहेंसिव बिल है लेकिन मुझे यह बात समझ में नहीं आई कि जब यह समस्या किसी एक नगर विशेष की समस्या नहीं है, सारे देश की समस्या है, सभी प्रांतों और सूबों की समस्या है तो केवल पार्ट सी स्टेट्स में ही यह बिल क्यों लागू किया जा रहा है । यह कहा जा सकता है कि दूसरी स्टेटों में चिल्ड्रेन्स एक्ट (Children's Act) बने हुये हैं । मैं कहना चाहती हूं कि अव्वल तो सारे स्टेट्स में यह बिल पास हुआ नहीं और यदि किन्हीं स्टेट्स में पास हुआ भी हो तो उन पर कोई अमल नहीं हो रहा है और उनका होना न होने के बराबर है । तो इस दृष्टि से कितना अच्छा होता जो यह व्यापक बिल सदन में लाया जा रहा है वह सारे देश के लिये, सारे स्टेट्स के लिये होता । अभी शिक्षा मंत्री जी ने इस सम्बन्ध में कहा था कि यह वैधानिक नहीं होता अतः यदि इस प्रकार की वैधानिक कठिनाई है तो मैं शिक्षा मंत्री जी से यह प्रार्थना अवश्य करूंगी कि वह यह देखें कि जिस प्रकार का बिल वह पार्ट सी स्टेट्स के लिये लाये हैं उसी नमूने का, उसी तरह का व्यापक और सुन्दर बिल हर स्टेट्स में लाया जाय । मैं यह कहना चाहती हूं कि उत्तर प्रदेश में चिल्ड्रेन्स बिल पास हो चुका है लेकिन बहुत थोड़े लोग हैं जो उसके बारे में जानते हैं । उसका कारण यह है कि वह अभी तक केवल कागज पर ही है । दो तीन महीने पूर्व देहरादून में इस सम्बन्ध के एक आफिसर से मेरी भेंट हुई और मैंने उनसे इसके सम्बन्ध में पूछा तो जो कुछ उन्होंने बताया वह अत्यंत निराशाजनक था । यह बात केवल उत्तर प्रदेश की ही नहीं है बल्कि सभी स्टेट्स में यही हालत है । बम्बई और मद्रास की बात को छोड़ दीजिये, ये स्टेट्स आगे बढ़ी हुई हैं, प्रगतिशील हैं और वहां कुछ अमल हो रहा है, कुछ चिल्ड्रेन होम्स हैं परन्तु जहां पांच हजार अनाथ और लावारिस बच्चे हों, वहां सौ, दो सौ बच्चों के लिये एक आध घर सरकार की तरफ से खोले जाने से तो समस्या हल होती नहीं । इसलिये यह मानना ही पड़ेगा कि यह समस्या केवल सरकार द्वारा स्वतंत्र रूप से हल नहीं की जा सकती । थोड़ी सी गैरसरकारी संस्थाओं द्वारा तो काम होता ही रहेगा,

आज भी हो रहा है और सरकार से ज्यादा हो रहा है लेकिन इस तरह काम चल नहीं सकता । मैंने देहली स्टेट के बारे में पता लगाया है । यहां पर कोई १४ या १५ बच्चों के लिये होम्स हैं जो कि लगभग सभी स्वतंत्र रूप से चलाये जा रहे हैं । मैं इस सम्बन्ध में आपका ध्यान विशेष रूप से प्राइवेट रूप से चलाये जाने वाले होम्स की तरफ आकर्षित करना चाहती हूं । ये अपने कुप्रबंध के लिये विख्यात हैं । ये अच्छे उद्देश्य को लेकर चलायें गये हैं, इसमें शक नहीं है, लेकिन जो सलूक वहां के बच्चों के साथ आज हो रहा है उस पर वास्तव में हमें विचार करना चाहिये । कुप्रबन्ध का एक विशेष कारण यह भी है कि इन संस्थाओं के पास न तो कोई ज्यादा फंड है, न कोई शिक्षा की सुविधा है, न मनोरंजन की और न उचित देखभाल की सुविधा है और एक कारण यह भी है कि आज इनके ऊपर कोई नियंत्रण नहीं है । नियंत्रण न होने के कारण बजाय इसके कि होम्स के बच्चों को उत्तम व्यक्ति बनायें, उनका चरित्र निर्माण करें, उन्हें समाज के लिये उपयोगी बनाये, वहां के प्रबन्धक उनको अपनी ही स्वार्थ-सिद्धि के लिये काम में लाते हैं और जैसा कि अभी बहन सावित्री ने कहा था, उनसे भीख मंगवाते हैं. उनको एक्सप्लायट (exploit) करते हैं । इसलिये मैं चाहती हूं कि जब आज इस समस्या पर विचार हो रहा है तो इस पर भी विचार होना चाहिये कि ये जो प्राइवेट होम्स चल रहे हैं उनको किस प्रकार से नियंत्रण में रखा जाय जिससे कि वे बच्चों को एक्सप्लायट न कर सकें और बच्चे उत्तम नागरिक बन सकें ।

दूसरी बात जो मुझे कहनी है वह डेलि- क्वेंट चिल्ड्रेन (delinquent children) के बारे में है । ये अपराधी बच्चे ऐसे हैं जिनकी समस्या बहुत जटिल है और इसको हर कोई समझ भी नहीं सकता । ये वे बच्चे होते हैं, जो असाधारण रूप से अपराध करने की ओर रहते हैं, जिनकी मनोवृत्ति दूषित और मारबिड टाइप (morbid type) की होती है, जो कि साधारण बच्चों से भिन्न होती है । इन बच्चों को उत्तम नागरिक बनाना एक कठिन परन्तु बहुत ही आवश्यक समस्या है । इस बिल के द्वारा इस समस्या का हल करने का मनोवैज्ञानिक ढंग से प्रयत्न किया गया है । वह वास्तव में एक प्रशंसनीय प्रयास है और उसके लिये मैं फिर शिक्षा मंत्री जी को बधाई देती हू ।

साथ ही साथ आज इस अवसर पर शिक्षा मंत्री जी का ध्यान एक और विषय की ओर भी आकर्षित करना चाहती हूं और वह है जुवेनाइल डेलिक्वेंट्स (juvenile delinquents) की समस्या। यह केवल नगरों तक ही सीमित नहीं है। जो स्कूल के टीचर्स हैं उनके लिये यह एक विशेष समस्या है। जो अपराधी बच्चे हैं वे शिक्षक के लिये एक बड़ा भारी सिरदर्द हैं, वे उनके लिये एक बड़ा भारी हेडेक (headache) बने हुये हैं और वे समझ नहीं पाते हैं कि उसका क्या हल निकाला जाय। ये अपराधी बच्चे सारे वातावरण को दूषित करने में बहुत अधिक भाग लेते हैं और जब इन बच्चों को दूसरे साधारण बच्चों के साथ स्कूल में पढ़ने के लिये भेज दिया जाता है, तो जो साधारण बच्चे हैं उनकी बहुत ज्यादा हानि होने की सम्भावना होती है क्योंकि उनकी जो दूषित मनोवृत्ति है, उसका प्रभाव साधारण बच्चों पर पड़े बिना नहीं रहता। इसलिये मैं शिक्षा मंत्री जी से अनुरोध करूंगी कि स्कूलों में जो डेलिक्वेंट चिल्ड्रेन हैं उनकी ओर भी ध्यान दें और उनके लिये विशेष स्कूलों को खोलने की भी व्यवस्था करें।

इन शब्दों के साथ मैं एक बार फिर शिक्षा मंत्री को और शिक्षा मंत्रालय को हार्दिक बधाई देती हूं।

Dr. S.K. Bhuyan (Assam): Mr. Deputy Chairman, I rise to give my wholehearted support to this measure. The present Government of India has enacted several laws for the social and economic uplift of the country. But it appears to me that of all those measures, this present piece of legislation, the Children Bill, is the noblest and the most humanitarian enactment which is going to be put on the statute book. Perhaps its companion measure will be the Bill for the removal of untouchability which we are told, will be coming before Parliament soon.

In every place and mostly in towns and factory areas, there are large numbers of riff-raff children who are destitute and neglected, mainly because their parents are too uneducated and too poor. Many have perhaps no proper parents, nor elders or guardians to look after them, and in many cases they are orphans having none to supervise their conduct and career. These young children are employed by unscrupulous men for the purpose of joining pick-pocket gangs. They are given regular training for this trade and....

Shri Rajendra Pratap Sinha: Sir, do we have a quorum?

Dr. S.K. Bhuyan: May I speak, Sir,

Mr. Deputy Chairman: Yes.

Dr. S.K. Bhuyan: And those boys are given regular training in the use of scissors for cutting open pockets, and to watch for careless passengers and visitors in important thoroughfares. They are also taught how to enter into rooms at night by squeezing themselves through iron bars of windows. Unfortunately enough some of these children are also employed to play the part of pimps.

I, therefore, feel that it has been a very good thing that the Government of India has been able to bring forward a Bill like this and to take steps for bringing up these destitute children by giving them proper education, and proper training so that they may become useful citizens of this country.

Similar measures were taken several decades ago by a poor Roman Catholic priest whose heart bled at the sight of these hapless children. He felt for them and he worked incessantly for their reclamation. He erected homes and schools in several places where these unfortunate boys were brought up and looked after on proper lines. They were given regular training in several vocations, such as printing, carpentry, smithy, etc. Such homes gradually sprang up everywhere. At present, there are more than 300 such homes all over the world, with their headquarters at Turin in Italy. This man was Saint Don Bosco, who founded the Salesian order. And when he died he was canonized by the Roman Catholic Church. Similarly, I am quite sure our Education Minister, Maulana Abul Kalam Azad, the father of this Bill and the present Government will be held in great respect by posterity, and they will hereafter be called "Garibonka Ma-Bap."

Sir, this is a good measure and I hope the whole country will extend its support in the working of it. This public co-operation is most essential for the successful and effective working of this measure. The officers will, of course, be there to find out and look after delinquent and neglected children. But unless the public also co-operate with this work in a whole-hearted manner, by tracing them out, by giving proper training and by establishing proper schools under this scheme, this measure will not be a success. In the first instance, the Bill is meant only for Part C States. But if the scheme is found to work successfully there, I am sure other States will also introduce similar measures in their respective areas.

Sir, I wish this measure every success and I give it all my support, and I express the gratitude of the country to the Government for taking such a wholesome step and for bringing forward this legislation.

Shri T.S. Pattabiraman (Madras): Mr. Deputy Chairman, the Education Minister of the Government of India deserves our heartiest congratulations for bringing forward this Bill. Sir, the motion has been moved for reference of this Bill to a Select Committee. Sir, the object and reasons for bringing forward this Bill have been clearly put in the Bill itself and also in the speech of the learned Education Minister.

The Bill is a very good one. One complaint is that it is too good. The Bill contains certain very good provisions, but I am afraid it will not at all be possible to work it out successfully. And why I say so I shall explain. There are two aspects to this question. We are going to deal with certain types of children and the entire Bill covers all sections of these chilren. It would had been better if the Bill had been confined to only, what may be called, the social side of the whole picture, rather than the political and the economic sides of it. The various provisions of the Bill are clearly for giving a certain preferential treatment to these children and there can be no doubt that such treatment is necessary. Nobody will be aagainst that. But the question is whether the Bill will be able to solve the problems that will arise or that are arising. Are they going to solve the problem of the neglected children and the delinquent children? Or is it only an attempt to deal with the external side of the problem? If one goes through the provisions of this Bill one will find that the children are to be classified as "neglected children", "uncontrollable children" and the "juvenile delinquents". With regard to the neglected children and also the uncontrolled children, whether we will be able to successfully solve the problem presented by them by this Bill becoming an Act is doubtful. The problem is not a social one. I would say it is an economic problem. And if you are not going to deal with the economic situation of the children, the Bill will be a failure. For example, here we have said that if a child is neglected, the child will be taken to the court and the court may order that he should be kept in an observation home or in a children's home for a period till he attains the age of sixteen. But after he attains the age of sixteen, what is to happen to him? That has not been provided for in this Bill. After attaining the age of sixteen, or when he attains the age of eighteen, he is to be left to the mercy of nature and again he becomes a vagabond. So I say, this measure does not go far enough to solve the problem of the child much less of the youth.

It may not be possible for the State to act up to this Bill even if it is passed by the House. Parliament is able to legislate only for Part C Stats and even Part C States are not likely to give effect to it immediately. Later on it may turn out that some Part C States may be able to implement it. But it is left to the other States either to enact this Bill *in toto* or with any modification that is necessary. I wonder whether the Government has given serious consideration to the question whether the implementation of this Bill *in toto* by the State Governments will be possible in the near future. An estimate of cost of one such institution has been given at the end of the Bill and in the finanical memorandum it has been mentioned that one such institution will cost Rs. 62,000 per year and I am sure, Sir, that every tehsil will have to have one such institution. If every tehsil has to have such an institution, how many tehsils are in a State, and the point is whether the State will be at all able to have such institutions with its crumbling finances. I am sure, Sir, that with the best of intentions of this Government this Bill will not see the light of a day nor will it be enforced in any of the States in the manner that we want. The provisions that have been made are rather very excessive. I am sure the Select Committee will go into the question and find out whether such provisions are necessary at all. Sir, even at the Select Committee stage, it will be better if a distinction is made between two sets of questions: one is the case of the juvenile delinquent. He must be treated separately. The provisions that are contained in this Bill with regard to neglected children or uncontrollable children, are very good. I am sure the provisions, relating to the delinquent children should be treated on a separate level. There is one objectionable feature of this Bill and I have very many misgivings about it and that is that it tries to completely overhaul or completely change or completely ignore the existing Criminal Procedure Code in many sections. Sir, the Criminal Procedure Code is sought to be ousted from the jurisdiction of the operation of this Bill. Whether it will be desirable or whether it is necessary will have to be deeply gone into by the Select Committee. Sir, clause 23 of the Bill deals with that. It says that there should be no joint trial of an adult and a child. After this Bill becomes law, no joint trial can be there when a child and an adult are co-charged in the same case. Sir, whether this may be possible or practicable is a point to be considered. Even now there are certain provisions whereby if an adult and a child are co-charged, both of them are tried by special Magistrates who have been empowered to try children. Sir, if that is so, the Bill now says that there must be separate trial; does the Bill contemplate that there must be two separate trials, evidence to be separately tendered in each trial? What will be the fate of the other trial? For example, there are two courts which will have to go into this one case. Would not the finding of one court prejudice that of the other? Will it not be said in the other court that already the case has been decided in one case and is this not certainly likely to prejudice the other case? This will be creating complications and it will also be undesirable and I do not know whether it will stand the test of law.

I come to clause 21 which deals with adjournment *sine die*. "Notwithstanding anything contained in this Act or any other law, the competent court may adjourn *sine die* any inquiry regarding a child alleged to have committed an offence and may, on additional grounds or materials being placed before it, re-open the inquiry at the stage at which it was left when adjourned." Sir, this is a very serious clause and I am sure the Select Committee will go into the question. There are already complaints in the courts and in Parliament also that criminal justice is being unnecessarily delayed and that criminal justice should be speeded up. In these cases adjournment *sine die* is sought to be given and I do not know whether this is right or whether it is proper or whether it is reasonable at all to say that criminal proceedings will remain in cold storage.

Sir, these are certain clauses, which appear, to my mind, not necessary. I wonder whether the Government should really have a separate legislation for many of the clauses are already existing. I wonder whether for separate courts a separate Bill at all is necessary. In Madras there are certain Special Magistrates, First Class Magistrates, who are empowered to try children who commit offences. These children get symapthetic consideration at the hands of the court. The Criminal Procedure Code can be amended to the same effect that any child brought up for an offence under the Criminal Procedure Code should be tried in the presence of two assessors, one being a Probation Officer and the other being a competent social worker who is on a panel for each district. That will be making justice also cheaper and that will be making justice easier. If instead of having separate courts you empower First Class Magistrates to try children with the help of two assessors, one a Probation Officer and the other a social worker, that will carry out the spirit of the legislation and will also minimise delays to a great extent. So, I would like the Select Committee to consider whether it is not desirable to amend the Criminal Procedure Code in a very simple manner and still get the effect of the provisions that are being sought to be included in this Bill with regard to the delinquent children.

Thirdly, there are certain provisions in this Bill which, I am sure, are greatly objectionable and I do not know whether they will be able to stand the test of the law, for example clause 29(2) which reads as follows: "No Order of a competent court shall be invalidated merely by any subsequent proof that the person in respect of whom the order has been made is not a child, and the age presumed or declared by the competent court to be the age of the person so brought before it shall, for the purposes of this Act, be deemed to be the true age of that person." Sir, this Bill, if it becomes law, will give power to the court to proceed under this law only when the child is 16 years of age while it is proved that the child is above 16 years of age even then a mistake of fact will not nullify the decision. This will be going against the spirit and quite contradictory to the Act and I also doubt whether it will stand the test of the judicial courts. This also goes against and is contradictory and I am sure that it may not be quite legal. I am only submitting it for the consideration of the Select Committee.

Similar is the case with clause 33 which prohibits the publication of names of children involved in any proceedings in this case. It says, "No report in any newspaper, magazine or news sheet of any inquiry regarding a child under this Act shall disclose the name, address or school or any other particulars calculated to lead to the identification of the child, nor shall any picture of any such child be published". Sir, this is a serious violaiton of the liberty that has been granted to the press under the Fundamental Rights. The Press, under the Fundamental Rights, has a right to publish the correct proceedings, authorised proceedings of the court. So, this clause will come in the way of the Fundamental Right that has been guaranteed to the Press and this clause also deserves serious consideration as to whether it is absolutely necessary or whether it is absolutely legal and whether the Government has the right to include any such clause in this Bill.

Going through the various clauses of the Bill it is clear that the authors of the Bill have very good intentions but it may not be possible for them to carry them out. For example, with regard to a neglected child clause 42 provides for the contributions to be made by parents.

Under section 488 of the Criminal Procedure Code there is already provision existing for the maintenance of a child if it is proved that it has been neglected by a parent. I wonder why a separate clause is necessary. If a careful scrutiny of the Criminal Procedure Code is made it will found that many existing sections are applicable to children. The only thing is to enforce them. It is also possible that such an enactment can be made applicable at once throughout the country, not only in Part C States. By amending certain sections of the Criminal Procedure Code it may be possible to fit in many of the provisions of this Bill and it can be done easily also.

The other day the Home Minister said that there is going to be a revision of the Criminal Procedure Code which is going to be done very soon. It will be rather beneficial to us and it will also be good for us to refer this matter to the body which would revise the Criminal Procedure Code and find out whether certain changes in the Criminal Procedure Code will be beneficial and they could also be made applicable to children throughout the country.

Finally, Sir, the Bill has a very laudable object and there can be no doubt about it. The States are to maintain the neglected children, children who have been ill-treated by the parents. There is no doubt about that but whether it is possible for the States to undertake this is a point. The problem is an economic one in the first instance, for a neglected child means, a child who —

> (i) is found in any street or place or public resort begging or receiving alms, or for the purpose of so begging or receiving alms, whether or not there is any pretence of singing, playing, performing, offering anything for sale, or otherwise; ..."

and it goes on enumerating in four sub-clauses. Sir, it is known now that due to poverty and due to the economic problems there are a large number of people in the whole of the countryside and throughout the country whose children are not being maintained properly. Sir, if the children have not been fed properly, if the children have not been maintained properly and have been neglected it is not due to unwillingness on the part of the parents but the incapacity of the parents to provide them sufficient food and shelter. Are you going to penalise the parents because they are not able to support their children and bring them up comfortably for want of money? No parent will neglect his child. The mother will not and the father will not unless they are by circumstances forced to neglect their children. This point should be taken into consideration. When this Bill becomes law you will be bringing a hornets' nest about your ears. I know in Madras that thousands are begging in the streets; they are under-nourished and ill-clad. Is it possible for the State Government and have they enough funds to bring into existence a sufficient number of children's homes? If that could be done certainly we would have achieved a laudable object. Can you take these children to the villages and give them employment? It is certainly a very good idea. Of course the State is bound to do it. But in the present circumstances with their poor finances can the States do it? No doubt the Bill has been introduced by the Government of India with good intentions but the Government of India must also find the finances for it. For example the Centre will have to pay at least four or five crores of rupees to Madras alone and if the Centre can find the money it is very good, it will be excellent, it is a welcome Bill and I am for it.

Shri H.P. Saksena: This Bill is meant for the Part 'C' States.

Shri T.S. Pattabiraman: I know this is intended for Part 'C' States but you have a very pious hope that the other States will also follow it and pass a Bill *in toto* or with modifications. With all the good intentions, for all I know of the financial condition of the Madras State, the Madras State and other similarly placed States will not pass such a Bill for centuries to come. What is the fun of passing such legislation if it canot be implemented in practice? It is a pious hope and it will remain a pious hope. It is no use throwing the responsibility on the State Governments and no use blaming the State Governments. The International Children's Convention has suggested this and so the Government of India thinks that it has followed it and has done its duty by introducing this Bill. The State Governments cannot pass such a Bill because they will not be able to implement it and the bottleneck is finance. My appeal to the Ministry of Education who is piloting this Bill is to see that it becomes operative not only in Part 'C' States but throughout the country by providing the funds for it. Sir, the problem is more economic and unless you are going to solve the economic problems of the country this Bill may never become a reality. If the economic condition of the country improves, if unemployment is relieved there will be no necessity for these homes and schools. So, Sir, while supporting this Bill I should tell the Government that it should not think that its duty is over by merely passing this Bill and I appeal to them to find the necessary financial resources for the States so that they might pass like Bills in their legislatures and implement the objects of the Bill in letter and spirit.

Shri P.T. Leuva (Bombay): After listening to the speech of Shri T.S. Pattabiraman I was rather provoked. It appears that he has not read the Bill at all. He does not know what are the provisions in the Bill. He must know that this Bill is primarily meant not for the punishment of children but this Bill is designed to re-educate the children who, by force of circumstances, have become delinquents, or are neglected by their parents or guardians.

Now, Sir, these cases used to be dealt with by the ordinary criminal courts. There are cases in English history that even children of even 10 or 11 years used to be sentenced to death merely for committing a petty offence of theft. There are cases also that children have spent their lives for about ten years in penal servitude. But, as time passed on, it was found necessary to take the view that the problem of a child is quite different from the problem of an adult criminal, because the adult criminal commits the offence after knowing the full consequences of it. But a child, by mere force of circumstances, sometimes commits an offence and therefore, Sir, it was decided practically in each and every country that the treatment of a juvenile should be different from that of an adult criminal.

Now my hon. friend Shri T.S. Pattabiraman has referred to various things regarding the Criminal Procedure Code. The main principle of this Bill is that the child is not to be treated as a criminal but he is to be treated as a person who requires to be re-educated. He should be kept away from evil influences and evil surroundings. That is the main reason for which this Bill has been designed, also that there shall be a special court for the trial of offences in which a child is involved. What is the reason? A child may become a delinquent because of social factors or he might be under the influence of parents who may themselves have criminal propensities. He may be living in an association where there might be such influence which may lead to a juvenile committing an offence. There are certain cases in which a child commits an offence because he is of a particular mental make-up. He may commit an offence under a temporary temptation. Now if you have such children tried before a regular criminal court of law, you are not going to improve him but you are....

Shri T.S. Pattabiraman: Even when tried by a criminal court, the criminal children are sent only to reformatory schools.

Shri P.T. Leuva: I know what reformatory schools are. I will come to it later. My hon. friend does not know what reformatory schools are. There are children who for having committed an offence have to be brought to the court. There are certain Acts under which they are brought to court and tried. Under the Municipal Act especially a child who is selling without a licence is also criminally liable because the Municipal Act provides it. Such a child though tried by an ordinary criminal court is sent to the reformatory school. It is a question of how you are going to treat this whole problem. The greatest advance that we have made in this direction is that we have removed this particular subject from the purview of the Home Department. Ordinarily the treatment of any criminals would come under the Home Department. There is a welcome departure and it is this that the Government of India has realised that in case of children it is not a question of 'criminal' but it is a quesion of education and rehabilitation of the children who are neglected and who commit offences because they are under evil influences. That is the reason why this law is being passed and it is a very healthy principle.

Now, Sir this Bill has been more or less designed on the recommendations contained in several international conferences. As far back as 1937, Sir, the League of Nations prepared a model Bill and in that model Bill they suggested various things and this Bill, in my opinion, more or less follows all the recommendations of that Bill.

Now, Sir, coming to the Bill itself, the Bill has made a distinction between two things. Those children who commit any contravention of any law have been classified as juvenile delinquents. There is a special reason for that also and I will come to that later on. The other class is those children who do not commit any contravention of the law but– merely because of the poor circumstances of their parents they are not looked after or even neglected – are living under the influence of certain bad associations or bad character and are becoming morally bad. These are the two categories, but most of them will come under the category of juvenile delinquents.

Now, Sir, the problem of the neglected child and the problem of juvenile delinquency are quite distinct. The juvenile delinquent requires a different type of treatment from that of a neglected child. For that very reason a provision has been made in the Bill that for juvenile delinquents there shall be, what they have called, special schools and for the neglected children they have made provision for children's homes. The treatment that you require for a juvenile delinquent is quite different from that required for a neglected child. The juvenile delinquent has already shown signs of criminal intentions, while the neglected child does not show that propensity. If you have had only one type of treatment for these categories of children, then the likelihood is that the neglected child might later on become a juvenile delinquent. Therefore it is necessary that there should be two different types of institutions. Even in juvenile delinquency there are stages of criminality. A juvenile delinquent might have committed an offence for the first time. It might be due to association. There might be certain juvenile deinquents who might have committed repeated offences and they might have become hardened criminals. Now it would be very unwise to put both these classes of juvenile delinquents in one and the same school, because if they remained together the hardened type of criminal juvenile might by association train the first-comer who comes for the first time into the home and he might also likely be the victim of the influence of the hardened criminal juveniles. Therefore the main principle is that for every child you have to think individually; you have to decide what type of treatment the child requires. Therefore these two separate institutions have been designed in this Bill.

Now, Sir, I will come to the next question regarding the trial of the offences in which children might be involved. Now in this Bill there is a provision that there shall be special courts. They are known as competent courts. It is absolutely essential that in the trial of these cases you should not have person to try such offences unless and until that person has knowledge about juvenile delinquency, otherwise the purpose for which this Bill is designed would be frustrated. A person who deals with a juvenile delinquent must have special knowledge about the problems which give rise to juvenile delinquency, because then and then only will he be in a position to find out what type of treatment is necessary for each particular child. Now, we have got criminal courts and those magistrates who are concerned with criminal cases might be quite competent to decide those questions but when a juvenile delinquent or a neglected child is brought before a court, different considerations apply. Therefore, Sir, in this Bill itself a provision has been made that the person who is presiding over this particular type of court must be a person who has got special knowledge and training about junvenile delinquency and child welfare. It is a difficult problem to be solved. It is not very easy to find competent persons to look after this type of work. This was visualised by the framers of the Bill and that is the reason why they have made a provision that there might be a Bench of Magistrates who might deal with such cases. But in that also they have made a very healthy provision that one of the judges should have special knowledge about juvenile delinquency and child welfare. From this Bill you will find, Sir, that greater emphasis has been laid on the educative principle in the treatment of children. It is not a question of punishing a child. That is why a special court has been provided. My hon. friend, Shri Pattabiraman, has referred to the question of finance. It is no doubt true that finance is the most important factor in this. But if the States have a will they can do it. In Bombay, Sir, I am intimately connected with this particular type of courts. In the Bombay City itself, the Bombay Government spends Rs. 8 lakhs per year on the juvenile delinquents. It is not that they cannot spend more money, it is the question of will. Therefore, so far as I am concerned, I feel that this Bill is capable of being properly implemented. But the question is that there must be a law to do it; there must be the obligation also on the Government to do it.

This Bill applies only to Part C States. There is the constitutional difficulty and so Parliament could not legislate so far as other States are concerned. In most of the States, so far as I know, Bombay, Madras, United Provinces and West Bengal and also Madhya Pradesh, the same type of legislation has been in existence.

Sir, the next question is regarding the children's after-care organisation. The delinquents are committed to the courts and if they satisfy the requirements of the case the courts commit them to a particular Home. After the child has attained a certain age, say 16 or 18, after the period of custody is over, what is to happen? If the hon. Members have taken pains to read the clause they would see that in these particular after-care organisations a particular type of education is given, industrial education, to the juvenile delinquents. They are given industrial training. The main point is that after he leaves the Home or the Institution, the juvenile delinquent should be able to obtain his livelihood by himself. That is why the juvenile delinquent is put in a special school and is given a special kind of training. Therefore, the fear entertained by my hon. friend Shri Pattabiraman is not of particular value.

The other thing is that these juvenile delinquents are to be brought before a court. There must be some machinery whereby juvenile delinquents can be prevented from coming under the influence of such courts. There might be very petty offences and if you bring such a child before a court, there is likely to be an emotional disturbance. He is likely to have a fear in his mind regarding the formality of courts. Therefore, Sir, in certain countries, and especially in Scotland, there is a particular type of system where a Public Prosecutor is appointed specially for this work. If he finds from the materials before him, if he comes to the conclusion that the child should not be sent to the court, he has the right to decide that; and then the child would not be brought before the court. Similarly, Sir, I would suggest that this is a system worthy of consideration, because there are many many petty types of offences in which a child should not be made to undergo the formal trial of the court. In Bombay City, we have started very recently a separate section of the Police Department. This section is called the 'Juvenile Section of the Police Department'. This is specially designed to see that the children are looked after properly. They try to find out the nature of the cases in which children are tried before a court. I would also suggest that such a type of machinery as there is in Scotland should be designed so that such a type of machinery as there is in Scotland should be designed so that children may not be unnecessarily brought before the courts, and in this way this problem could be lightened.

Now, Sir, there are one or two points regarding this Bill to which I would like to make a reference. Now there is one point that the court has got the power to amend or alter an order passed by itself at any time. That is clause 37 which reads as follows:

> "Without prejudice to the provisions for appeal and revision under this Act, any competent court may, either on its own motion or on an application received in this behalf, amend any order as to the institution to which a child is to be sent or as to the person under whose care or supervision a child is to be placed under this Act."

Now this power has been given to the court for various reasons. The court may hand over the child to any person. But a similar power has been given to the State Government. My own fear is that there might be a conflict between the Government and the court itself, because in clause 37 there is no limitation placed upon the court and the court can pass this order at any time. Supposing in the meantime the State Government has also passed an order transferring the child from one institution to another, then what happens? The power of the court is still in existence. Then the question would arise whether the court has still got the power to amend the order passed by the Government. I would, therefore, submit, Sir, that this is an important point which should be considered by the Select Committee, and they should try to find out whether there can be any suitable reconciliation so that there may not be any conflict between the power exercisable by the court and the State Government.

Now, Sir, there is another clause which is there. That is clause 39. It says:

> "Where it appears to the State Government that any child kept in a special school or children's home in pursuance of this Act is a leper or of unsound mind, the State Government may order his removal to a leper asylum or mental hospital or other place of safe custody for being kept there for the remainder of the term for which he has to be kept in custody under the orders of the competent court or for such further period as may be certified by a medical officer to be necessary for the proper treatment of the child."

Now, Sir, under the provisions of this Bill the court has only got the jurisdiction to keep a child in custody till he attains the age of 15. The power of the court is limited to that extent and the State Government also cannot possibly extend that power regarding custody. But if you read, Sir, the provisions of this clause – clause 39 – you will find that there is no limitation provided at all. The moment a child has been sent by the State Government to a mental hospital or a leper asylum, the power becomes unlimited unless and until there is a specific mention that the State Government also cannot keep a child in custody beyond 18 years of age. But unfortunately, Sir, the State Government has been given an unlimited power. According to me, Sir, unless and until this clause is amended, it is likely that the State Government might interpret it in a way so as to give them the unlimited power of confining a child in a mental hospital or a leper asylum for an unlimited period of time.

Now, Sir, my hon. friend, Shri Pattabiraman, referred to section 488 of the Criminal Procedure Code. Now under that section, Sir, the criminal courts have a right to pass a maintenance order for an illegitimate child. Now there is no question of suppression of that power conferred by the Criminal Procedure Code. This section only refers to the contribution which is to be paid to the juvenile court for the purpose of maintaining a child. So the question of awarding maintenance by a juvenile court does not arise under the Bill.

Now, for this purpose, I would read the clause:

> "Provided that where the child is illegitimate and an order for his maintenance has been made under section 488 of the Code of Criminal Procedure, 1898 (Act V of 1898), the competent court shall not ordinarily make an order for contribution

> aginst the putative father, but may order the whole or any part of the sums accruing due under the said order for maintenance to be paid to such person as may be named by the competent court and such sum shall be paid by him towards the maintenance of the child."

The question of the order being passed by the juvenile court does not arise at all. It is only a question of asking for a contribution from the amount which has been already ordered to be paid by a criminal court. My hon. friend, Mr. Pattabiraman, said that these juvenile courts have been given the power of passing such an order. I think that he may not have read this particular provision.

Shri T.S. Pattabiraman: On a point of explanation. I said that under the existing provisions of section 488 a parent is compelled to pay for maintenance.

Shri P.T. Leuva: These courts have only got jurisdiction to ask for contribution from that amount which has already been passed by an order. So, there is no question of any additional amount.

Shri T.S. Pattabiraman: There is a provision already in the Criminal Procedure Code, whereby a parent can be forced to contribute wherever the child may be. So, I thought that this might not be necessary, in view of the existing law.

Shri P.T. Leuva: So far as I know the law, under section 488, generally these orders are made at the instance of the mother. The mother is the applicant, and she has the right to receive that amount from the court, and not the child. The child cannot claim that contribution from the court. Therefore, for that reason, there cannot be increased liability on the parent.

Shri T.S. Pattabiraman: Section 488 says:

> "If any person having sufficient means neglects or refuses to maintain his wife or his legitimate or illegitimate child unable to maintain itself, a District Magistrate, a Presidency Magistrate may pass an order....

So, the section is clear. My friend may not have read it.

Shri P.T. Leuva: What I was saying is that they can ask for a contribution only from the amount which has already been ordered to be paid. The order has already been passed by the criminal court. Let the juvenile court take that money from that court. Why should the parent be unnecessarily asked to pay a double amount? The mother would still be taking the money from the court which has already passed the order. Why should the parent again contribute for the maintenance of the child? It is only for the purpose of avoiding this, this provision has been incorporated.

Sir, I have got one more difficulty in this particular provision. It says:

> "The person liable to maintain a child shall, for the purposes of sub-section (1), include, in the case of illegitimacy, his putative father:"

Now, Sir, if you read this section, it provides in effect that the juvenile court will have jurisdiction to revise an order passed by another court. Section 488 empowers an ordinary criminal court to determine which particular person is the putative father and pass an order against that person. Now there may be a case where an ordinary criminal court might have passed an order deciding that a particular person is not the putative father. But if subsequently such an illegitimate child is brought before the Juvenile Court, then according to this section the Juvenile Court has got power to decide who is the illegitimate father. Now this might lead to great conflicts. It may be that the matter might have gone to the High Court and the High Court might have given a decision and if you give the Juvenile Court power to revise the order which has been already passed, I think it would go against the basic principles of criminal jurisprudence that once a decision has been given by a criminal court, the court of coordinate jurisdiction should not be allowed to revise that order. I would therefore submit that it is necessary that this provision also should be reconsidered and suitable amendments must be made; otherwise there is a likelihood that conflicts might arise. So far as the other provisions are concerned, the question of after-care is a very important problem. After-care organisations are generally voluntary in character but after-care organisations will not be able to do their duty properly and adequately unless and until they are provided with sufficient finances. Now the question of finance will vary from State to State but that does not mean that the State should not take up such type of legislation. Now in other countries they make a distinction between a child who has attained the age of sixteen and a child who is in a children's home or certified school between the ages of sixteen and eighteen. There the treatment is slightly different. In order that the child might become independent and might get used to the new surroundings, they have got the system of hostels. Now in these hostels the children are kept between the ages of sixteen and eighteen and they are encouraged to go out of the hostels and earn their livelihood. But there is only one condition that after their work is finished, they should return to the hostels. There the provision has been made for shelter and food. I would also like the Government to think on those lines so that after the children come out of such institutions, they are in a position to earn their own livelihood. Another question which I wanted to refer to was regarding the child delinquency. Those cases don't refer to juvenile cases but those cases are more or less individual in character. In early life a child might show signs of delinquency but he may not be actually delinquent; but if proper steps are taken, if proper treatment is given to the child, then such cases can be avoided and a potential juvenile delinquent ceases to be a juvenile delinquent. Therefore, in Bombay City I think the Tata Institute of Social Science runs some child guide clinics and officers attend to such clinics and examine children who show signs which are likely to lead to delinquent life. Before they embark on their careers, the children are psycho-analysed. The family is given proper direction and I know of an instance of a very bright girl who suddenly became indifferent to her studies and the question arose as to how she becane indifferent. She was sent to a child clinic and it was discovered that the mother was making a discrimination between the daughter and the son and that led to an emotional disturbance in her mind and labouring under that particular type of injustice, she became indifferent. But when proper treatment was given to her, she became quite normal. Therefore in order to prevent the spread of juvenile delinquents, the most essential thing is prevention rather than cure. No treatment can ever be adequate to solve any problem. The problem of juvenile delinquency cannot be completely solved by any Government. It has not been possible in any part of the world. We are only making a beginning but the beginning which we are making is on the right lines and that is the reason why I want to congratulate the Education Ministry for taking up this particular type of Bill in their jurisdiction because they have realized that this problem is a problem relating to the education of children. Now this problem is of such a complicated character that we cannot successfully solve it unless and until we have got the proper type of machinery. In this problem we have to find out proper and suitable magistrates who know not only to find out whether an offence has been committeed but they will have to find out the circumstances under which the offence was committed and then they will have to deal with the child with sympathy and understanding.

Therefore largely the question will depend upon the type of magistrates that we are able to recruit. Then there is the question of separate institution.The success of an institution will largely depend upon the persons who are incharge of it. The question of children is a delicate one. The children have to be treated with understanding and sympathy. Unless and until we get those persons who are incharge of such institutions, unless and until we get enthusiastic persons who will look upon this work as a matter of public service and unless and until they work in a missionary spirit, this problem cannot be solved at all. Sir, it is not a question of money alone. Money might be forthcoming but the main problem is for us to find out proper persons to look after this question who will solve the problems relating to juvenile delinquency. Then the larger question is that it is much better to have prevention rather than cure and what is the cure? The cure is that we have to create conditions in this country so that the children may not have the necessity or the compulsion to take recourse to criminal activities. As we progress this problem would lose its importance. Because if the economic conditions are improved, then largely the problem of neglected children and of juvenile delinquents would diminish. Therefore with the passage of time, I have great hope that this problem will diminish gradually. This problem is not in the rural areas. This problem is generally concentrated only in urban cities and mostly in industrialised cities. Therefore the question of finance would not be of very great importance in view of the fact that these problems would be located in certain areas only and therefore the question of finance should not frighten the Government. With these words, Sir, I support this Bill.

Mr. Deputy Chairman: Dr. Shrimali.

Shri K.B. Lall (Bihar): May I not speak?

Mr. Deputy Chairman: I have called Dr. Shrimali to reply. We have got two more Bills. This is coming up again after the Select Committee. Then you can have your full say.

The Parliamentary Secretary to the Minister for Education (Dr. K.L. Shrimali): Mr. Deputy Chairman, I do not like to take much time of the hon. Members now because the Bill is going to be referred to the Select Committee and I am quite sure that the Select Committee and I am quite sure that the Select Committee will give full consideration to the valuable suggestions which have been made by hon. Members. There is only one point to which I wish to refer. During the last few years, there has been a good deal of research in the matter of juvenile delinquency.

It is high time that we introduced some kind of legislation in our own country to reclaim the large number of juvenile delinquents who have become delinquents not because of any inherent defect but because of social conditions. All the researches in recent times indicate that one of the major factors for juvenile delinquency is the environmental condition. A broken home or poverty or ill-health – these are some of the conditions which lead to all kinds of emotional difficulties and emotional disturbances which ultimately lead to delinquency. If such children are put in proper environmental conditions or placed in an educative atmosphere they change their outlook and all those anti-social characteristics disappear. In all civilised countries, there are legislations for reclaiming such children at an early age and I think, Sir, that it is high time that we also introduce this legislation in our own country.

I, therefore, move that the motion which has been moved by the hon. Education Minister to refer the Children Bill to a Select Committee might be passed.

Shri K.B. Lall: Sir, on a point of order.....

Mr. Deputy Chairman: There is no point of order, Mr. Lall.

Shri K.B. Lall: I am standing on a point of order, Sir.

Mr. Deputy Chairman: There is no point of order, Mr. Lall. I am putting the question to the House.

Shri K.B. Lall: Sir, this is a Money Bill and I want to know whether we have got the right to initiate it here. That was the point I was going to make.

Mr. Deputy Chairman: There is no point of order, Mr. Lall. Order, order. You have to resume your seat, Mr. Lall. Both of us cannot stand together.

Shri K.B. Lall: I know, Sir; I was raising a point of order. You may rule that it is not a point of order but....

Mr. Deputy Chairman: Order, order. Will the Hon. Member resume his seat?

Shri K.B. Lall: .....you must at least hear me first.

Mr. Deputy Chairman: I want you to resume your seat, Mr. Lall. Both of us cannot be standing in this House. Please resume your seat.

Shri K.B. Lall: I am resuming my seat, Sir, but I want to know whether I am going to be heard.

Mr. Deputy Chairman: All that was required was the President's recommendation and it has been obtained. Please look at the last page. There is no point of order.

Mr. Deputy Chairman: The question is:

"That the Bill to provide for the care, protection, maintenance, welfare, training, education and rehabilitation of neglected children and juvenile delinquents in Part C States be referred to a Select Committee consisting of the following members:

Shrimati Rukmini Arundale,

Dr. Shrimati Seeta Parmanand,

Shrimati Violet Alva,

Kunwarani Vijaya Raje,

Shri Onkar Nath,

Shri Lavji Lakhamshi,

Shri J.N. Kaushal,

Shri T.R. Deogirikar,

Shri Rahmath-Ullah,

Maulana M. Faruqi,

Shri Indra Vidyavachaspati,

Shri S.D. Misra,

Dr. K.L. Shrimali,

Shri Kishori Ram,

Shri H.C. Mathur,

Shri Kishen Chand,

Shri S.N. Mazumdar,

Shri Abdul Razak,

Shri Amolakh Chand,

Shri K.D. Malaviya, and The Mover."

The motion was adopted.

Shri Rajendra Pratap Sinha: Sir, I would like to make a statement.

Mr. Deputy Chairman: Not at this stage.

Shri Rajendra Pratap Sinha: A certain clarification I would like to make.

Mr. Deputy Chairman: What is it about? We have got other business to go through.

Shri Rajendra Pratap Sinha: I will take hardly two minutes, with your permission.

Mr. Deputy Chairman: What is it about, I want to know first.

Shri Rajendra Pratap Sinha: It is regarding the allegation made by the other side, Sir, that the Opposition has been inconsistent with regard to...

Mr. Deputy Chairman: All that is not necessary, Mr. Sinha.

Shri Rajendra Pratap Sinha: They have said that we are participating in the Select Committee but we are not participating in the debate. Sir. There is nothing inconsistent about it, inasmuch as we are in full agreement with the principle of the Bill.

Mr. Deputy Chairman: You have said that. The motion is over.

Shri Rajendra Pratap Sinha: I want to make it clear, Sir.

Mr. Deputy Chairman: Not at this stage. Even before you have made that statement for not participating in the debate, which is enough.

Who's Who

Azad, Bhagvat Jha	: Leading Congress leader of Bihar and former Chief-Minister.
Bedi, M.S.	: An eminent Urdu writer, Poet and Scholar
Birla, G.D.	: Well Known Indian industrialist, follower of Mahatma Gandhi, financed Congress Movement several times.
Curzon, Lord	: British Viceroy to India in 1905.
Deshmukh, P.R.	: An Eminent Journalist and Editor of the Statesman.
Faruqi, M.	: Well-known Communist leader and former Member of Parliament.
Gadgil, N.V.	: Front-ranking Congress leader of Maharashtra; was appointed a Minister in Union Cabinet, headed by Pt. Jawaharlal Nehru.
Jain, A.P.	: Well-known Congress leader of U.P. and a member of Nehru's Cabinet.
Kalidas	: An eminent Scholar of ancient age.
Sachar, Bhimsen	: A leading Congressman of Punjab; was a Minister in the State Government till 1947, headed by K. Hyat Khan, became Finance Minister of PEPSU (1947-49) and later on Chief Minister of Punjab.
Singh, Karan	: Son of Thakur Hari Singh, the king of Kashmir who became the Head of State of Jammu and Kashmir in 1949.
Singh, T.N.	: An eminent statesman of U.P. who became Chief Minister of S.V.D. Government of Uttar Pradesh in 1970
Sinha, S.N.	: Leading Congressman of Bihar and a member of Union Cabinet, headed by Pt. Nehru.
Tandon, P.D.	: Front-ranking Congress leader of U.P.; was elected President of Indian National Congress in 1950.
Zaidi, B.H.	: Former Prime Minister of Rampur State.

Glossary

Chaprasi	: Attendant
Diara	: A dried up river-bed
Gitanjali	: A best poetry book of R.N. Tagore
Fakir	: A man of renunciation
Farman	: Administrative order
Inquilab	: Revolution
Nawab	: A petty ruler
PEPSU	: Erstwile Patiala and East Punjab States Union
Qanun	: Urdu (Persian) term of law
Sadar-i-Riyasat	: Head of State
Yuvaraj	: Heir Apparent

Chronology of Events

(1953-1954)

1953 January	5	:	Inaugurated session of the seminar on the contribution of Gandhian outlook and technique to the solution of tension between and within Nation, in New Delhi.
	28	:	Delivered speech of welcome at the inauguration of the Indian Academy of Dance, Drama and Music in New Delhi.
February	1	:	Declared opened the National Library, Alipur.
	8	:	Presided over the Eighth meeting of the All India Council for Technical Education in New Delhi.
March	30	:	Delivered speech in the House of People for the Demands for Grants.
April	11	:	Presided over the conference of State Education Ministers and Vice-Chancellors of the Universities in New Delhi.
	12	:	Declared open the Central Building Research Institute at Roorkee.
June	29	:	Delivered speech at the President's reception to members of the British Everest Expedition in Rashtrapati Bhavan.
September	8	:	Declared edcuational programme in the House of People.
	21	:	Delivered speech at the laying of the foundation stone of the 12th National Institute, Pilani.
November	9	:	Delivered speech at the 20th annual meeting of Central Advisory Board of Education held at New Delhi.

	December 28	:	Presided over the first meeting of the University Grants Commission.
1954	August 5	:	Inaugurated the first session of the Lalit Kala Academy.
	October 30	:	Presided over the 9th annual meeting of the All India Council for Technical Education in New Delhi.

Index

D

E

F

G

W

Y

Z